D0065520

GUIDE TO FINANCIAL MARKETS

GUIDE TO FINANCIAL MARKETS

FOURTH EDITION

Marc Levinson

BLOOMBERG PRESS

NEW YORK

THE ECONOMIST IN ASSOCIATION WITH
PROFILE BOOKS LTD

Published in the United States and Canada by Bloomberg Press
Published in the U.K. by Profile Books Ltd, 2006

Printed in the United States of America
3 5 7 9 10 8 6 4
ISBN-13: 978-1-57660-201-0

The Library of Congress has cataloged the earlier printing as follows:

Levinson, Marc
    Guide to financial markets / Marc Levinson.-- 4th ed.
        p. cm. -- (The Economist)
Includes index.
    ISBN 1-57660-201-x (alk. paper)
    1. Finance. I. Title. II. Series: Economist series.

HG173.L485 2006   2005036426
332.64--dc22

Contents

1 Why markets matter

THE EURO is slightly higher against the yen. The Dow Jones Industrial Average is off 18 points in active trading. A Chinese airline loses millions of dollars with derivatives. Following the Bank of England's decision to lower its base rate, monthly mortgage payments are set to fall. All these events are examples of financial markets at work. That markets exercise enormous influence over modern life comes as no news. But although people around the world speak glibly of "Wall Street", "the bond market" and "the currency markets", the meanings they attach to these time-worn phrases are often vague and usually out of date. This book explains the purposes different financial markets serve and clarifies the way they work. It cannot tell you whether your investment portfolio is likely to rise or to fall in value. But it may help you understand how its value is determined, and how the different securities in it are created and traded.

In the beginning

The word "market" usually conjures up an image of the bustling, paper-strewn floor of the New York Stock Exchange or of traders motioning frantically in the futures pits of Chicago. But formal exchanges such as these are only one aspect of the financial markets, and far from the most important one. There were financial markets long before there were exchanges and, in fact, long before there was organised trading of any sort.

Financial markets have been around ever since mankind settled down to growing crops and trading them with others. After a bad harvest, those early farmers would have needed to obtain seed for the next season's planting, and perhaps to get food to see their families through. Both of these transactions would have required them to obtain credit from others with seed or food to spare. After a good harvest, the farmers would have had to decide whether to trade away their surplus immediately or to store it, a choice that any 20th-century commodities trader would find familiar. The amount of fish those early farmers could obtain for a basket of cassava would have varied day by day, depending upon the catch, the harvest and the weather; in short, their exchange rates were volatile.

The independent decisions of all of those farmers constituted a basic financial market, and that market fulfilled many of the same purposes as financial markets do today.

What do markets do?

Financial markets take many different forms and operate in diverse ways. But all of them, whether highly organised, like the London Stock Exchange, or highly informal, like the money changers on the street corners of many African capitals, serve the same basic functions.

- **Price setting.** The value of an ounce of gold or a share of stock is no more, and no less, than what someone is willing to pay to own it. Markets provide price discovery, a way to determine the relative values of different items, based upon the prices at which individuals are willing to buy and sell them.
- **Asset valuation.** Market prices offer the best way to determine the value of a firm or of the firm's assets, or property. This is important not only to those buying and selling businesses, but also to regulators. An insurer, for example, may appear strong if it values the securities it owns at the prices it paid for them years ago, but the relevant question for judging its solvency is what prices those securities could be sold for if it needed cash to pay claims today.
- **Arbitrage.** In countries with poorly developed financial markets, commodities and currencies may trade at very different prices in different locations. As traders in financial markets attempt to profit from these divergences, prices move towards a uniform level, making the entire economy more efficient.
- **Raising capital.** Firms often require funds to build new facilities, replace machinery or expand their business in other ways. Shares, bonds and other types of financial instruments make this possible. Increasingly, the financial markets are also the source of capital for individuals who wish to buy homes or cars, or even to make credit-card purchases.
- **Commercial transactions.** As well as long-term capital, the financial markets provide the grease that makes many commercial transactions possible. This includes such things as arranging payment for the sale of a product abroad, and providing working capital so that a firm can pay employees if payments from customers run late.
- **Investing.** The stock, bond and money markets provide an

Table 1.1 **Amounts raised in financial markets ($bn, net of repayments)**

	1996	1998	2000	2002	2004
International bank loans	405	115	714	540	1,343
International bonds and notes	499	669	1,148	1,014	1,560
International money-market instruments	41	10	87	2	61
Domestic bonds and notes	1,497	1,600	865	1,672	2,461
Domestic money-market instruments	401	377	377	103	774
International equity issues	83	125	318	103	214
Domestic equity issues	438	472	901	320	593
Total excluding domestic loans	3,364	3,368	4,410	3,754	7,006

Sources: Bank for International Settlements; World Federation of Exchanges

opportunity to earn a return on funds that are not needed immediately, and to accumulate assets that will provide an income in future.

◢ **Risk management.** Futures, options and other derivatives contracts can provide protection against many types of risk, such as the possibility that a foreign currency will lose value against the domestic currency before an export payment is received. They also enable the markets to attach a price to risk, allowing firms and individuals to trade risks until they hold only those that they wish to retain.

The size of the markets

Estimating the overall size of the financial markets is difficult. It is hard in the first place to decide exactly what transactions should be included under the rubric "financial markets", and there is no way to compile complete data on each of the millions of sales and purchases occurring each year. Total capital market financing was approximately $7 trillion worldwide in 2004, excluding purely domestic loans that were not resold in the form of securities (see Table 1.1).

The figure of $7 trillion for 2004, sizeable as it is, represents only a single year's activity. Another way to look at the markets is to estimate the value of all the financial instruments they trade. When measured in this way, the financial markets accounted for $109 trillion of capital in 2004 (see Table 1.2 on the next page). Large as it is, this figure excludes many important financial activities, such as insurance underwriting,

Table 1.2 **The world's financial markets ($trn)**

	1996	1998	2000	2002	2004
International bonds and notes	3.1	4.1	6.1	8.8	13.2
International money-market instruments	0.2	0.2	0.3	0.4	0.7
Domestic bonds and notes	21.2	23.8	23.8	27.9	35.9
Domestic money-market instruments	4.5	5.2	6.0	6.3	8.2
International bank loans	8.3	8.2	8.3	10.1	13.9
Domestic equities	19.6	25.4	31.1	22.8	37.2
Total value outstanding	56.9	66.9	75.6	76.3	109.1

Source: Bank for International Settlements

bank lending to individuals and small businesses, and trading in financial instruments such as futures and derivatives that are not means of raising capital. If all of these other financial activities were to be included, the total size of the markets would be much larger.

Cross-border measure

Another way of measuring the growth of finance is to examine the value of cross-border financing. Cross-border finance is by no means new, and at various times in the past (in the late 19th century, for example) it has been quite large relative to the size of the world economy. The period since 1990 has been marked by a huge increase in the amount of international financing broken by financial crises in Asia and Russia in 1998 and the recession in the United States in 2001. The total stock of cross-border finance in 2005, including international bank loans and debt issues, was more than $30 trillion, according to the Bank for International Settlements.

Looking strictly at securities provides an even more dramatic picture of the growth of the financial markets. A quarter of a century ago, cross-border purchases and sales of securities amounted to only a tiny fraction of most countries' economic output. Today, annual cross-border share and bond transactions are several times larger than GDP in a number of advanced economies – Japan being a notable exception.

International breakdown

The ways in which firms and governments raise funds in international markets have changed substantially. In 1993, bonds accounted for 59%

Table 1.3 **Financing on international capital markets, by type of instrument ($bn)**

	1996	1998	2000	2002	2004
Bonds and money-market instruments	543	678	1,241	1,009	1,621
Equities	83	125	317	102	214
Syndicated loans	901	902	1,485	1,300	1,807
Total	1,527	1,705	3,043	2,411	3,642

Source: Bank for International Settlements

of international financing. By 1997, before the financial crises in Asia and Russia shook the markets, only 47% of the funds raised on international markets were obtained through bond issues. Equities became an important source of cross-border financing in 2000, when share prices were extremely high, but bonds and loans regained importance in the low-interest-rate environment of 2002–05. Table 1.3 lists the amounts of capital raised by the main instruments used in international markets.

Turn-of-the-century slowdown

By all of these measures, financial markets grew extremely rapidly during the 1990s. At the start of the decade, active trading in financial instruments was confined to a small number of countries, and involved mainly the same types of securities, bonds and equities that had dominated trading for two centuries. By the first years of the 21st century, however, financial markets were thriving in dozens of countries, and new instruments accounted for a large proportion of market dealings.

The expansion of financial-market activity paused in 1998 in response to banking and exchange-rate crises in a number of countries. The crises passed quickly, however, and in 1999 financial-market activity reached record levels following the inauguration of the single European currency, interest-rate declines in Canada, the UK and continental Europe, and a generally positive economic picture, marred by only small rises in interest rates, in the United States. Equity-market activity slowed sharply in 2000 and 2001, as share prices fell in many countries, but bond-market activity was robust. Trading in foreign-exchange markets fell markedly at the turn of the century. Bond markets remained very active through 2005.

The general increase in financial-market activity can be traced to four main factors:

- **Lower inflation.** Inflation rates around the world have fallen sharply since the 1980s. Inflation erodes the value of financial assets and increases the value of physical assets, such as houses and machines, which will cost far more to replace than they are worth today. When inflation is high, as was the case in the United States, Canada and much of Europe during the 1970s and throughout Latin America in the 1980s, firms avoid raising long-term capital because investors require a high return on investment, knowing that price increases will render much of that return illusory. In a low-inflation environment, however, financial-market investors require less of an inflation premium, as general increases in prices will not devalue their assets and the prices of many physical assets are stable or even falling.
- **Pensions.** A significant change in pension policies is under way in many countries. Since the 1930s, and even longer in some countries, governments have operated pay-as-you-go schemes to provide income to the elderly. These schemes, such as the old age pension in the UK and the social security programme in the United States, tax current workers to pay current pensioners and therefore involve no saving or investment. Changes in demography and working patterns have made pay-as-you-go schemes increasingly costly to support, as there are fewer young workers relative to the number of pensioners. This has stimulated interest in pre-funded individual pensions, whereby each worker has an account in which money must be saved, and therefore invested, until retirement. Although these personal investment accounts have to some extent supplanted firms' private pension plans, they have also led to a huge increase in financial assets in countries where private pension schemes were previously uncommon.
- **Stock and bond market performance.** Many countries' stock and bond markets performed well during most of the 1990s. The rapid increase in financial wealth feeds on itself: investors whose portfolios have appreciated are willing to reinvest some of their profits in the financial markets. And the appreciation in the value of their financial assets gives investors the collateral to borrow additional money, which can then be invested.

◼ **Risk management.** Innovation has generated many new financial products, such as derivatives and asset-backed securities, whose basic purpose is to redistribute risk. This has led to enormous growth in the use of financial markets for risk-management purposes. To an extent unimaginable a few years ago, firms and investors are able to choose which risks they wish to bear and use financial instruments to shed the risks they do not want, or, alternatively, to take on additional risks in the expectation of earning higher returns. The risk that the euro will trade above $1.40 during the next six months, or that the interest rate on long-term US Treasury bonds will rise to 6%, is now priced precisely in the markets, and financial instruments to protect against these contingencies are readily available. The risk-management revolution has thus resulted in an enormous expansion of financial-market activity.

The investors

The driving force behind financial markets is the desire of investors to earn a return on their assets. This return has two distinct components:

◼ **Yield** is the income the investor receives while owning an investment.
◼ **Capital gains** are increases in the value of the investment itself, and are often not available to the owner until the investment is sold.

Investors' preferences vary as to which type of return they prefer, and these preferences, in turn, will affect their investment decisions. Some financial-market products are deliberately designed to offer only capital gains and no yield, or vice versa, to satisfy these preferences.

Investors can be divided broadly into two categories:

◼ **Individuals.** Collectively, individuals own a small proportion of financial assets. Most households in the wealthier countries own some financial assets, often in the form of retirement savings or of shares in the employer of a household member. Most such holdings, however, are quite small, and their composition varies greatly from one country to another. In 2000, equities accounted for nearly half of households' financial assets in France, but only about 8% in Japan. The great majority of individual investment is

7

controlled by a comparatively small number of wealthy households. Nonetheless, individual investing has become increasingly popular. In the United States, bank certificates of deposit accounted for more than 10% of households' financial assets in 1989 but only 3.1% in 2001, as families shifted their money into securities.

◪ **Institutional investors.** Insurance companies and other institutional investors (see below) are responsible for most of the trading in financial markets. The assets of institutional investors based in the 30 member countries of the OECD totalled about $35 trillion in 2001. They grew almost 12% per year between 1990 and 1999, then declined in 2000 and 2001. The size of institutional investors varies greatly from country to country, depending on the development of collective investment vehicles. Investment practices vary considerably as well. In 2001, for example, US institutional investors kept 44% of their assets in the form of shares and 35% in bonds, whereas British institutional investors held 65% of assets in shares. In Japan, 56% of institutional investors' assets were bonds, despite extremely low interest rates, and only 16% were shares.

Mutual funds

The fastest-growing institutional investors are investment companies, which combine the investments of a number of individuals with the aim of achieving particular financial goals in an efficient way. Mutual funds and unit trusts are investment companies that typically accept an unlimited number of individual investments. The fund declares the strategy it will pursue, and as additional money is invested the fund managers purchase financial instruments appropriate to that strategy. Investment trusts, some of which are known in the United States as closed-end funds, issue a limited number of shares to investors at the time they are established and use the proceeds to purchase financial instruments in accordance with their strategy. In some cases, the trust acquires securities at its inception and never sells them; in other cases, the fund changes its portfolio from time to time. Investors wishing to enter or leave the unit trust must buy or sell the trust's shares from stockbrokers.

Hedge funds

A third type of investment company, a hedge fund, can accept invest-

Table 1.4 **Financial assets of institutional investors (% of GDP)**

	1990	1996	1999	2001
Australia	49.3	92.3	125.8	129.7
Canada	58.1	93.2	111.5	115.8
France	54.8	86.6	124.2	131.8
Germany	36.5	50.6	76.9	81.0
Italy	13.4	39.0	99.5	94.0
Japan	81.7	88.4	98.9	94.7
Mexico	8.8	4.6	8.3	11.7
Netherlands	133.4	167.5	212.7	190.9
Sweden	85.7	115.8	167.9	153.5
Switzerland	119	164.2	116.9	232.7
Turkey	0.6	1.7	3.4	4.4
UK	114.5	172.0	227.7	190.9
US	123.8	162.9	207.8	191.0

Source: OECD

ments from only a small number of wealthy individuals or big institutions. In return it is freed from most types of regulation meant to protect consumers. Hedge funds are able to employ extremely aggressive investment strategies, such as using borrowed money to increase the amount invested and focusing investment on one or another type of asset rather than diversifying. If successful, such strategies can lead to very large returns; if unsuccessful, they can result in sizeable losses and the closure of the fund.

All investment companies earn a profit by charging investors a fee for their services. Some, notably hedge funds, may also take a portion of any gain in the value of the fund. Hedge funds have come under particular criticism because their fee structures may give managers an undesirable incentive to take large risks with investors' money, as fund managers may share in their fund's gains but not its losses.

Insurance companies
Insurance companies are the most important type of institutional investor, owning one-third of all the financial assets owned by institutions. In the past, most of these holdings were needed to back life insurance policies. In recent years, a growing share of insurers' business has

consisted of annuities, which guarantee policy holders a sum of money each year as long as they live, rather than merely paying their heirs upon death. The growth of pre-funded individual pensions has benefited insurance companies, because on retirement many workers use the money in their accounts to purchase annuities.

Pension funds

Pension funds aggregate the retirement savings of a large number of workers. Typically, pension funds are sponsored by an employer, a group of employers or a labour union. Unlike individual pension accounts, pension funds do not give individuals control over how their savings are invested, but they do typically offer a guaranteed benefit once the individual reaches retirement age. Pension-fund assets total about $10 trillion worldwide. Three countries, the United States, the UK and Japan, account for the overwhelming majority of this amount. Pension funds, although huge, are slowly diminishing in importance as individual pension accounts gain favour.

Other types of institutions, such as banks, foundations and university endowment funds, are also substantial players in the markets.

The rise of the formal markets

Every country has financial markets of one sort or another. In countries as diverse as China, Peru and Zimbabwe, investors can purchase shares and bonds issued by local companies. Even in places whose governments loudly reject capitalist ideas, traders, often labelled disparagingly as speculators, make markets in foreign currencies and in scarce commodities such as petrol. The formal financial markets have expanded rapidly in recent years, as governments in countries marked by shadowy, semi-legal markets have sought to organise institutions. The motivation was in part self-interest: informal markets generate no tax revenue, but officially recognised markets do. Governments have also recognised that if businesses are to thrive they must be able to raise capital, and formal means of doing this, such as selling shares on a stock exchange, are much more efficient than informal means such as borrowing from moneylenders.

Investors have many reasons to prefer formal financial markets to street-corner trading. Yet not all formal markets prosper, as investors gravitate to certain markets and leave others underutilised. The busier ones, generally, have important attributes that smaller markets often lack:

- **Liquidity**, the ease with trading can be conducted. In an illiquid market an investor may have difficulty finding another party ready to make the desired trade, and the difference, or "spread", between the price at which a security can be bought and the price for which it can be sold, may be high. Trading is easier and spreads are narrower in more liquid markets. Because liquidity benefits almost everyone, trading usually concentrates in markets that are already busy.
- **Transparency**, the availability of prompt and complete information about trades and prices. Generally, the less transparent the market, the less willing people are to trade there.
- **Reliability**, particularly when it comes to ensuring that trades are completed quickly according to the terms agreed.
- **Legal procedures** adequate to settle disputes and enforce contracts.
- **Suitable investor protection and regulation.** Excessive regulation can stifle a market. However, trading will also be deterred if investors lack confidence in the available information about the securities they may wish to trade, the procedures for trading, the ability of trading partners and intermediaries to meet their commitments, and the treatment they will receive as owners of a security or commodity once a trade has been completed.
- **Low transaction costs.** Many financial-market transactions are not tied to a specific geographic location, and the participants will strive to complete them in places where trading costs, regulatory costs and taxes are reasonable.

The forces of change

Today's financial markets would be almost unrecognisable to someone who traded there only two or three decades ago. The speed of change has been accelerating as market participants struggle to adjust to increased competition and constant innovation.

Technology

Almost everything about the markets has been reshaped by the forces of technology. Abundant computing power and cheap telecommunications have encouraged the growth of entirely new types of financial instruments and have dramatically changed the cost structure of every part of the financial industry.

Deregulation

The trend towards deregulation has been worldwide. It is not long since authorities everywhere kept tight controls on financial markets in the name of protecting consumers and preserving financial stability. But since 1975, when the United States prohibited stockbrokers from setting uniform commissions for share trading, the restraints have been loosened in one country after another. Although there are great differences, most national regulators agree on the principles that individual investors need substantial protection, but that dealings involving institutional investors require little regulation.

Liberalisation

Deregulation has been accompanied by a general liberalisation of rules governing participation in the markets. Many of the barriers that once separated banks, investment banks, insurers, investment companies and other financial institutions have been lowered, allowing such firms to enter each others' businesses. The big market economies, most recently Japan and South Korea, have also allowed foreign firms to enter financial sectors that were formerly reserved for domestic companies.

Consolidation

Liberalisation has led to consolidation, as firms merge to take advantage of economies of scale or to enter other areas of finance. Almost all of the UK's leading investment banks and brokerage houses, for example, have been acquired by foreigners seeking a bigger presence in London, and many of the medium-sized investment banks in the United States were bought by commercial banks wishing to use new powers to expand in share dealing and corporate finance.

Globalisation

Consolidation has gone hand in hand with globalisation. Most of the important financial firms are now highly international, with operations in all the major financial centres. Many companies and governments take advantage of these global networks to issue shares and bonds outside their home countries. Investors increasingly take a global approach as well, putting their money wherever they expect the greatest return for the risk involved, without worrying about geography.

This book

The following chapters examine the most widely used financial instruments and discuss the way the markets for each type of instrument are organised. Chapter 2 establishes the background by explaining the currency markets, where exchange rates are determined. The money markets, where euro-commercial paper and domestic commercial paper are among the instruments used for short-term financing, are discussed in Chapter 3. The bond markets, the most important source of financing for companies and governments, are the subject of Chapter 4. Asset-backed securities, complicated but increasingly important instruments that have some characteristics in common with bonds but also some important differences, receive special attention in Chapter 5. Chapter 6 deals with offshore markets, including the market for euro-notes. Chapter 7 discusses the area that may be most familiar to many readers, shares and equity markets. Chapter 8 covers exchange-traded futures, and Chapter 9 discusses other sorts of derivatives. The markets for syndicated loans and other kinds of bank credit are beyond the scope of this book, as are insurance products of all sorts.

2 Foreign-exchange markets

IN EVERY COUNTRY prices are expressed in units of currency, either that issued by the country's central bank or a different one in which individuals prefer to denominate their transactions. The value of the currency itself, however, can be judged only against an external reference. This reference, the exchange rate, thus becomes the fundamental price in any economy. Most often, the references against which a currency's value is measured are other currencies. Determining the relative values of different currencies is the role of the foreign-exchange markets.

The foreign-exchange markets underpin all other financial markets. They directly influence each country's foreign-trade patterns, determine the flow of international investment and affect domestic interest and inflation rates. They operate in every corner of the world, in every single currency. Collectively, they form the largest financial market by far. Hundreds of thousands of foreign-exchange transactions occur every day, with an average turnover totalling $1.9 trillion a day.

Foreign-exchange trading dates back to ancient times, and has flourished or diminished depending on the extent of international commerce and the monetary arrangements of the day. In medieval times, coins minted from gold or silver circulated freely across the borders of Europe's duchies and kingdoms, and foreign-exchange traders provided one form of coinage in trade for another to comfort people worried that unfamiliar coins might contain less precious metal than claimed. By the late 14th century bankers in Italy were dealing in paper debits or credits issued in assorted currencies, discounted according to the bankers' judgment of the currencies' relative values. This allowed international trade to expand far more than would have been possible if trading partners had to barter one shipload of goods for another or to physically exchange each shipment of goods for trunks of precious metal.

Yet foreign-exchange trading remained a minor part of finance. When paper money came into widespread use in the 18th century, its value too was determined mainly by the amount of silver or gold that the government promised to pay the bearer. As this amount changed infrequently, businesses and investors faced little risk that exchange-rate movements would greatly affect their profits. There was little need to trade foreign currencies except in connection with a specific transaction, such as an export sale or the purchase of a company abroad.

Even after the main economies stopped linking their currencies to gold in the 1920s and 1930s, they tried to keep their exchange rates steady. The new monetary arrangements created at the end of the second world war, known as the Bretton Woods system after the American resort where they were agreed, were also based on fixed rates. These arrangements began to break down in the late 1960s, and in 1972 the governments of the largest economies decided to let market forces determine exchange rates. The resulting uncertainty about the level of exchange rates led to dramatic growth in currency trading.

The amount of trading declined in the late 1990s for two principal reasons. First, the introduction of the euro as the currency of 12 European countries eliminated all exchange-market activity among those currencies. Second, consolidation in the banking industry worldwide greatly reduced the number of firms with a significant presence in the market. Currency trading rebounded in 2003–04 as institutional investors, especially hedge funds, speculated in foreign-exchange markets in hopes of generating greater yields than were available on stagnant stockmarkets.

How currencies are traded

The foreign-exchange markets comprise four different markets, which function separately yet are closely interlinked.

The spot market

Currencies for immediate delivery are traded on the spot market. A tourist's purchase of foreign currency is a spot-market transaction, as is a firm's decision immediately to convert the receipts from an export sale into its home currency. Large spot transactions among financial institutions, currency dealers and large firms are arranged mainly on the telephone, although electronic broking services have gained considerable importance. The actual exchange of the two currencies is handled through the banking system and generally occurs two days after the trade is agreed, although some trades, such as exchanges of US dollars for Canadian dollars, are settled more quickly. Small spot transactions often occur face to face, as when a moneychanger converts individuals' local currency into dollars or euros.

The futures market

The futures markets allow participants to lock in an exchange rate at certain future dates by purchasing or selling a futures contract. For example, an American firm expecting to receive SFr10m might purchase Swiss franc futures contracts on the Chicago Mercantile Exchange. This would effectively guarantee that the francs the firm receives can be converted into dollars at an agreed rate, protecting the firm from the risk that the Swiss franc will lose value against the dollar before it receives the payment. The most widely traded currency futures contracts, however, expire only once each quarter. Unless the user receives its foreign-currency payment on the precise day that a contract expires, it will face the risk of exchange-rate changes between the date it receives the foreign currency and the date its contracts expire. (Futures markets are discussed in Chapter 8.)

The options market

A comparatively small amount of currency trading occurs in options markets. Currency options, which were first traded on exchanges in 1982, give the holder the right, but not the obligation, to acquire or sell foreign currency or foreign-currency futures at a specified price during a certain period of time. (Options contracts are discussed in Chapter 9.)

The derivatives market

Most foreign-exchange trading now occurs in the derivatives market. Technically, the term derivatives describes a large number of financial instruments, including options and futures. In common usage, however, it refers to instruments that are not traded on organised exchanges. These include the following:

- **Forward contracts** are agreements similar to futures contracts, providing for the sale of a given amount of currency at a specified exchange rate on an agreed date. Unlike futures contracts, however, currency forwards are arranged directly between a dealer and its customer. Forwards are more flexible, in that they can be arranged for precisely the amount and length of time the customer desires.
- **Foreign-exchange swaps** involve the sale or purchase of a currency on one date and the offsetting purchase or sale of the same amount on a future date, with both dates agreed when the transaction is initiated. Swaps account for about 56% of all foreign-exchange trading. Normally, these are short-term deals, lasting a week or less.
- **Forward rate agreements** allow two parties to exchange

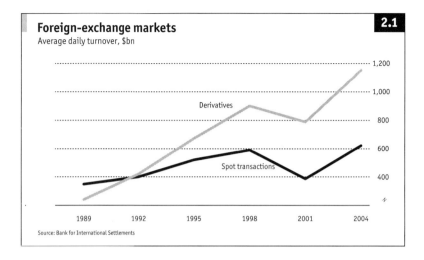

Foreign-exchange markets
Average daily turnover, $bn

2.1

Source: Bank for International Settlements

interest-payment obligations, and if the obligations are in different currencies there is an exchange-rate component to the agreement.

◪ **Barrier options** and collars are derivatives that allow a user to limit its exchange-rate risk.

Although large-scale derivatives trading is a recent development, derivatives have supplanted the spot market as the most important venue for foreign-exchange trading, as shown in Figure 2.1. (Derivatives are discussed further in Chapter 9.)

Currency markets and related markets

In most cases, foreign-exchange trading is closely linked with the trading of securities, particularly bonds and money-market instruments. An investor who believes that a particular currency will appreciate will not want to hold that currency in cash form, because it will earn no return. Instead, the investor will buy the desired currency, invest it in highly liquid interest-bearing assets, and then sell those assets to obtain cash at the time the investor wishes to sell the currency itself.

Gearing up

Investors often wish to increase their exposure to a particular currency without putting up additional money. This is done by increasing leverage or gearing. The simplest way for a currency-market investor to gain leverage is to borrow money to purchase additional foreign currency. Levering spot-market transactions is usually not worthwhile, as the interest that must be paid on the borrowed money can easily exceed the investor's gain from exchange-rate changes. Futures and options contracts allow investors to take larger bets on exchange-rate movements relative to the amount of cash that is required upfront. Large firms and institutional investors may take highly leveraged positions in the derivatives market, making large gains if the exchange rate between two currencies moves as anticipated but conversely suffering large losses if the exchange rate moves in the opposite direction.

The players

Participants in the foreign-exchange markets can be grouped into four categories.

Exporters and importers

Firms that operate internationally must pay suppliers and workers in the local currency of each country in which they operate, and may receive payments from customers in many different countries. They will eventually convert their foreign-currency earnings into their home currency. Historically, supporting international trade and travel has been the main purpose of currency trading. In modern times, however, the volume of currency dealing has swamped the volume of trade in goods and services.

Investors

Many businesses own facilities, hold property or buy companies in other countries. All these activities, known as foreign direct investment, require the investor to obtain the currency of the foreign country. Much larger sums are committed to international portfolio investment – the purchase of bonds, shares or other securities denominated in a foreign currency. The investor must enter the foreign-exchange markets to obtain the currency to make a purchase, to convert the earnings from its foreign investments into its home currency, and again when it terminates an investment and repatriates its capital.

Speculators

Speculators buy and sell currencies solely to profit from anticipated changes in exchange rates, without engaging in other sorts of business dealings for which foreign currency is essential. Currency speculation is often combined with speculation in short-term financial instruments, such as treasury bills. The biggest speculators include leading banks and investment banks, almost all of which engage in proprietary trading using their own (as opposed to their customers') money, as well as hedge funds and other investment funds.

Governments

National treasuries or central banks may trade currencies for the purpose of affecting exchange rates. A government's deliberate attempt to alter the exchange rate between two currencies by buying one and selling the other is called intervention. The amount of currency intervention varies greatly from country to country and time to time, and depends mainly on how the government has decided to manage its foreign-exchange arrangements.

The main trading locations

The currency markets have no single physical location. Most trading occurs in the interbank markets, among financial institutions which are present in many different countries. Trading formerly occurred mainly in telephone conversations between dealers, but trading over computerised systems accounted for 55% of London currency trading – and 76% of spot business – in 2004. These systems work in different ways, but in general a party seeking to exchange, say, €10m for yen will enter the request into a computer, and any interested banks will respond with offers of the exchange rates at which they propose to transact the trade.

Despite the legal and technological ability to trade currencies from anywhere, most banks conduct their spot-market currency trading in the same centres where other financial markets are located. London has emerged as the dominant location, with New York a considerable distance behind. Tokyo, which once challenged London and New York as a centre for currency trading, now lags far behind. A handful of huge international banks is responsible for most currency dealing worldwide. In London, ten banks handled 61% of spot-market trading and 79% of currency derivatives trading in 2004.

Table 2.1 on the next page lists the biggest national markets for trading in traditional foreign-exchange products, including spot-market transactions and simple types of exchange-rate derivatives. The amount of average daily trading reported in Table 2.1 far exceeds the amount of spot-market trading shown in Figure 2.1 on page 17, because some of the instruments considered traditional can be categorised as derivatives.

Table 2.1 **Geographic distribution of traditional currency trading**[a]

| | ——— April 1989 ——— | | ——— April 1998 ——— | | ——— April 2004 ——— | |
	Average daily turnover ($bn)	% share	Average daily turnover ($bn)	% share	Average daily turnover ($bn)	% share
UK	184.0	26	637.3	32	753	31.3
US	115.2	16	350.9	18	461	19.2
Japan	110.8	15	148.6	8	199	8.3
Singapore	55.0	8	139.0	7	125	5.2
Germany	n/a	n/a	94.3	5	118	4.9
Hong Kong	48.8	7	78.6	4	102	4.2
Australia	28.9	4	46.6	2	81	3.4
Switzerland	56.0	8	81.7	4	79	3.3
France	23.2	3	71.9	4	63	2.6
Canada	15.0	2	37.0	2	54	2.2

a Traditional products include spot transactions, forwards and foreign-exchange swaps.
Source: Bank for International Settlements

The pattern of currency futures trading is quite different. Exchange-rate futures were invented at the Chicago Mercantile Exchange. Almost all trading in exchange-rate futures now occurs either there or on the Brazilian exchange in São Paulo. In contrast, no exchange-rate futures contracts are traded on the main exchanges in the European Union or Japan. Many exchanges elsewhere do trade currency futures contracts, usually based on the exchange rate between the local currency and the dollar, the euro or the yen. However, trading volume in most of these contracts is extremely small.

Worldwide trading in currency futures peaked at 99.6m contracts in 1995. It then declined substantially as investors favoured derivatives that are not traded on exchanges, including forward contracts and swaps. Currency futures regained popularity in 2004 and 2005; total worldwide volume in 2004 was 83m contracts, double the figure for 2001. Table 2.2 lists the most heavily traded currency futures contracts.

Like exchange-rate futures contracts, currency options contracts have been popular mainly in the United States and Brazil. The leading exchanges for currency options are the Chicago Mercantile Exchange, the Bolsa de Mercadorias & Futuros and the Philadelphia Stock Exchange. Currency options are also traded on several other exchanges.

Table 2.2 **Largest exchange-rate futures contracts, 2004**

Contract	Exchange	Number traded
US dollars	Bolsa de Mercadorias & Futuros, Brazil	24,741,990
Euro	Chicago Mercantile Exchange	20,456,672
Japanese yen	Chicago Mercantile Exchange	7,395,322
Canadian dollars	Chicago Mercantile Exchange	5,611,328
Pounds sterling	Chicago Mercantile Exchange	4,676,512
Swiss francs	Chicago Mercantile Exchange	4,067,767
Mexican pesos	Chicago Mercantile Exchange	3,247,322

Source: Exchange reports

In most cases, contracts are based on the exchange rate between the local currency and the dollar, although some contracts use the yen, the euro or the pound sterling. Total trading volume worldwide peaked at 26.3m contracts in 1996, and was only half that level in 2004. Options are expected to become even less important in foreign-exchange trading as investors shift from exchange-traded instruments to over-the-counter derivatives, which can be designed to suit a particular investor's needs more precisely.

Trading in over-the-counter currency options also has rebounded after lagging in the late 1990s and early 2000s. The market value of over-the-counter currency options outstanding was $149 billion in September 2004, compared with $96 billion in 1998. According to a 2004 survey, the most important location for this business is the UK, which had a 33% market share, followed by the United States and Japan.

Favourite currencies

In the traditional market, the most widely traded currency is the US dollar, which has accounted for 40–45% of all spot trading since the first comprehensive survey in 1989. Table 2.3 on the next page lists the most widely traded currencies, by share of total trading in April 2004, when the most recent survey of currency-trading activity was conducted by central banks. The most popular currency trade, the exchange of US dollars and euros, accounted for 28% of currency-market activity, with dollar/yen trades accounting for 17%. Trades involving the euro and currencies other than the dollar accounted for only 8% of all turnover in the foreign-exchange market.

Table 2.3 **Traditional foreign-exchange trading, by currency[a], April 2004**

	% of average daily turnover[b]
US dollar	44.4
Euro	18.6
Japanese yen	10.2
Pound sterling	8.5
Swiss franc	3.1
Australian dollar	2.8
Canadian dollar	2.1
Swedish krona	1.2
Hong Kong dollar	1.0

a Traditional includes spot transactions, forwards and foreign-exchange swaps.
b Published figures double-count transactions; figures in this table represent half of official totals.
Source: Bank for International Settlements

The US dollar is more dominant in derivatives trading than in spot-market trading. About 27% of all over-the-counter currency derivatives traded in 2004 involved the dollar and the euro, and 18% involved the dollar and the Japanese yen. Euro/yen and euro/sterling trades each accounted for less than 3% of all trading in currency derivatives.

London is unusual among currency-trading centres in that its own currency, the pound sterling, has a comparatively minor role in the market. Only 14% of London trading in April 2004 involved sterling, whereas 90% of trades had one side denominated in US dollars. In London currency-derivative trading, 78% of deals involve the dollar. The main trades handled in London's spot and forward markets are listed in Table 2.4.

The location and composition of currency trading have been altered significantly by the launch of the single European currency, the euro, in January 1999. The volume of trading in many European centres, including Paris, Brussels and Rome, has fallen dramatically since the euro's introduction. The creation of the euro has also reduced the amount of trading in US dollars because many exchanges between smaller European currencies were formerly arranged by swapping into and then out of dollars; now, dealings between businesses in the euro-zone countries require no such complicated arrangements. Meanwhile, trading in some less prominent currencies, including those of Canada, Australia and the Scandinavian countries, has increased.

Table 2.4 **Development of the London market, share of spot and forward turnover (%)**

	1989	1992	1995	1998	2001	2004
Dollar/D-mark	22	24	22	22	...	...
Dollar/euro	...	...	...	...	34	33
Sterling/dollar	27	17	11	14	20	23
Dollar/yen	15	12	17	13	15	12
Dollar/Swiss franc	10	6	5	6	5	4
Dollar/Australian dollar	2	2	2	2	3	4
Dollar/French franc	2	3	5	5	...	...
Sterling/D-mark	3	5	3	3	...	...
Sterling/euro	...	...	...	...	3	3

Source: Bank of England

Trading in emerging-market currencies amounts to a tiny share of total daily trading. Almost all of this trading involves exchanges between the dollar and currencies from eastern Europe, Asia and Latin America. Trading in smaller currencies may decline further as east European countries seek to adopt the euro.

Settlement

Once two parties have agreed upon a currency trade, they must make arrangements for the actual exchange of currencies, known as settlement. At the retail level, settlement is simple and immediate: one party pushes Mexican banknotes through the window at a foreign-exchange office and receives US $20 bills in return. Trades on options and futures exchanges are settled by the exchange's own clearing house, so market participants face no risk that the other party will fail to comply with its obligations.

Large trades in the spot and derivatives markets, however, are another matter. When two parties have agreed a trade, they turn to banks to arrange the movement of whatever sums are involved. Each large bank is a member of one or more clearing organisations. These ventures, some government owned and others owned co-operatively by groups of banks, have rules meant to assure that each bank lives up to its obligations. This cannot be guaranteed, however. The total amount of a large bank's pending currency trades at any moment – its gross position – may be many times its capital. Its net position, which subtracts the amount the bank is expecting to receive from the amount it is expecting to pay, is always far smaller. But if for some reason not all of those trades are settled promptly, the bank could suddenly find itself in serious difficulty.

Herstatt risk

The greatest risk arises from the fact that trading often occurs across many time zones. If a bank in Tokyo agrees a big currency trade with one in London, the London bank's payment will reach the Tokyo bank during Japanese business hours, but the Japanese bank's payment cannot be transferred to the London bank until the British clearing organisation opens hours later. If the Japanese bank should fail after it has received a huge payment from the UK but before it has made the reciprocal payment, the British bank could suffer crippling losses, and its failure could in turn endanger other banks unconnected with the original trade. This is known as Herstatt risk, after a German bank that failed in 1974 with $620m of partially completed trades. Reducing Herstatt risk by speeding up the settlement process has become a major preoccupation of bank regulators around the world, but it has proved difficult to eliminate the risk altogether.

Why exchange rates change

In the very short run exchange rates may be extremely volatile, moving in response to the latest news. Investors naturally gravitate to the currencies of strong, healthy economies and avoid those of weak, troubled economies. The defeat of proposed legislation, the election of a particular politician or the release of an unexpected bit of economic data may all cause a currency to strengthen or weaken against the currencies of other countries.

Real interest rates

In the longer run, however, exchange rates are determined almost entirely by expectations of real interest rates. A country's real interest rate is the rate of interest an investor expects to receive after subtracting inflation. This is not a single number, as different investors have different expectations of future inflation. If, for example, an investor were able to lock in a 5% interest rate for the coming year and anticipated a 2% rise in prices, it would expect to earn a real interest rate of 3%.

Covered interest arbitrage

The mechanism whereby real interest rates affect exchange rates is called covered interest arbitrage. To understand covered interest arbitrage, assume that an investor in the UK wishes to invest £100 risk-free for one year, and can do so with no transaction costs. One possibility is for the investor to buy a one-year British government bond. Alternatively, the investor could exchange the £100 into a foreign currency, invest the foreign currency in a one-year government bond, and at the end of the year reconvert the proceeds into sterling. Which choice would leave the investor better off? That depends on the spot exchange rate; interest rates in sterling and in the foreign currency; inflation expectations; and the forward exchange rate for a date 12 months hence.

Suppose, to take a simple example, that the British interest rate is 5%, the US interest rate is 7%, the spot exchange rate is £1 = $1.60 and the one-year forward exchange rate is £1 = $1.61. Suppose further, for the sake of clarity, that the investor expects no inflation in either country, It would face the following choice:

Investment in the UK	Investment in the United States
Initial capital = £100	Initial capital = £100 × $1.60/£1 = $160.00
Sterling interest rate = 5%	Dollar interest rate = 7%
Capital after 1 year = £105.00	Capital after 1 year = $171.20
	$171.20 × £1/$1.61 = £106.34

With this combination of exchange rates, expected inflation rates and interest rates, the investor is guaranteed to earn a higher profit on US bonds than on British ones. The risk of buying US bonds is no higher than the risk of buying British bonds, as the investor can buy a forward contract entitling it to convert $171.20 into pounds at a rate of £1 = $1.61 in precisely one year, eliminating any need to worry about exchange-rate movements in the interim.

Covered interest parity

This guaranteed profit, however, will be fleeting. Many investors, whose computers are constantly scanning the markets for price anomalies, will spot this unusual opportunity. As they all seek to sell pounds for dollars in the spot market and dollars for pounds in the forward market in order to invest in the United States rather than in the UK, the pound will fall in the spot market and rise on the forward market. Eventually, market forces might lower the spot sterling/dollar rate to £1 = $1.59, and push the one-year forward rate to just above $1.62 = £1. At these exchange rates investors would no longer rush to exchange sterling for dollars to invest in the United States, because the one-year return from either investment would be the same. The two currencies will then have reached covered interest parity.

In the real world, of course, market interest rates and inflation expectations in all countries change by at least a small amount every day. For traders with hundreds of millions of dollars to invest, even the tiniest changes can create profitable opportunities for interest arbitrage for periods as brief as one day. Their efforts to obtain the highest possible return inevitably drive exchange rates in the direction of covered interest parity.

Managing exchange rates

Governments' decisions about exchange-rate management continue to be the single most important factor shaping the currency markets. Many different exchange-rate regimes have been tried. All fall into one of three basic categories: fixed, semi-fixed or floating. Each has its advantages, but all have disadvantages as well, as exchange-rate management is intimately related to the management of a country's domestic economy.

Fixed-rate systems

There are various types of fixed-rate systems.

◢ **Gold standard.** The oldest type of fixed-rate regime is a metallic standard. The most famous example is the gold standard, introduced by the UK in 1840 and adopted by most other countries by the 1870s. Under a gold standard a country's money supply is directly linked to the gold reserves owned by its central bank, and notes and coins can be exchanged for gold at any time. If several countries adopt the gold standard, the exchange rates among them will be stable. In the late 19th and early 20th centuries, for example, the British standard set £100 equal to about 22oz troy of gold and the American standard set $100 equal to 4.5oz, so £1 could be exchanged for $4.86.

This system was thought to be self-correcting. If a country ran a current-account deficit because, for example, it imported more than it exported, foreigners acquired more of its currency than they wanted to hold. The central bank could not eliminate the current-account deficit by devaluation, reducing the amount of gold that a unit of currency bought and thereby making exports cheaper and imports dearer, as the gold standard precluded devaluation. Instead, as foreigners exchanged currency for gold the central bank's gold stores dwindled, forcing it to reduce the amount of money in circulation. The shrinkage of the money supply would throw the economy into recession, bringing the current account into balance by reducing demand for imports. This proved to be a painful method of correcting current-account imbalances, and the era of the gold standard was marked by prolonged depressions, or panics, in a number of countries. A true gold standard has not been used since the end of the first world war.

◤ **Bretton Woods.** An alternative type of fixed-rate regime is that established at Bretton Woods, which was based on foreign currencies as well as gold. The Bretton Woods system tried to solve the problems of the gold standard by allowing countries with persistent balance-of-payments deficits to devalue under certain conditions. A new organisation, the International Monetary Fund (IMF), could lend members gold or foreign currencies to help them deal with short-term balance-of-payments crises and avert devaluation. In 1969 the IMF even created its own currency, special drawing rights (SDRs), which countries can use to settle their debts with one another. SDRs are distributed to central banks to increase their reserves. The value of SDR1 has arbitrarily been set equal to 58.2 US cents plus €0.3519 plus ¥27.2 plus 10.5 UK pence, so its value against any single currency fluctuates. The fixed-rate regime collapsed in the late 1960s and early 1970s for many of the same reasons as the gold standard.

◤ **Pegs.** Another form of fixed exchange rates is a pegged rate. This means that a country decides to hold the value of its currency constant in terms of another currency, usually that of an important trading partner. Denmark, for example, pegs to the euro, as it trades overwhelmingly with the 12 euro-zone countries. A peg is always subject to change, and the knowledge that this could happen can itself destabilise the currency.

A currency board is a particular type of peg designed to avoid destabilisation. The board, which takes the place of a central bank, issues currency only to the extent that each unit of currency is backed by an equivalent amount of foreign-currency reserves. This assures that any person wishing to exchange domestic currency for foreign currency at the official rate will be able to do so. If investors sell domestic currency, the currency board's reserves decline and it automatically reduces the domestic money supply by an equal amount, forcing interest rates higher and quickly slowing the economy. A currency board is able to stabilise the currency only to the extent that the government can resist the objections of those hurt when interest rates rise. The main difference between a currency board and a simple peg, aside from the mandatory reserves, is that changing the exchange rate under a currency board requires passing a law. Hong Kong has a currency board that pegs its currency to the US dollar. Estonia has a currency board that pegs to the euro.

Fixed-rate shortcomings

Despite their differences, all fixed-rate systems have the same short-comings. As long as people are free to move money into and out of a country, interest rates must rise high enough for investors to want to hold its currency because they can earn an attractive return. The country's central bank is therefore forced to use its monetary powers solely for the purpose of keeping the exchange rate stable. This means that the central bank cannot pursue other goals, such as fighting inflation or lowering interest rates to revive a depressed economy.

Argentina's fixed peg to the US dollar, backed by a currency board, collapsed in January 2002. Again, the system's inflexibility was at fault. Argentina's government, having surrendered control of monetary policy in the interest of a fixed exchange rate, was unable to lower interest rates to combat a depression. High and rising unemployment and falling economic output led to a political backlash that forced the resignation of the government and the abandonment of the one-to-one exchange rate between the peso and the dollar. Many Argentinian businesses that had contracted debts in dollars were forced to default on their obligations, because their income in devalued pesos was insufficient to service their dollar-denominated obligations.

A fixed exchange rate also creates a riskless opportunity for investors to borrow in a foreign currency that has lower interest rates than their own, and this can lead to financial crises. To see why, assume that country A, where the one-year interest rate is 10%, pegs its currency to that of country B, where the one-year rate is 5%. An investor from country A can borrow at 5% in country B, exchange the foreign currency for its domestic currency, invest the money domestically at a 10% return, and after one year obtain the foreign currency to repay the loan at the same exchange rate. Earning this riskless profit is sensible from the point of view of an individual borrower, but if many firms follow the same strategy, country A's central bank may lack the foreign-currency reserves to meet the demand for country B's currency at the fixed rate. It may have to abandon the fixed rate, making it more costly for borrowers to buy the foreign currency to repay their loans and forcing some of them into default. This was the cause of crises in Indonesia, South Korea, Thailand and other East Asian countries in 1997.

Semi-fixed systems

The practical problems with fixed-rate regimes have led to hybrid systems meant to provide exchange-rate stability, leaving the government more flexibility to pursue other economic goals. Because all these systems leave room for currency fluctuations, they lead to much more trading in foreign-exchange markets than fixed-rate systems. Most of these systems involve a managed float, in which a government allows the currency's value to change as market forces determine, but actively seeks to guide the market. Variations include the following:

◪ **Bands.** The European Exchange Rate Mechanism, to which most EU countries adhered before adopting the new single currency in 1999, involved agreement that exchange rates against the German mark would stay within certain bands. So long as a currency remained within its band, it was allowed to float. If, however, a currency lost or gained considerable value against the mark and reached the top or bottom of its band, the country's central bank was obliged to adjust interest rates to keep the exchange rate within the band. Unfortunately, this system of managed floating did not prove as stable as its designers had hoped. In 1992 and 1993 the mark appreciated strongly against the pound sterling, the Italian lira, the Swedish krona and several other currencies in the system, requiring these countries to raise interest rates sharply in order to keep their exchange rates within their bands. The UK eventually withdrew from the system and allowed its currency to float freely. Several other countries stayed within the system only after accepting large devaluations and setting new bands for their currencies.

- **Target zones.** These are similar to bands except that governments' commitments are non-binding. A government might proclaim its desire for its currency to trade within a certain range against another currency, but might not commit itself to acting to keep the exchange rate within that range. As with bands, one government might unilaterally set a target zone for its currency against another currency, or target zones might be agreed multilaterally by a group of countries.
- **Pegs and baskets.** A third variant of managed float is for a country to peg to a basket of foreign currencies, rather than to just one. If a country pegs to a single currency and that currency then rises relative to a third currency, imports from the third country will become cheaper and exports to that country harder to sell. This can lead to a balance-of-payments crisis. Setting the peg as the average exchange rate against several currencies, rather than just one, insulates the country from such problems to some extent. The government can manage the currency simply by changing the weights assigned to each of the foreign-exchange currencies in the basket. Singapore and Turkey are among the countries that manage their currencies against baskets of foreign currencies. In Singapore's case, the composition of the basket is secret and is thought to change from time to time; in Turkey's, the basket is known publicly. China announced in 2005 that it would value its currency against a basket of currencies rather than the US dollar alone, and it disclosed the currencies in the basket but not their weights.
- **The crawling peg.** This is a mechanism for adjusting an exchange rate, usually in a pre-announced way. A central bank might, for example, announce that it will allow its currency's exchange rate with the dollar to depreciate by 1% per month over the coming year. This is less rigid than a fixed exchange rate, but it entails the same basic commitment: the central bank must use its monetary policy to keep the currency depreciating at the desired rate, rather than for other ends. If investors judge that the exchange rate is depreciating too slowly, they may exchange their domestic currency for foreign currency *en masse*, causing the central bank to run short of foreign reserves and forcing a devaluation, just as occurs with a fixed rate. In the wake of such a crisis in 1994–95, Mexico abandoned its crawling peg against the US dollar and allowed its peso to float.

Floating rates

In a floating-rate system, exchange rates are not the target of monetary policy. Governments and central banks use their policies to achieve other goals, such as stabilising domestic prices or stimulating economic growth, and allow exchange rates to move with market forces. The world's main currencies now float freely against one another, creating a large demand for currency trading. Several important countries, including Mexico, Brazil and South Korea, have recently adopted floating rates after crises made managed exchange rates impossible to sustain. It would be incorrect, however, to say that exchange rates float completely freely. From time to time, one or more governments act, often without disclosing their intentions, to nudge a particular exchange rate in a certain direction. This usually occurs only when a currency is far cheaper or more expensive than economic fundamentals would seem to indicate.

The majority of countries manage exchange rates in one way or another. The lion's share of the world's economic activity, however, occurs in countries with floating rates.

Comparing currency valuations

How can markets and policymakers judge whether a currency is extremely overvalued or undervalued? This is not a simple question. Some would answer never, arguing that the current market price is the only good indicator of a currency's value. There is, however, considerable empirical evidence that foreign-exchange markets frequently overshoot. This means that when political or economic news causes a particular currency to rise or fall sharply, it moves further than careful analysis might indicate as many investors simultaneously act in the same way. Once the markets realise that the currency has overshot, it will partially retrace its movements and settle at an intermediate level.

Indications of overshooting

There are three different indications that a currency may be seriously misvalued. First, its exchange rates with other currencies may not be moving towards covered interest parity, suggesting that the markets expect a sharp rise or fall in the immediate future. Second, a country may run a large and persistent balance-of-payments deficit or surplus. Although it is not uncommon for a country to have a balance-of-payments deficit or surplus for many years, an extremely large deficit or surplus can indicate that the currency is far too strong or weak relative to the currencies of major trading partners.

The third indication of misvaluation is when the before-tax prices of traded goods in one country are very different from the prices in another. This approach draws on the theory of purchasing power parity, which holds that a given amount of money should be able to purchase similar amounts of traded goods in different countries. One simple guide to purchasing power parity is *The Economist's* Big Mac Index, which uses the cost of a hamburger in different countries, expressed in dollars, to estimate whether currencies are overvalued or undervalued relative to the dollar. More exhaustive analyses, which study the prices of various products in different countries, are published by the World Bank and private firms.

Managing floating rates

When they decide that exchange rates have veered far from levels they deem appropriate, governments and their central banks may endeavour to move the market. This is not difficult. If a government or a central bank manages to reduce investors' expectations of inflation, its currency will strengthen. If the central bank is able to reduce short-term interest rates while keeping inflation in check, the country's currency will weaken relative to the currencies of countries whose real interest rates have not declined.

In many cases, however, a government or central bank wishes to alter exchange rates without making fundamental changes in economic policy. It might deem its interest-rate policy appropriate for reducing unemployment, for example, even as it makes known its dissatisfaction with exchange rates. Trying to move exchange rates under such circumstances is more a psychological exercise than an economic one. The effort is bound to fail, because an economic policy can be used to achieve only one target at a time. If monetary policy is being used to achieve the goal of lowering unemployment, it cannot simultaneously be used to achieve a desired exchange rate.

In these circumstances, authorities often resort to intervention to support a currency that has been falling or drive down a currency that has been rising. Intervention, which is always done in secret, usually involves the use of a country's foreign-currency reserves to buy domestic currency in the markets, thereby strengthening the domestic currency's price. In some cases, central banks have intervened by purchasing their currency in the forward markets rather than in the spot market. Either method can inflict heavy losses on investors and traders who have bet aggressively that the currency will fall. Knowing of this danger, the foreign-exchange markets are extremely sensitive to the slightest hints from government officials that they would like to see exchange rates change.

The amount of money central banks can spend on intervention, however, is small relative to the amount of currency traded each day. It is also finite, limited by the amount of the country's reserves. As a result, neither intervention nor official comments that hint at intervention will affect exchange rates for long unless the country's economic policies are changed as well. Otherwise, traders will quickly sense that the central bank is losing its desire to intervene or is running short of reserves, and exchange rates will resume their previous course.

Obtaining price information

Except when a government supports a fixed exchange rate, there is no single posted price at which currencies are traded. Banks, electronic information systems such as Reuters and electronic currency-trading systems display price quotations on customers' screens. Normally, a dealer provides both a buy price, giving the amount of one currency it will pay for each unit of another, and a higher sell price at which customers may obtain currency. The spread between the buy and sell prices provides the dealer's profit and covers the cost of running the trading operation. The prices any dealer offers on screen, however, are strictly indicative; recent trades may or may not have occurred at these prices, and a customer may not be able to obtain a quoted price. Most dealers offer much more favourable rates on large trades than on small ones.

Many daily newspapers offer currency-price tables. These contain exchange rates drawn from those offered by dealers on the previous trading day, so they do not necessarily represent rates that will be available on the day of publication. These are normally rates offered on large commercial transactions, and are much more favourable than those available to the tourists who read them closely. Table 2.5 on the next page offers an extract from a typical newspaper currency-price table.

This table was published in the United States, and therefore states all prices in terms of US dollars; in other countries, the table would normally quote prices in the local currency. The countries listed are those whose currencies trade most actively against the dollar. Prices are reported in two different ways: columns two and three give the number of dollars required to buy one unit of the relevant currency on the last two trading days, and columns four and five give the number of units of the other currency that could be purchased for $1.

Table 2.5 **Typical newspaper currency prices**

Country	Exchange rate ($ equivalent)		Currency per $	
	Tuesday	Monday	Tuesday	Monday
Argentina (peso)	0.5263	0.5263	1.9000	1.9000
Australia (dollar)	0.5195	0.5152	1.9249	1.9410
Bahrain (dinar)	2.6525	2.6532	0.3770	0.3769
Brazil (real)	0.4227	0.4227	2.3655	2.3650
Canada (dollar)	0.6215	0.6203	1.6090	1.6121
1-month forward	0.6219	0.6209	1.6079	1.6105
3-months forward	0.6217	0.6207	1.6084	1.6112
6-months forward	0.6217	0.6206	1.6084	1.6113
Chile (peso)	0.001491	0.001494	670.55	669.15
UK (pound)	1.4288	1.4373	0.6999	0.6957
1-month forward	1.4256	1.4352	0.7015	0.6968
3-months forward	1.4205	1.4299	0.7040	0.6993
6-months forward	1.4201	1.4278	0.7043	0.7010

Forward rates

As well as spot rates, Table 2.5 also gives forward rates for the most heavily traded currencies, the pound sterling and the Canadian dollar. These represent the prices an investor would pay for currency to be delivered in one, three or six months. For the Canadian dollar, the forward rates barely differ from the spot rates, indicating that investors expect Canada's real interest rates to remain stable compared with US interest rates over the coming months, causing exchange rates to be stable as well. The pound sterling is expected to weaken slightly against the US dollar over the next six months.

Cross rates

A different kind of table is required to report currency cross rates. Table 2.6 lists the identical currencies across the top and down the left-hand side. The individual cells in the table offer each country's exchange rate with respect to the other country, without requiring that either currency be converted into a third currency, such as dollars. Hence, 10 Danish krone would purchase 2.148 Swiss francs on this date, while one Swiss franc would buy 4.655 krone. In practice, however, cross-trading is limited to the most heavily traded currencies. A Japanese

Table 2.6 **Currency cross-rates**

	C$	DKr	€	¥	NKr	SKr	SFr	£	US$
Canada (C$)		4.673	0.628	74.5	5.185	5.514	1.004	0.414	0.669
Denmark (Dkr)	2.140		1.345	159.4	11.100	11.800	2.148	0.885	1.432
Euro (€)	1.592	7.438		118.6	8.252	8.777	1.598	0.659	1.065
Japan (¥)	1.342	6.272	0.843		6.959	7.401	1.347	0.555	0.898
Norway (NKr)	1.929	9.013	1.212	143.7		10.640	1.936	0.798	1.290
Sweden (SKr)	1.814	8.474	1.139	135.1	9.402		1.820	0.750	1.213
Switzerland (SFr)	0.996	4.655	0.626	74.2	5.165	5.494		0.412	0.666
UK (£)	2.417	11.300	1.519	180.1	12.530	13.330	2.426		1.617
US ($)	1.495	6.985	0.939	111.4	7.750	8.243	1.501	0.618	

Note: Danish kroner, Norwegian krone and Swedish krona per 10; yen per 100.

firm would have no difficulty exchanging yen directly for euros. A Malaysian firm wishing to purchase Polish zlotys however, would first have to exchange ringgit for a major currency, such as euros or dollars, and then exchange these for zlotys.

Currency indexes
Evaluating changes in the exchange rate between two currencies is simple enough. Evaluating how a particular currency has performed over time, however, is much trickier, as the performance of that currency against many other currencies must be considered.

Trade-weighted exchange rate
The most widely used method for doing this is constructing a trade-weighted exchange rate, which is an index incorporating a currency's performance against a basket containing the currencies of all of its trading partners. The weighting is done based on the share of the country's trade that can be attributed to each trading partner. For example, Mexico's trade-weighted exchange rate depends heavily on the exchange rate between the peso and the dollar, as the United States accounts for about four-fifths of Mexico's foreign trade; and about half of the Czech Republic's trade-weighted exchange rate is determined by the exchange rate between the koruna and the euro. The index is arbitrarily set equal to 100 in some base year, and then measures how the currency has subsequently fared.

Figure 2.2 on the next page shows the weighted exchange rates for

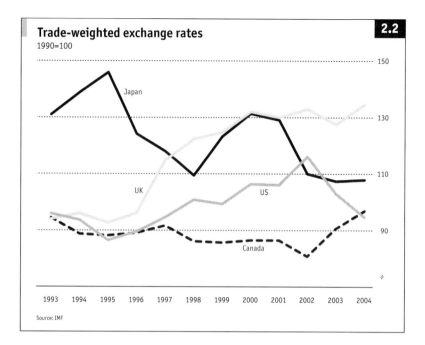

Trade-weighted exchange rates `2.2`
1990=100

Source: IMF

four currencies prepared by the IMF on the basis of their trade in manufactured goods with rich economies. Other methods of calculating trade weights would produce different changes in the currencies' measured performance.

These indexes suffer from problems common to all indexes, such as failing to accommodate changes in trade patterns since the start date. Nonetheless, they make clear two basic facts of life in the currency markets. First, no currency is strong forever, so buy and hold is not a profitable strategy in foreign-exchange markets. Second, currencies can fluctuate greatly over comparatively brief periods of time, offering potentially huge gains to investors who are astute enough to guess which way the markets will go.

3 Money markets

THE TERM "MONEY MARKET" refers to the network of corporations, financial institutions, investors and governments which deal with the flow of short-term capital. When a business needs cash for a couple of months until a big payment arrives, or when a bank wants to invest money that depositors may withdraw at any moment, or when a government tries to meet its payroll in the face of big seasonal fluctuations in tax receipts, the short-term liquidity transactions occur in the money market.

The money markets have expanded significantly in recent years as a result of the general outflow of money from the banking industry, a process referred to as disintermediation. Until the start of the 1980s, financial markets in almost all countries were centred on commercial banks. Savers and investors kept most of their assets on deposit with banks, either as short-term demand deposits, such as cheque-writing accounts, paying little or no interest, or in the form of certificates of deposit that tied up the money for years. Drawing on this reliable supply of low-cost money, banks were the main source of credit for both businesses and consumers.

Financial deregulation has caused banks to lose market share in both deposit gathering and lending. This trend has been encouraged by legislation, such as the Monetary Control Act of 1980 in the United States, which allowed market forces rather than regulators to determine interest rates. Investors can place their money on deposit with investment companies that offer competitive interest rates without requiring a long-term commitment. Many borrowers can sell short-term debt to the same sorts of entities, also at competitive rates, rather than negotiating loans from bankers. The money markets are the mechanism that brings these borrowers and investors together without the comparatively costly intermediation of banks. They make it possible for borrowers to meet short-run liquidity needs and deal with irregular cash flows without resorting to more costly means of raising money.

There is an identifiable money market for each currency, because interest rates vary from one currency to another. These markets are not independent, and both investors and borrowers will shift from one currency to another depending upon relative interest rates. However, regulations limit the ability of some money-market investors to hold foreign-currency instruments, and most money-market investors are concerned to minimise any risk of loss as a result of exchange-rate fluctuations. For these reasons, most money-market transactions occur in the investor's home currency.

The money markets do not exist in a particular place or operate according to a single set of rules. Nor do they offer a single set of posted prices, with one current interest rate for money. Rather, they are webs of borrowers and lenders, all linked by telephones and computers. At the centre of each web is the central bank whose policies determine the short-term interest rates for that currency. Arrayed around the central bankers are the treasurers of tens of thousands of businesses and government agencies, whose job is to invest any unneeded cash as safely and profitably as possible and, when necessary, to borrow at the lowest possible cost. The connections among them are established by banks and investment companies that trade securities as their main business. The constant soundings among these diverse players for the best available rate at a particular moment are the force that keeps the market competitive.

The Bank for International Settlements, which compiles statistics gathered by national central banks, estimates that the total amount of money-market instruments in circulation worldwide at December 2004 was $8.2 trillion, compared with $6 trillion in 2001 and $4 trillion at the end of 1995.

What money markets do

There is no precise definition of the money markets, but the phrase is usually applied to the buying and selling of debt instruments maturing in one year or less. The money markets are thus related to the bond markets, in which corporations and governments borrow and lend based on longer-term contracts. Similar to bond investors, money-market investors are extending credit, without taking any ownership in the borrowing entity or any control over management.

Yet the money markets serve different purposes from the bond markets, which are discussed in Chapter 4. Bond issuers typically raise money to finance investments that will generate profits – or, in the case of government issuers, public benefits – for many years into the future. Issuers of money-market instruments are usually more concerned with cash management or with financing their portfolios of financial assets.

A well-functioning money market facilitates the development of a market for longer-term securities. Money markets attach a price to liquidity, the availability of money for immediate investment. The interest rates for extremely short-term use of money serve as benchmarks for longer-term financial instruments. If the money markets are active, or "liquid", borrowers and investors always have the option of engaging in a series of short-term transactions rather than in longer-term transactions, and this usually holds down longer-term rates. In the absence of active money markets to set short-term rates, issuers and investors may have less confidence that longer-term rates are reasonable and greater concern about being able to sell their securities should they choose. For this reason, countries with less active money markets, on balance, also tend to have less active bond markets.

Investing in money markets

Short-term instruments are often unattractive to investors, because the high cost of learning about the financial status of a borrower can outweigh the benefits of acquiring a security with a life span of six months. For this reason, investors typically purchase money-market instruments through funds, rather than buying individual securities directly.

Money-market funds

The expansion of the money markets has been fuelled by a special type of entity, the money-market fund, which pools money-market securities, allowing investors to diversify risk among the various company securities in the fund. Retail money-market funds cater for individuals, and institutional money-market funds serve corporations, foundations, government agencies and other large investors. The funds are normally required by law or regulation to invest only in cash equivalents, securities whose safety and liquidity make them almost as good as cash.

Money-market funds are a comparatively recent innovation. They reduce investors' search costs and risks. They are also able to perform the role of intermediation at much lower cost than banks, because money-market funds do not need to maintain branch offices, accept accounts with small balances and otherwise deal with the diverse demands of bank customers. The spread between the rate money-market funds pay investors and the rate at which they lend out these investors' money is normally a few tenths of a percentage point, rather than the 2–4 percentage point spread between what banks pay depositors and charge borrowers.

The shift of short-term capital into investment funds rather than banks is most advanced in the United States, which began deregulat-

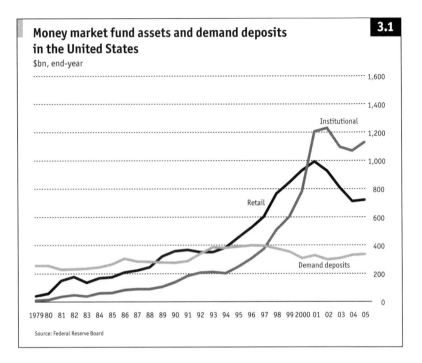

Money market fund assets and demand deposits in the United States

$bn, end-year

3.1

Source: Federal Reserve Board

ing its financial sector earlier than most other countries. The flow of assets into money-market funds is related to the gap between short-term and long-term interest rates; assets in US money-market funds fell between 2001 and 2005, as extremely low short-term interest rates encouraged investors to put their money elsewhere. Figure 3.1 illustrates the shift.

Investors in US money-market funds, which had $1.8 trillion in assets in 2005, own nearly one-quarter of all the money-market instruments in the world. Similar funds are gaining popularity in Europe, where equity investment trusts (mutual funds), all but unknown until recently, are becoming widely used investment vehicles. In Canada, assets of money-market funds fell from C$67 billion (US$42 billion) in 2001 to C$50 billion in mid-2005 because of the low interest rates on offer.

Individual sweep accounts

The investment companies that operate equity funds and bond funds usually provide money-market funds to house the cash that investors wish to keep available for immediate investment. People with large amounts of assets often invest in money-market instruments through sweep accounts. These are multipurpose accounts at banks or stockbrokerage firms, with the assets used for paying current bills, investing in shares and buying mutual funds. Any uncommitted cash is automatically "swept" into money-market funds or overnight investments at the end of each day, in order to earn the highest possible return.

Institutional investors

Money-market funds are by no means the only investors in money-market instruments. All sizeable banks maintain trading departments that actively speculate in short-term securities. Investment trusts (mutual funds) that mainly hold bonds or equities normally keep a small proportion of their assets in money-market instruments to provide flexibility, in part to meet investors' requests to redeem shares in the trust without having to dispose of long-term holdings. Pension funds and insurers, which typically invest with extremely long time horizons, also invest a proportion of their assets in money-market instruments in order to have access to cash at any time without liquidating long-term positions. Businesses in the United States owned $323 billion of money-market instruments, including commercial paper and shares in money-market funds, in mid-2005. Certain types of money-market instruments, particularly bank certificates of deposit, are often owned directly by individual investors.

Interest rates and prices

Borrowers in the money markets pay interest for the use of the money they have borrowed. Most money-market securities pay interest at a fixed rate, which is determined by market conditions at the time they are issued. Some issuers prefer to offer adjustable-rate instruments, on which the rate will change from time to time according to procedures laid down at the time the instruments are sold. Because of their short maturities, most money-market instruments do not pay periodic interest during their lifetimes but rather are sold to investors at a discount to their face value. The investor can redeem them at face value when they mature, with the profit on the redemption serving in place of interest payments.

The value of money-market securities changes inversely to changes in short-term interest rates. Because money-market instruments by nature are short term, their prices are much less volatile than the prices of longer-term instruments, and any loss or gain from holding the

Table 3.1 **Domestic money-market instruments worldwide ($bn, end-year)**

	1994	1996	1998	2000	2002	2004
Commercial paper	857.6	1,072.7	1,473.3	2,089.4	1,911.4	2,015.0
Treasury bills	1,993.2	1,965.4	1,826.2	1,888.2	2,318.3	3,413.2
Other short-term paper	1,385.7	1,610.6	1,860.1	1,930.8	2,064.1	2,743.9
Total	4,236.5	4,648.7	5,159.6	5,908.5	6,293.8	8,172.1

Source: Bank for International Settlements

security in the short time until maturity rather than investing at current yields is small.

Types of instruments

There are numerous types of money-market instruments. The best known are commercial paper, bankers' acceptances, treasury bills, government agency notes, local government notes, interbank loans, time deposits and paper issued by international organisations. The amount issued during the course of a year is much greater than the amount outstanding at any one time, as many money-market securities are outstanding for only short periods of time.

Commercial paper

Commercial paper is a short-term debt obligation of a private-sector firm or a government-sponsored corporation. In most cases, the paper has a lifetime, or maturity, greater than 90 days but less than nine months. This maturity is dictated by regulations. In the United States, most new securities must be registered with the regulator, the Securities and Exchange Commission, prior to issuance, but securities with a maturity of 270 days or less are exempt from this requirement. Commercial paper is usually unsecured, although a particular commercial paper issue may be secured by a specific asset of the issuer or may be guaranteed by a bank.

The market for commercial paper first developed in the United States in the late 19th century. Its main advantage was that it allowed financially sound companies to meet their short-term financing needs at lower rates than could be obtained by borrowing directly from banks. At a time when US bank deposits were not insured, short-term corporate debt was not necessarily a riskier investment choice for savers than

Table 3.2 **Commercial paper outstanding in the United States
($bn, seasonally adjusted, end-year)**

	Financial	*Non-financial*	*Total*
1990	421	150	571
1992	407	146	553
1994	444	165	609
1996	601	187	788
1998	936	227	1,163
2000	1,206	398	1,606
2002	1,101	269	1,370
2004	1,268	120	1,388

Source: Federal Reserve Board

a bank deposit. In the wake of the Great Depression, during which the government created a deposit-insurance scheme, the popularity of commercial paper declined. By the early 1980s, annual issuance of commercial paper in the United States was only about one-fifth the annual volume of bank lending.

Commercial paper became hugely more popular in the 1980s. At a time of high inflation and soaring short-term interest rates, regulations limited the interest that banks could pay depositors. Money-market funds enabled investors to earn higher rates than banks could offer, and strong non-banking firms discovered that they could raise money more cheaply by selling commercial paper to money-market funds than by borrowing from banks. These events caused the commercial paper market to thrive. It has continued to grow rapidly, with occasional interruptions due to conditions in the financial markets, as shown in Table 3.1. Issuance declined from 2001 to 2005, as some companies took advantage of low long-term interest rates to borrow in the bond market, and others were unable to sell additional commercial paper because of the deterioration of their financial condition.

Because financial deregulation came earlier in the United States than elsewhere, the US commercial paper market was the first to develop. However, commercial paper markets have developed rapidly in other countries, and the US share of worldwide issuance has declined.

In recent years, financial firms have become the most important issuers, as shown in Table 3.2. This category includes, for example, firms that finance industrial equipment, aircraft leasing companies and the financing subsidiaries of automobile manufacturers. These firms, which compete with banks, often find it profitable to use commercial paper to fund loans to individual borrowers without the expense and regulatory complications of becoming a bank and gathering deposits.

Commercial paper was slow to develop in most other countries, which lacked a legal framework for it. The exception is Canada, where there was C\$123 billion (\$99 billion) outstanding in mid-2005. Japan, the UK and the euro-zone countries have developed liquid markets for commercial paper, giving companies an alternative to bank borrowing or long-term funds.

In addition to domestic issues, \$495 billion of commercial paper was outstanding on international markets at June 2005. This amount refers to paper that was sold outside the issuer's country and was not denominated in the currency of the country where it was issued. Approximately half of international commercial paper was denominated in euros, one-quarter in dollars and most of the remainder in sterling. The share of international commercial paper denominated in euros has been increasing, as it can now be traded in the 12 countries of the euro zone with no currency risk. The largest single source of international commercial paper issuance is Germany, reflecting the difficulty of issuing such securities on the German domestic markets, followed by the United States, the UK, the Netherlands and Spain.

Many large companies have continual commercial paper programmes, bringing new short-term debt on to the market every few weeks or months. It is common for issuers to roll over their paper, using the proceeds of a new issue to repay the principal of a previous issue. In effect, this allows issuers to borrow money for long periods of time at short-term interest rates, which may be significantly lower than long-term rates. The short-term nature of the obligation lowers the risk perceived by investors. Thus, although gross issuance of commercial paper in the UK in 2004 came to £171 billion, net issuance, after repayment of previously outstanding paper, was only £4.5 billion.

These continual borrowing programmes are not riskless. If market conditions or a change in the firm's financial circumstances preclude a new commercial paper issue, the borrower faces default if it lacks the cash to redeem the paper that is maturing. This occurred to several major American and European companies in 2001 and 2002: the credit-rating agencies lowered their ratings, making it impossible for them to sell new commercial paper and thus confronting them with dire shortages of cash. Some of the companies were able to avert bankruptcy thanks to last-minute loans from banks, but others were forced to declare themselves bankrupt. The use of commercial paper also creates a risk that if interest rates should rise, the total cost of successive short-term borrowings may be greater than had the firm undertaken longer-term borrowing when rates were low.

Bankers' acceptances

Before the 1980s, bankers' acceptances were the main way for firms to raise short-term funds in the money markets. An acceptance is a promissory note issued by a non-financial firm to a bank in return for a loan. The bank resells the note in the money market at a discount and guarantees payment. Acceptances usually have a maturity of less than six months.

Bankers' acceptances differ from commercial paper in significant ways. They are usually tied to the sale or storage of specific goods, such as an export order for which the proceeds will be received in two or three months. They are not issued at all by financial-industry firms. They do not bear interest; instead, an investor purchases the acceptance at a discount from face value and then redeems it for face value at maturity. Investors rely on the strength of the guarantor bank, rather than of the issuing company, for their security.

In an era when banks were able to borrow at lower cost than other types of firms, bankers' acceptances allowed manufacturers to take advantage of banks' superior credit standing. This advantage has largely disappeared, as many other big corporate borrowers are considered at least as creditworthy as banks. Although bankers' acceptances are still a significant source of financing for some companies, their importance has diminished considerably as a result of the greater flexibility and lower cost of commercial paper. The amount outstanding in the United States peaked at $74 billion in 1974, and declined steadily to near zero by 2000. They are more extensively issued in some other countries, notably Canada.

Treasury bills

Treasury bills, often referred to as T-bills, are securities with a maturity of one year or less, issued by national governments. Treasury bills issued by a government in its own currency are generally considered the safest of all possible investments in that currency. Such securities account for a larger share of money-market trading than any other type of instrument.

The mix of money-market and longer-term debt issuance varies considerably from government to government and time to time. The US government sought to reduce the average length of its borrowing, starting in 1996, to reduce interest costs, but then announced in 2005 that it would resume issuance of 30-year bonds to finance an increased national debt. Approximately $900 billion in treasury bills with a maturity of one year or less was outstanding at the end of 2005, amounting to one-fifth of the public debt. The government of Japan had until recently exhibited a strong preference for long-term bonds, but sharply increased its issuance of short-term securities after 2001. The German government makes relatively little use of money-market instruments, relying more heavily on longer-term borrowings. France emphasised short-term government debt in 2004, but then replaced much of it with longer-term debt in 2005. The UK has traditionally avoided issuing short-term treasury securities, but it expanded the stock of short-term Treasury debt from £2 billion in 2001 to £20 billion in 2005.

In cases where a government is unable to convince investors to buy its longer-term obligations, treasury bills may be its principal source of financing. This is the main reason for the steep growth in treasury-bill issuance by the governments of emerging-market countries during the 1980s. Many of these countries have histories of inflation or political instability that have made investors wary of long-term bonds, forcing governments as well as non-government borrowers to use short-term instruments. As countries develop reputations for better economic and fiscal management, they are often able to borrow for longer terms rather than relying exclusively on short-term instruments. At the end of 1999, for example, 53% of the Brazilian government's debt was due within one year, but by 2005 only 30% was short-term.

Some emerging-market countries have issued treasury bills denominated in foreign currencies, mainly dollars, in order to borrow at lower rates than prevail in their home currency. This strategy requires frequent refinancing of short-term foreign-currency debt. When a sudden decline in the value of the currency raises the domestic-currency cost of refinancing that debt, the government may not be able to meet its obligations unless foreign investors are willing to purchase new treasury-bill issues to repay maturing issues. This caused debt crises in Mexico in 1995, Russia in 1998 and Brazil in 1999.

The overall size of the treasury-bill market changes considerably from year to year, depending upon the status of governments' fiscal policies. The market shrank in the late 1990s as a result of the shift from

Table 3.3 **Domestic treasury bills outstanding at year-end**

	$bn
	$bn
1996	2,002
1997	1,827
1998	1,826
1999	1,922
2000	1,833
2001	2,006
2002	2,317
2003	2,974
2004	3,413

Source: Bank for International Settlements

budget deficits to budget surpluses, which reduced government debt outstanding in the United States, Canada, most EU countries and some emerging markets, but then expanded after 2000 as many governments increased their budget deficits to combat recession (see Table 3.3).

Government agency notes
National government agencies and government-sponsored corporations are heavy borrowers in the money markets in many countries. These include entities such as development banks, housing finance corporations, education lending agencies and agricultural finance agencies.

Agencies of the US government have become some of the most important money-market borrowers. As shown in Table 3.4 on the next page, their issuance of short-term debt increased dramatically during the 1990s.

These figures include the paper of such agencies as the Tennessee Valley Authority, an electric utility, and Sallie Mae, a lender to students. Much of this issuance was of extremely short duration. For example, the Federal Home Loan Bank System, the central authority for savings institutions, issued some $6.6 trillion in paper during 2004.

Local government notes
Local government notes are issued by state, provincial or local governments, and by agencies of these governments such as schools authorities and transport commissions. The ability of governments at this level

Table 3.4 **Short-term debt issuance by US government agencies**

	$bn
1990	581
1992	817
1994	2,098
1996	4,246
1998	5,757
2000	8,745
2002	9,236
2004	10,422

Source: Bond Market Association

to issue money-market securities varies greatly from country to country. In some cases, the approval of national authorities is required; in others, local agencies are allowed to borrow only from banks and cannot enter the money markets.

One common use for short-term local government securities is to deal with highly seasonal tax receipts. Such securities, called tax anticipation notes, are issued to finance general government operations during a period when tax receipts are expected to be low, and are redeemed after a tax payment deadline. Local governments and their agencies may also issue short-term instruments in anticipation of transfers from a higher level of government. This allows them to proceed with spending plans even though the transfer from higher authorities has not yet been received.

The total size of the market for the short-term debt securities of state and local governments is difficult to estimate. In the United States, short-term borrowings represented 14–16% of such governments' debt issuance in 2003–04, but many local governments shifted to longer-term financing in 2005 as short-term rates rose and longer-term rates declined. About $60 billion of short-term local government securities were outstanding at the end of 2004. State and local governments in many other countries, notably Brazil, Canada and Italy, are frequent money-market borrowers as well.

Interbank loans
Loans extended from one bank to another with which it has no affilia-

tion are called interbank loans. Many of these loans are across international boundaries and are used by the borrowing institution to re-lend to its own customers. As of March 2005, banks had $12.6 trillion outstanding to banks in other countries, with almost all of this amount maturing with one year.

Banks lend far greater sums to other institutions in their own country. Overnight loans are short-term unsecured loans from one bank to another. They may be used to help the borrowing bank finance loans to customers, but often the borrowing bank adds the money to its reserves in order to meet regulatory requirements and to balance assets and liabilities.

The interest rates at which banks extend short-term loans to one another have assumed international importance. Many financial instruments have interest rates tied to LIBOR (the London Inter-Bank Offer Rate), which is the average of rates charged by important banks in the UK for overnight loans to one another. A newer interest rate, EURIBOR, the rate at which European banks lend to each other, fulfils the same function for financial instruments denominated in euros. In the United States the Fed funds rate, the rate at which banks with excess reserves lend to those that are temporarily short of reserves, is the primary policy lever of the Federal Reserve Board, and hence a closely watched economic indicator. Each of these rates is applied only to loans to healthy, creditworthy institutions. A bank that believes another bank to be in danger of failing will charge sharply higher interest rates or may refuse to lend at all, even overnight, lest the unsecured loan be lost if the borrower fails.

Time deposits

Time deposits, another name for certificates of deposit or CDs, are interest-bearing bank deposits that cannot be withdrawn without penalty before a specified date. Although time deposits may last for as long as five years, those with terms of less than one year compete with other money-market instruments. Deposits with terms as brief as 30 days are common. Large time deposits are often used by corporations, governments and money-market funds to invest cash for brief periods. Banks in the United States held $1.4 billion in large time deposits in 2005.

International agency paper

International agency paper is issued by the World Bank, the Inter-American Development Bank and other organisations owned by member governments. These organisations often borrow in many different currencies, depending upon interest and exchange rates.

Repos

Repurchase agreements, known as repos, play a critical role in the money markets. They serve to keep the markets highly liquid, which in turn ensures that there will be a constant supply of buyers for new money-market instruments.

A repo is a combination of two transactions. In the first, a securities dealer, such as a bank, sells securities it owns to an investor, agreeing to repurchase the securities at a specified higher price at a future date. In the second transaction, days or months later, the repo is unwound as the dealer buys back the securities from the investor. The amount the investor lends is less than the market value of the securities, a difference called the haircut, to ensure that it still has sufficient collateral if the value of the securities should fall before the dealer repurchases them.

For the investor, the repo offers a profitable short-term use for unneeded cash. A large investor whose investment is greater than the amount covered by bank insurance may deem repos safer than bank deposits, as there is no risk of loss if the bank fails. The investor profits in two different ways. First, it receives more for reselling the securities than it paid to purchase them. In effect, it is collecting interest on the money it advances to the dealer at a rate known as the repo rate. Second, if it believes the price of the securities will fall, the investor can sell them and later purchase equivalent securities to return to the dealer just before the repo must be unwound. The dealer, meanwhile, has obtained a loan in the cheapest possible way, and can use the proceeds to purchase yet more securities.

In a reverse repo the roles are switched, with an investor selling securities to a dealer and subsequently repurchasing them. The benefit to the investor is the use of cash at an interest rate below that of other instruments.

Repos and reverse repos allow dealers, such as banks and investment banks, to maintain large inventories of money-market securities while preserving their liquidity by lending out the securities in their portfolios. They have therefore become an important source of financing for dealers in money-market instruments. Many dealers and investors also take positions in the repo market to profit from anticipated interest-rate changes, through matched book trading. This might entail arranging a repo in one security and a reverse repo in another, both to expire on the same day, in the expectation that the difference in the prices of the two securities will change.

Investors like repos partly because of their flexibility. The average maturity of a repo is only a few days, but it is possible to arrange one for any desired term. An investor can arrange an overnight repo, which carries the lowest interest rate but must be repaid the following day; a term repo, which is settled on a specific date usually three to six months hence and carries a slightly higher rate; or an open repo, which continues until one or the other party demands its termination at a rate close to the overnight repo rate. Any type of security can be used, although in practice the overwhelming majority of repos involve national government notes or, in the United States, the notes of federally sponsored agencies.

The repo market was originally a result of government regulations limiting the interest banks can pay on short-term deposits. It has grown rapidly in the United States, the largest single market. The British repo market was slower to develop, and was not officially recognised by the Bank of England until January 1996. Since then the market has grown significantly.

Repos have historically been discouraged in France, where the legal basis for them was unclear before 1993, and in Germany, where banks were forced to set aside reserves for repo transactions until 1997, making such transactions uneconomic. Much trading in repos on German securities still occurs in London, for legal reasons. The French repo market has become quite large, but in Italy the market has remained small because of unfavourable regulations. In Japan, *gensaki*, repos with Japanese government bonds, have been traded since 1976. The *gensaki* market declined during the 1980s as a result of the increased use of commercial paper and a tax on transactions. By 1998 the average amount of *gensaki* outstanding was only about $90 billion. As part of its 1998 financial-market reform programme the Bank of Japan, the central bank, announced its intention to revive the Japanese repo market.

Futures and the money markets

Investors in the money markets also utilise futures contracts on money-market rates for a variety of purposes, including hedging and cash management. By buying or selling a futures contract on a short-term interest rate or a short-term debt security, an investor can profit if the relevant rate is above or below the chosen level on the contract's expiration date. Interest-rate futures can also be used to cover, or hedge, the risk that money-market instruments will decline in value owing to interest-rate changes. Futures markets in many countries trade contracts based on three-month government securities, and there are also contracts based on overnight bank lending rates. Institutional investors use futures contracts, along with short-term notes and commercial paper, as an integral part of their money-market strategies. (Futures markets are discussed in Chapter 8.)

How trading occurs

Trading in money-market instruments occurs almost entirely over telephone links and computer systems. The banks and non-bank dealers in money-market instruments sign contracts, either with one another or with a central clearing house, committing themselves to completing transactions on the terms agreed.

Some clearing houses are government entities, such as the Central Moneymarkets Office of the Bank of England, whereas others, such as the Depository Trust Company in New York and Euroclear in Brussels, are co-operative institutions owned by the banks and dealers active in the market. When a trade occurs, one or both parties is responsible for reporting the event electronically to the clearing house, which settles the trade by debiting the bank account of the dealer responsible for the purchase and crediting the account of the selling dealer. Most money-market instruments exist only in electronic book-entry form and are held by the clearing house at all times; after a trade, the clearing house simply holds the instrument on behalf of the new owner instead of the previous one. The clearing house thus reduces counterparty risk – the risk that the parties to a transaction might not live up to their obligations. It generally does not serve as an investigative or enforcement agency, so if there is a dispute between the putative buyer and seller as to the terms of a trade it must be resolved by the parties themselves or in the legal system.

Because of the large amounts of money involved, the collapse of an important bank or securities dealer with many unsettled trades could pose a threat to other banks and dealers as well. For this reason, clearing houses have been striving to achieve real-time settlement, in which funds and securities are transferred as quickly as possible after the transaction has been reported.

Credit ratings and the money market

Ratings agencies are private firms that offer opinions about the credit-

Table 3.5 **Short-term credit ratings**[a]

	Moody's	S&P	Fitch IBCA
Very strong capacity to pay	Prime-1	SP-1+	F1, F1+
Strong capacity to pay	Prime-2	SP-1	F2
Adequate ability to pay	Prime-3	SP-2	F3
Speculative ability to pay	Not prime	SP-3	B, C
In default			D

a Exact definitions used by agencies may differ.
Source: Ratings agencies

worthiness of borrowers in the financial markets. The issuers of treasury bills, agency notes, local government notes and international
agency paper usually obtain ratings before bringing their issues to
market. Some commercial paper issues are rated, although in many
cases the ratings agency expresses its view of an issuer's multi-year commercial paper programme rather than judging each issue separately.
Participants in interbank lending and buyers of bankers' acceptances
look for a rating not of the particular deal, but of the financial institutions involved.

Three firms, Moody's Investor Services, Standard & Poor's (s&p) and
Fitch IBCA, rate money-market issuers around the world. Their ratings
scales for short-term corporate debt appear in Table 3.5. Some of these
agencies maintain separate scales for rating short-term government
debt, commercial paper and banks' strength. Many other ratings agencies specialise in individual industries or countries.

Tier importance

These ratings have a great impact on the market. In the United States,
money-market funds invest overwhelmingly in Tier 1 commercial
paper, defined as paper having the highest short-term ratings from at
least two ratings agencies. Funds are prohibited from investing more
than 5% of their assets in Tier 2 paper, defined as paper that does not
qualify for Tier 1. As a result, comparatively little commercial paper is
issued by firms that cannot qualify for Tier 1, and there is almost no
below-investment-grade paper available in the market. Similarly, banks
that do not have high financial strength ratings will have difficulty
attracting certificates of deposit, and the lowering of a bank's rating by

any of the ratings agencies will cause depositors to demand higher interest rates or to flee altogether.

Money markets and monetary policy

The money markets play a central role in the execution of central banks' monetary policy in many countries. Until recently, the job of national central banks, which indirectly seek to regulate the amount of credit in the economy in order to manage economic growth and inflation, involved mainly purchasing and selling government debt to government-securities dealers in open-market operations. These operations involve adding money to or draining money out of the banking system, which encourages or constrains banks' lending and thereby affects spending and demand in the economy.

These days, however, central banks in countries with well-developed financial systems often manage monetary policy through the repo market rather than with direct purchases and sales of securities. Under this system, the central bank enters into a repurchase agreement with a dealer. The money it pays the dealer passes to the dealer's bank, adding reserves to the banking system. When the repo matures the dealer returns the money to the central bank, draining the banking system of reserves unless the central bank enters into new repo transactions to keep the reserves level unchanged.

If the central bank wishes to drain reserves from the system, it engages in a matched sale-purchase transaction, selling securities from its portfolio to dealers with agreements to repurchase them at future dates.

Central bank interest rates

In many countries, central banks can also lend directly to the money markets by providing credit to financial institutions at posted rates. Such loans are mainly for the purpose of helping institutions that have experienced sudden withdrawals of funds or otherwise face a lack of liquidity. Central bank loan rates are often less attractive than those available in the private sector, so as to encourage financial institutions to borrow in the money markets before turning to the central bank. Central bank rates change much less frequently than rates in the money markets. The main central bank loan rate in the United States and Japan is called the discount rate. The corresponding rate in the UK is the base rate and in Canada the Bank of Canada rate. The rate at which the European Central Bank (ECB) lends to banks in the euro zone is its marginal lending rate.

Open-market operations have a direct impact on interest rates in the money markets. A central bank is not able to exert direct influence over medium-term and long-term rates, but its use of money-market rates to accelerate or retard economic growth affects investors' expectations of inflation, which in turn influence longer-term rates.

Watching short-term interest rates

Central banks, governments and investors pay close attention to short-term interest rates.

Spreads

In particular, spreads, the differences in interest rates on different instruments, are highly sensitive indicators of market participants' expectations.

One important set of spreads is that between uncollateralised loans and repos. As repos are fully collateralised, there is almost no risk that repayment will be disrupted. Uncollateralised loans among banks, however, are at risk if a bank should fail. The spread between these two types of lending thus reflects perceived creditworthiness. Comparing spreads in various countries is instructive. During winter 1998, for example, the average spread between uncollateralised three-month loans and three-month repos was 21 basis points (hundredths of a percentage point) in the UK, 5.6 basis points in the United States, 8 basis points in France and 58 basis points in Japan, the much wider spread reflecting the general view that many Japanese banks were extremely weak.

The spreads between different categories of commercial paper are closely watched by the Federal Reserve in the United States and by the Bank of Canada. The spread between paper rated AA and that with a weaker A2-P2 rating is usually 15–20 basis points. A widening may indicate that investors are worried about a deteriorating economy, which would be more likely to cause financial distress for issuers of A2-P2 paper than for issuers of stronger AA-rated paper. A spread between top-rated commercial paper issued by financial companies and that issued by non-financial companies also indicates anxiety in the markets, as in good times paper from financial and non-financial issuers bears similar interest rates. The ECB's reliance on repos to implement monetary policy means that the two-week euro repo rate has become an important indicator. The spread between two-week repos on German government securities and short-term notes also receives considerable attention in the markets.

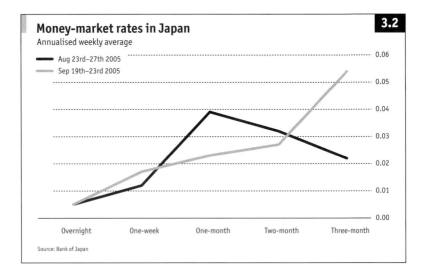

3.2

Money-market rates in Japan
Annualised weekly average

— Aug 23rd–27th 2005
— Sep 19th–23rd 2005

0.06
0.05
0.04
0.03
0.02
0.01
0.00

Overnight One-week One-month Two-month Three-month

Source: Bank of Japan

Overnight rates

Rates paid on overnight bank deposits also receive close attention. In some countries this is known as the call rate; in the euro-zone countries it is called EONIA (euro overnight index average). Differences in rates for money-market instruments of different maturities are among the most sensitive economic indicators. Consider Japan, where in 2005, after several years of poor economic growth and deepening problems in the banking sector, the economy began to show signs of recovery. Interest rates were extremely low throughout the year. In late August 2005, the closely watched call rate on overnight bank deposits earned interest at an average annual rate close to zero, and money placed on deposit for three months earned an average of 0.02%. One month later, as shown in Figure 3.2, the overnight rate was still negligible, but the rate on three-month deposits had begun to move up as borrowers increased their demand for funds.

In more technical language, the yield curve, which traces the interest-rate yields of securities of different maturities from the same issuer, steepened during the month, at least at the long end. Why? An investor with a three-month time horizon can choose to make 91 consecutive overnight investments rather than a single investment for three months. The three-month rate can therefore be thought of as a forecast of overnight rates for the coming three months. It is usually higher than the overnight rate to compensate for inflation, which could erode the value of the investor's principal over time. The drop in the three-month rate during December indicates that at the end of the month investors no longer expected overnight rates to rise as much as they had thought likely at the start of December. As overnight rates are strongly influenced by the policies of the central bank, this suggests that investors thought it less likely that the Bank of Japan would push up interest rates soon, presumably because economic conditions had not improved as much as had been expected. (The yield curve is discussed in more detail in Chapter 4.)

The prime rate

The prime rate was established decades ago as the interest rate charged by banks in the United States to their best corporate borrowers, and it receives a great deal of attention in the news media. Although big corporate borrowers are no longer affected by the prime rate, it is the basis for a large proportion of variable-rate consumer credit, including credit-card loans and home-equity loans. Thus a rise in the prime rate often curtails consumer spending. The rate, however, changes only infrequently and by increments of 0.25%, rather than daily in response to immediate money-market conditions. Another US money-market rate, that for US treasury securities adjusted to an average maturity of one year, is used as the basis for many adjustable-rate mortgage loans. Its economic impact has increased as more Americans have taken out adjustable-rate mortgages, although in the United States, unlike some other countries, interest rates on individual mortgages of this type change only once a year.

UK mortgage rates

Changes in the variable mortgage rates in the UK, in contrast, are passed on to homeowners within a matter of weeks and therefore have an almost immediate impact on the economy. These rates usually change in increments of 0.25%, and lenders are free to alter them, along with the mortgage payments they govern, as often as desired. This has made mortgage rates one of the UK's most sensitive economic indicators.

4 Bond markets

THE WORD "BOND" means contract, agreement, or guarantee. All these terms are applicable to the securities known as bonds. An investor who purchases a bond is lending money to the issuer, and the bond represents the issuer's contractual promise to pay interest and repay principal according to specified terms. A short-term bond is often called a note.

Bonds were a natural outgrowth of the loans that early bankers provided to finance wars starting in the Middle Ages. As governments' financial appetites grew, bankers found it increasingly difficult to come up with as much money as their clients wanted to borrow. Bonds offered a way for governments to borrow from many individuals rather than just a handful of bankers, and they made it easier for lenders to reduce their risks by selling the bonds to others if they thought the borrower might not repay. The earliest known bond was issued by the Bank of Venice in 1157, to fund a war with Constantinople.

Today, bonds are the most widely used of all financial instruments. The total size of the bond market worldwide at end-2004 was approximately $50 trillion, of which roughly $37 trillion traded on domestic markets, and another $13 trillion traded outside the issuer's country of residence.

In the United States, the largest single market, over $400 billion worth of bonds change hands on an average day, and the value of outstanding bonds at March 2005 exceeded $13 trillion. Table 4.1 shows the countries with the largest domestic debt markets.

Bonds are generally classified as fixed-income securities. They are often thought of as dull, low-risk instruments for conservative investors, as defensive vehicles for preserving capital in unsettled markets. Before the 1970s these stereotypes were true, but bond markets have changed dramatically over the past two decades. Some bonds do not guarantee a fixed income. Many bear a high degree of risk. All that bonds have in common is that they are debt securities which entitle the owner to receive interest payments during the life of the bond and repayment of principal, without having ownership or managerial control of the issuer.

Why issue bonds?

Bonds are never an issuer's only source of credit. All the businesses and

Table 4.1 **Outstanding amounts of domestic debt securities**[a]**, December 2004**

Country	$trn
US	24.7
Japan	15.7
Italy	3.9
Germany	3.4
France	3.3
UK	1.7
Canada	1.3
Spain	1.3
Netherlands	0.9
Belgium	0.8
China	0.8
Brazil	0.7

a Excludes asset-backed and money-market instruments.
Source: Bank for International Settlements

government entities that choose to sell bonds have already borrowed from banks, and many have received financing from customers, suppliers or specialised finance companies. The principal reason for issuing bonds is to diversify sources of funding. The amount any bank will lend to a single borrower is limited. By tapping the vastly larger base of bond-market investors, the issuer can raise far more money without exhausting its traditional credit lines with direct lenders.

Bonds also help issuers carry out specific financial-management strategies. These include the following:

- **Minimising financing costs.** Leverage, the use of borrowed money, enables profit-making businesses to expand and earn more profit than they could using only the funds invested by their shareholders. Firms generally prefer bonds to other forms of leverage, such as bank loans, because the cost is lower and the funds can be repaid over a longer period. A bond issue may or may not increase the issuer's leverage, depending upon whether the bonds increase the total amount of borrowing or merely replace other forms of borrowing.
- **Matching revenue and expenses.** Many capital investments,

such as a toll bridge or a copper smelter, take years to complete but are then expected to produce revenue over a lengthy period. Bonds offer a way of linking the repayment of borrowings for such projects to anticipated revenue.

- **Promoting inter-generational equity.** Governments often undertake projects, such as building roads or buying park land, that create long-lasting benefits. Bonds offer a means of requiring future taxpayers to pay for the benefits they enjoy, rather than putting the burden on current taxpayers.
- **Controlling risk.** The obligation to repay a bond can be tied to a specific project or a particular government agency. This can insulate the parent corporation or government from responsibility if the bond payments are not made as required.
- **Avoiding short-term financial constraints.** Governments and firms may turn to the bond markets to avoid painful steps, such as tax increases, redundancies or wage reductions, that might otherwise be necessary owing to a lack of cash.

The issuers

Four basic types of entities issue bonds.

National governments

Bonds backed by the full faith and credit of national governments are called sovereigns. These are generally considered the most secure type of bond. A national government has strong incentives to pay on time in order to retain access to credit markets, and it has extraordinary powers, including the ability to print money and to take control of foreign-currency reserves, that can be employed to make payments.

The best-known sovereigns are those issued by the governments of large, wealthy countries. US Treasury bonds, known as Treasuries, are the most widely held securities in the world, with $4.5 trillion in private ownership in mid-2005. Other popular sovereigns include Japanese government bonds, called JGBS; the German government's *Bundesanleihen*, or Bunds; the gilt-edged shares issued by the British government, known as gilts; and OATS, the French government's *Obligations assimilables du trésor*. Governments of so-called emerging economies, such as Brazil, Argentina and Russia, also issue large amounts of bonds.

Another category of sovereigns includes bonds issued by entities, such as a province or an enterprise, for which a national government has agreed to take responsibility. Investors' enthusiasm for such bonds will depend, among other things, on whether the government has made a legally binding commitment to repay or has only an unenforceable moral obligation. In many countries the amount of debt for which the national government is potentially responsible is extremely high. In the United States, for example, federally sponsored agencies had $2.7 trillion in bonds outstanding as of 2005. Although much of this does not represent legal obligations of the US government, the government would come under heavy pressure to pay if one of the issuing agencies were to default.

Lower levels of government

Bonds issued by a government at the subnational level, such as a city, a province or a state, are called semi-sovereigns. Semi-sovereigns are generally riskier than sovereigns because a city, unlike a national government, has no power to print money or to take control of foreign exchange.

The best-known semi-sovereigns are the municipal bonds issued by state and local governments in the United States, which are favoured by some investors because the interest is exempt from US federal income taxes and income taxes in the issuer's state. About $2.1 trillion worth were outstanding in 2005. Canadian provincial bonds, Italian local government bonds and the bonds of Japanese regions and municipalities are also widely traded. Many countries, however, deliberately seek to keep subsovereign entities away from the bond markets. This serves to limit their indebtedness, but also has the less noble goal of providing a steady flow of loan business to banks. Germany's states, or *Länder*, have emerged as significant issuers, with €170 billion of bonds outstanding at the end of 2004 – a leap from only €59 billion of bond indebtedness in 1999. German local governments, however, had almost no bonds outstanding.

There are many categories of semi-sovereigns, depending on the way in which repayment is assured. A general-obligation bond gives the bondholder a priority claim on the issuer's tax revenue in the event of default. A revenue bond finances a particular project and gives bondholders a claim only on the revenue the project generates; in the case of a revenue bond issued to build a municipal car park, for example, bondholders cannot rely on the city government to make payments if the car park fails to generate sufficient revenue. Special-purpose bonds provide for repayment from a particular revenue source, such as a tax on hotel stays dedicated to service the bonds for a convention centre, but usually are not backed by the issuer's general fund.

Public-sector debt, including sovereign and semi-sovereign issues, accounts for about 60% of all domestic debt worldwide. The total amount of public-sector debt outstanding at June 2005 was almost $24 trillion, of which $22 trillion was issued by governments within their domestic bond markets and $1.4 trillion was issued internationally.

Corporations
Corporate bonds are issued by a business enterprise, whether owned by private investors or by a government. Large firms may have many debt issues outstanding at a given time. In issuing a secured obligation, the firm must pledge specific assets to bondholders. In the case of an electric utility that sells secured bonds to finance a generating plant, for example, the bondholders might be entitled to take possession of and sell the plant if the company defaults on its bonds, but they would have no claim on other generating plants or the revenue they earn. The holders of general-purpose debt have first claim on the company's revenue and assets if the firm defaults, save those pledged to secured bondholders. The holders of subordinated debt have no claim on assets or income until all other bondholders have been paid. A big firm may have several classes of subordinated debt. Mezzanine debt is a bond issue that has less security than the issuer's other bonds, but more than its shares.

Securitisation vehicles
An asset-backed security is a type of bond on which the required payments will be made out of the income generated by specific assets, such as mortgage loans or future sales. Some asset-backed securities are initiated by government agencies, others by private-sector entities. These sorts of securities are assembled by an investment bank, and often do not represent the obligations of a particular issuer. (Asset-backed securities are discussed in Chapter 5.)

The distinctions among the various categories of bonds are often blurred. Government agencies, for example, frequently issue bonds to assist private companies, although investors may have no legal claim against the government if the issuer fails to pay. National governments may lend their moral support, but not necessarily their full faith and credit, to bond issues by state-owned enterprises or even by private enterprises. Corporations in one country may arrange for bonds to be issued by subsidiaries in other countries, eliminating the parent's liability in the event of default but making payment dependent upon the policies of the foreign government.

Table 4.2 **Outstanding private-sector domestic debt securities ($bn)**

	1993	1998	2000	2002	2004
US	3,419	5,984	6,504	11,761	13,661
Japan	1,325	1,453	1,543	1,829	2,030
Germany	738	1,140	956	966	1,033
France	541	477	432	645	959
Italy	300	364	296	544	877
UK	134	388	470	290	367
Total	6,503	11,302	11,829	18,239	22,346

Source: Bank for International Settlements

Bond futures

Futures contracts on interest rates are traded on exchanges in many countries. These contracts allow investors to receive payment if an interest rate is above or below a specified level on the contract's expiration date. Large investors use such contracts as an integral part of their bond-investment strategies. (Futures contracts are discussed in Chapter 8; interest-rate options and forwards, which can also be used to manage the risk that interest rates will change, in Chapter 9.)

The biggest national markets

Corporate bonds and some asset-backed securities are the main components of the private-sector debt market. This market has been growing rapidly overall, although in a few countries, notably Japan and France, the value of outstanding bonds has diminished (see Table 4.2).

As Table 4.2 illustrates, a disproportionate share of the world's private-sector debt securities is issued in the United States. This is largely the result of deliberate efforts to retard the development of bond markets in many other countries. In Japan, the Bond Issue Arrangement Committee, a bankers' group encouraged by the government, controlled costs and the timing of issuance until 1987, and a bankers' cartel kept fees high. In Germany, regulations up to 1984 prohibited companies from selling bonds with terms of less than five years and required approval from the finance ministry for each issue. France barred corporate issues with terms of less than seven years before 1992, required Treasury approval of the details of each issue and required a committee of bankers and public officials to approve the timing so that private-sector issues would not interfere with the government's borrowing plans. Such restrictions encouraged the use of bank financing rather than bonds. The European corporate-bond market has grown rapidly since the introduction of a single currency in 12 EU countries created a large pool of investors who could purchase a bond denominated in euros without exposing themselves to the risk of exchange-rate changes.

Bond markets in many countries expanded rapidly in 2002–04. This was partly the result of low interest rates around the world, and partly the consequence of a more stable macroeconomic environment, which gave investors increased confidence in owning long-term obligations.

Issuing bonds

National regulations detail the steps required to issue bonds. Each issue is preceded by a lengthy legal document, variously called the offer document, prospectus or official statement, which lays out in detail the financial condition of the issuer; the purposes for which the debt is being sold; the schedule for the interest and principal payments required to service the debt; and the security offered to bondholders in the event the debt is not serviced as required. Investors scrutinise such documents carefully, because details specific to the issue have a great impact on the probability of timely payment. In some cases, regulators must review the offer document to determine whether the disclosures are sufficient, and may block the bond issue until additional information is provided. Issuers in the United States may file a shelf registration to obtain advance approval for a large volume of bonds, which can be sold in pieces, or tranches, whenever market conditions appear favourable. Most other countries have not adopted this innovation.

Underwriters and dealers

Issuers sell their bonds to the public with the help of underwriters and dealers. An issue may be underwritten by a single investment banking firm or by a group of them, referred to as a syndicate. Many syndicates include investment banks from different countries, the better to sell the bonds internationally. The issuer normally chooses one or two firms to be the lead underwriters. They are responsible for arranging the syndicate and for allocating a proportion of the bonds to each of the member firms. Formerly, dozens of firms competed in the underwriting business. However, mergers and acquisitions among banks have led to the creation of a handful of huge investment banks, most of them based in the United States, that dominate bond underwriting throughout the world.

The underwriters may receive a fee from the issuer in return for arranging the issue and marketing it to potential investors. Alternatively, they may purchase the bonds from the issuer at a discount and resell them to the public at a higher price, profiting from the mark-up. If the investment bankers underwrite the issue on a firm commitment basis, they guarantee the price the issuer will receive and take the risk of loss if purchasers do not come forward at that price. They may instead underwrite the bonds with only their best efforts, in which case the issuer receives whatever price investors will pay and the underwriter takes no risk if the bonds fail to sell at a particular price. The underwriters may sell bonds at a discount to dealers, who take no underwriting risk but handle sales to smaller investors.

National governments often distribute their bonds through primary dealers without the assistance of underwriters. Primary dealers have the obligation, and often the exclusive right, to participate in the government's bond sales, and then resell the bonds to investors.

Swaps

The fact that an issuer has sold a particular bond issue need not mean that the issuer is paying the expected amount of interest on that issue. Increasingly, issuers make use of interest-rate swaps to obtain the financing schedule they desire. For example, an issuer might issue $100m of five-year notes at a fixed interest rate, and then immediately enter into a swap transaction whereby an investment bank meets those fixed payments and the issuer makes floating-rate payments to the bank. Whether such a transaction saves costs or reduces risk for the issuer depends upon the swap spread – the difference between a fixed rate and the current floating rate for a swap of a given maturity.

Setting the interest rate

The interest rate on a bond issue can be determined by a variety of methods. The most common is for the underwriter to set the rate based on market rates on the day of issuance. This, however, involves a certain amount of guesswork, and can lead either to excessive costs for the issuer if the interest rate is set too high, or to the underwriter being stuck with unsold bonds if the rate is set too low. Most syndicates prohibit their members from selling the bonds at less than the agreed price for a certain period of time, to keep the syndicate members from competing against one another.

An alternative method of determining interest rates involves auctions. There are several auction techniques used in the bond markets. Competitive-bid auctions allow investors or dealers to offer a price for bonds being issued at particular interest rate (or, alternatively, to offer an acceptable interest rate for bonds being sold at par value). The offered price may go higher (or the offered rate lower) in successive rounds of bidding. The bonds may all be sold at the single highest price at which there are sufficient offers to sell the entire issue, or, in a multiple-price auction, each bidder that wins a share of the bonds will pay the last price it bid. In a sealed-bid action bids are submitted in writing. One popular type of sealed-bid auction is a Dutch auction, in which the issuer sets an interest rate and bidders then submit schedules stating how many bonds they would buy at various prices; the bonds are sold at the highest price at which the entire issue is taken up.

Selling direct

New technology has made it practical for some issuers to sell their bonds directly to investors over the internet, without the intermediation of underwriters or dealers. This is likely to lead to lower costs for some issuers, and to reduce the profits of investment banks and brokers that underwrite and sell bonds.

The first online issue was an offering of $55m by the city of Pittsburgh, Pennsylvania, in November 1999. Since then, volume has grown rapidly. So far, all of these sales have involved only institutional investors. The investors have been able to learn about the issues, read financial materials and submit "indications of interest" – tentative offers – over the internet, but the bonds have not actually been auctioned online.

Most electronic underwritings have involved well-known issuers. Investment banks have been involved in each bond issue, although it is believed that the banks receive smaller fees for distributing new issues online than for traditional underwritings.

No more coupons

In the past, bond purchasers were given certificates as proof of their ownership. The certificates would often come with coupons attached, one for each interest payment due on the bonds. The investor would detach the appropriate coupon and take it to the bank or securities broker in order to receive the payment.

Paper bonds are now less common. They are still used for some registered bonds, which are issued in the name of the holder, and for bearer bonds, which are not registered in a particular name and may be sold by whoever has physical possession. Most debt securities, however, are issued as book-entry bonds, existing only as electronic entries in the computer of the trustee, the bank that is responsible for making interest payments on behalf of the issuer and, eventually, for redeeming the bonds. Tax authorities increasingly insist that bonds be issued in the name of a specific bondholder, as interest payments on bearer bonds are difficult to tax.

The changing nature of the market

Until the 1970s the bond market was principally a primary market. This meant that investors would purchase bonds at the time of issuance and hold the bonds until the principal was repaid. Their highly predictable cash flow made bonds attractive assets to investors such as life insurance companies and pension funds, the obligations of which could be predicted far in advance. The basic investment strategy was to match assets and liabilities. An investor would estimate its financial requirements in a certain future year, often 10 or 20 years hence, and would then search for bonds of acceptable quality that would be repaid at that time. Successful bond investors were those who managed to buy bonds offering slightly higher yields than other bonds of similar quality.

Since the late 1970s, the reasons for investing in bonds have changed. Many investors now actively trade bonds to take advantage of price differences, rather than holding them over the long term. Two developments have brought about this change. First, computers have made it possible for traders to spot price differences quickly. Second, whereas investors previously valued all their bonds at the original purchase price until they were sold, accounting rules now require that under certain conditions bonds be valued at their current market value, or "marked to market". As this requires the owner to record any loss or gain during each reporting period regardless of whether a bond is sold, there may be no advantage in holding rather than selling it.

Secondary dealing

Some corporate bonds trade on stock exchanges, where brokers for buyers and sellers meet face-to-face. The vast majority of bond trading, though, occurs in the over-the-counter market, directly between an

investor and a bond dealer. Most trades are made over a telephone linking investor and dealer.

Whatever the system, an institutional investor wishing to purchase
or sell a bond makes its desire known, usually by calling several dealers.
Dealers which hold or are willing to hold inventories of that bond
respond with a bid price if they are offering to buy, or an asking price if
they are offering to sell. Government bonds are traded by many dealers,
and the spread between bid and ask prices is often razor-thin. Popular
corporate issues will be actively traded by a dozen or more dealers and
usually have wider bid-ask spreads than government bonds. Smaller
issues by corporations or sub-sovereigns can be difficult to trade, as
there may be only one or two dealers interested in buying or selling the
bonds. In some cases, it may not be possible to acquire a particular bond
as none is being offered in the market.

Electronic trading

Much effort and money has gone into building electronic trading systems. By 2002, 81 screen-based bond-trading systems were in operation, some belonging to a single dealer and others bringing many
dealers together. The market was unable to support so many competi-
tors and many of these nascent electronic bond exchanges have failed.
Electronic trading has been extremely successful in the government
bond market, where the number of different securities is small and liquidity – the amount available for investment – is high. Electronic systems accounted for about three-quarters of trading in European
government bonds in 2004. Most electronic systems also offer online
trading of commercial paper, emerging-market bonds and other fixed-
income products.

Trading of corporate and municipal bonds has proven surprisingly
difficult to automate because of three characteristics of these markets.
First, institutional investors often pursue strategies that require near-
simultaneous transactions. For example, an investor may wish to sell
the DaimlerChrysler bonds in its portfolio and purchase General Motors
bonds, which are currently cheaper. But this transaction is uninteresting
unless the investor can complete both legs – it does not wish to sell
DaimlerChrysler and then find that it cannot obtain the General Motors
bonds. Such transactions may be difficult to consummate without discussion with dealers, whose inventories of bonds allow them to assure
clients that the entire transaction can be completed.

Second, obtaining full price information is a persistent problem in bond trading. As comparatively little bond trading occurs on exchanges, there is no way to ensure that all trades are publicly reported. In the corporate-bond market, only the dealer and its customer know the price at which a particular bond has traded. The prices posted by dealers and released to financial information providers may or may not reflect the prices at which trades have actually occurred.

Third, the number of bonds issued by companies, and by local governments and their agencies, is vast. A large corporation may have dozens of different bonds outstanding, each with different characteristics. Most of these bonds are traded rarely, if ever, after initial issuance. An investor posting an electronic offer to buy or sell such a security is unlikely to find a taker – in market parlance, trading in such issues is illiquid. The investor may be better served by talking to a dealer, who may be willing to trade the bonds or may know of another investor prepared to buy or sell that specific issue.

Electronic trading is likely to lead to increased price transparency, at least for some types of securities, and this will help reduce investors' costs. As the technology develops, electronic trading systems may take on an important role in the dealing of large, heavily traded issues. However, they are unlikely to be an efficient way of buying and selling the millions of smaller bond issues outstanding. The existence of this enormous variety of bonds will continue to assure a role, albeit a lesser one, for bond dealers.

Settlement

Central banks have made considerable efforts to shorten the time between execution of a trade and the exchange of money and payment. The shorter the settlement time, in general, the lower is the risk that a bank or securities firm will be harmed by the collapse of another firm with which it has traded. Central banks in wealthier countries are encouraging traders in government securities to settle no later than the next business day. Such an effort in Japan has led to about three-quarters of all trades settling before 10am on the following day; in December 2001, only 240 of 161,796 trades failed to settle within 24 hours.

Types of bonds

An increasing variety of bonds is available in the marketplace. In some cases, an issuer agrees to design a bond with the specific characteristics required by a particular institutional investor. Such a bond is then privately placed and is not traded in the bond markets. Bonds that are issued in the public markets generally fit into one or more of the following categories.

Straight bonds

Also known as debentures, straight bonds are the basic fixed-income investment. The owner receives interest payments of a predetermined amount on specified dates, usually every six months or every year following the date of issue. The issuer must redeem the bond from the owner at its face value, known as the par value, on a specific date.

Callable bonds

The issuer may reserve the right to call the bonds at particular dates. A call obliges the owner to sell the bonds to the issuer for a price, specified when the bond was issued, that usually exceeds the current market price. The difference between the call price and the current market price is the call premium. A bond that is callable is worth less than an identical bond that is non-callable, to compensate the investor for the risk that it will not receive all of the anticipated interest payments.

Non-refundable bonds

These may be called only if the issuer is able to generate the funds internally, from sales or taxes. This prohibits an issuer from selling new bonds at a lower interest rate and using the proceeds to call bonds that bear a higher interest rate.

Putable bonds

Putable bonds give the investor the right to sell the bonds back to the issuer at par value on designated dates. This benefits the investor if interest rates rise, so a putable bond is worth more than an identical bond that is not putable.

Perpetual debentures

Also known as irredeemable debentures, perpetual debentures are bonds that will last forever unless the holder agrees to sell them back to the issuer.

Zero-coupon bonds

Zero-coupon bonds do not pay periodic interest. Instead, they are issued at less than par value and are redeemed at par value, with the difference serving as an interest payment. Zeros are designed to eliminate reinvestment risk, the loss an investor suffers if future income or principal payments from a bond must be invested at lower rates than those available today. The owner of a zero-coupon bond has no payments to reinvest until the bond matures, and therefore has greater certainty about the return on the investment.

STRIPS

STRIPS (an acronym for Separately Registered Interest and Principal of Securities) are an innovation related to zero-coupon bonds. STRIPS turn the payments associated with a bond into separate securities, one for each payment involved. Thus a ten-year bond with semi-annual interest payments could be restructured as up to 21 different securities, with 20 representing the right to each of the interest payments to be made over the bond's term and one the right to receive the principal when it is repaid. Each of these securities is effectively a zero-coupon bond, which is sold for less than the related payment and is redeemed at face value. Federal Reserve Banks will strip US Treasury bonds at the request of securities dealers, and the British government's debt-management office does the same with certain gilts. The Deutsche Bundesbank, the German central bank, also offers stripped securities. Investment banks may construct similar securities from any bond to meet the needs of particular investors.

Convertible bonds

Under specified conditions and strictly at the bondholder's option, convertible bonds may be exchanged for another security, usually the issuer's common shares. The prospectus for a convertible issue specifies the conversion ratio, the number of shares for which each bond may be exchanged. A convertible bond has a conversion value, which is simply the price of the common shares for which it may be traded. The buyer must usually pay a premium over conversion value, to reflect the fact that the bond pays interest until and unless it is converted. Convertibles often come with hard call protection, which prohibits the issuer from calling the bonds before the conversion date.

Adjustable bonds

There are many varieties of adjustable bonds. The interest rate on a floating-rate bond can change frequently, usually depending on short-term interest rates. The rate on a variable-rate bond may be changed only once a year, and is usually related to long-term interest rates. A step-up note will have an increase in the interest rate no more than once a year, according to a formula specified in the prospectus. Inflation-indexed bonds seek to protect against the main risk of bond investing: the likelihood that inflation will erode the value of both interest payments and principal. Capital-indexed bonds apply an inflation adjustment to interest payments as well as to principal. Interest-indexed bonds adjust interest payments for inflation, but the value of the principal itself is not adjusted for inflation. Indexed zero-coupon bonds pay an inflation-adjusted principal upon redemption.

Structured securities

Bonds that have options attached to them are called structured securities. Callable, putable and convertible bonds are simple examples of structured securities. Another traditional example is a warrant bond, a bond which comes with a warrant entitling the holder to buy a different bond under certain conditions at some future date. Many structured securities are far more complex, featuring interest rates that can vary only within given limits, can change at an exponential rate or can even cease to be payable altogether in certain circumstances. The prices of such instruments can be difficult to calculate and depend heavily on the value attached to the option features. (Options are discussed in more detail in Chapter 9.)

Properties of bonds

Every bond, irrespective of issuer or type, has a set of basic properties.

Maturity

This is the date on which the bond issuer will have repaid all of the principal and will redeem the bond. The number of years to maturity is the term. In practice, term and maturity are often used interchangeably. Bonds with maturities of 1–5 years are usually categorised as short-term, those with maturities of 5–12 years as medium-term and those with maturities exceeding 12 years as long-term. Few bonds are issued with maturities beyond 30 years, and in many countries the longest maturity is only 10 or 20 years.

Coupon

This is the stated annual interest rate as a percentage of the price at issuance. Once a bond has been issued, its coupon never changes. Thus a bond that was issued for $1,000 and pays $60 of interest each year would be said to have a 6% coupon. Bonds are often identified by their maturity and coupon, for example, "the 6.25s of '18".

Current yield

Current yield is the effective interest rate for a bond at its current market price. This is calculated by a simple formula:

$$\frac{\text{Annual dollar coupon interest}}{\text{current price}}$$

If the price has fallen since the bond was issued, the current yield will be greater than the coupon; if the price has risen, the yield will be less than the coupon. Suppose a bond was issued with a par value of €100 and a 6% coupon. Interest rates have fallen, and the bond now trades at €105. The current yield is:

$$\frac{€6}{€105} = 5.71\%$$

Yield to maturity

This is the annual rate the bondholder will receive if the bond is held to maturity. Unlike current yield, yield to maturity includes the value of any capital gain or loss the bondholder will enjoy when the bond is redeemed. This is the most widely used figure for comparing returns on different bonds.

Duration

Duration is a number expressing how quickly the investor will receive half of the total payment due over the bond's remaining life, with an adjustment for the fact that payments in the distant future are worth less than payments due soon. This complicated concept can be grasped by looking at two extremes. A zero-coupon bond offers payments only at maturity, so its duration is precisely equal to its term. A hypothetical ten-year bond yielding 100% annually lets the owner collect a great deal of money in the early years of ownership, so its duration is much shorter than its term. Most bonds fall in between. If two bonds have identical terms, the one with the higher yield will have the shorter duration, because the holder is receiving more money sooner.

The duration of any bond changes from one day to the next. The actual calculation can be complicated, and can be done in several different

Table 4.3 **What bond ratings mean**[a]

	Moody's	Standard & Poor's	Fitch IBCA
Highest credit quality; issuer has strong ability to meet obligations	Aaa	AAA	AAA
Very high credit quality; low risk of default	Aa1 Aa2 Aa3	AA+ AA AA–	AA
High credit quality, but more vulnerable to changes in economy or business	A1 A2 A3	A+ A A–	A
Adequate credit quality for now, but more likely to be impaired if conditions worsen	Baa1 Baa2 Baa3	BBB+ BBB BBB–	BBB
Below investment grade, but good chance that issuer can meet commitments	Ba1 Ba2 Ba3	BB+ BB BB–	BB
Significant credit risk, but issuer is presently able to meet obligations	B1 B2 B3	B+ B B–	B
High default risk	Caa1 Caa2 Caa3	CCC+ CCC CCC–	CCC CC C
Issuer failed to meet scheduled interest or principal payments	C	D	DDD DD D

a Firms' precise definitions of ratings vary.

ways. Different investors may have different views of a bond's duration: one of the critical numbers in the calculation, the discount rate that should be used to attach a current value to future payments, is strictly a matter of opinion; and another, the amounts that will be paid at specific dates, is not always certain.

Traders and investors pay close attention to duration, as it is the most basic measure of a bond's riskiness. The longer the duration, the more the price of the bond is likely to fluctuate before maturity. Divergent estimates of duration are an important reason that investors differ about bond prices: if there is a ten-year bond with a 6% coupon and semi-annual interest payments, an investor who estimates the duration to be 7.6 years would be willing to pay a higher price than one who estimates it to be 7.7 years.

Ratings of risk

Before issuing bonds in the public markets, an issuer will often seek a rating from one or more private ratings agencies. The selected agencies investigate the issuer's ability to service the bonds, including such matters as financial strength, the intended use of the funds, the political and regulatory environment, and potential economic changes. After completing its investigation, an agency will issue a rating that represents its estimate of the default risk, the likelihood that the issuer will fail to service the bonds as required. This rating is normally paid for by the issuer, although in some cases an agency will issue a rating on its own initiative.

Three well-known companies, Moody's Investors Service and Standard & Poor's, both based in New York, and Fitch IBCA, based in New York and London, dominate the ratings industry. The firms' ratings of a particular issue are not always in agreement, as each uses a different methodology. Table 4.3 interprets the default ratings of the three international firms. There are also many ratings agencies that operate in a single country, and several that specialise in a particular industry, such as banking.

All the ratings agencies emphasise that they rate only the probability of default, not the probability that the issuer will experience financial distress or that the price of its bonds will fall. Nonetheless, ratings are extremely important in setting bond prices. Bonds with lower ratings almost always have a greater yield than bonds with higher ratings. If an agency lowers its rating on a bond that has already been issued, the bond's price will fall. Government regulations or internal procedures restrict the amount many pension funds and insurance companies can invest in bonds that have a high probability of default, those rated as "below investment grade".

Ratings have increased in importance because of the growing number of bonds with "step-up" and acceleration provisions. Under a typical step-up, a bond might be issued with a 7% coupon, but if the issuer's credit rating is lowered, the coupon immediately increases to 7.25%. If the issue has an acceleration provision, the bonds could become repayable immediately upon a downgrade. In either case, the lowering of an issuer's credit rating can have serious adverse consequences, both for the issuer and for the investors who hold its securities.

Interpreting the price of a bond

The price of a bond is normally quoted as a percentage of the price at which the bond was issued, which is usually reported as 100. In most countries, prices are quoted to the second decimal place. Thus a bond trading at 94.75% of its issue price will be quoted at 94.75 in most countries, indicating that a bond purchased for $10,000 when issued is currently worth $9,475. A price exceeding 100 means that the bond is worth more now than at the time it was issued.

The prices of non-government bonds are often reported in terms of the spread between a particular bond and a benchmark. In the United States, confusingly, high-grade corporate bonds are usually quoted in terms of a spread over US Treasury yields at similar maturity; if the current yield on ten-year Treasuries is 5.20%, a bond quoted at +220 would yield 7.40% at its current price. High-yield bonds, however, are quoted as a percentage of the face value. For floating-rate instruments, the spread is often expressed in terms of the London Inter-Bank Offer Rate (LIBOR), a key rate in the London market. In some cases, both the bid and ask prices are quoted.

The interest rates on government bonds may be affected by the expectation that a particular bond issue will be repurchased rather than by economic fundamentals alone. This has made government bonds an increasingly unstable benchmark in some countries, and investors have been looking for other measures by which to judge the pricing of non-government bonds.

Interest rates and bond prices

Interest-rate changes within the economy are the single most important factor affecting bond prices. This is because investors can profit from interest-rate arbitrage, selling certain bonds and buying others to take advantage of small price differences. Arbitrage will quickly drive the prices of similar bonds to the same level.

Bond prices move inversely to interest rates. The precise impact of an interest-rate change depends upon the duration of the bond, using the basic formula:

$$\text{Price change} = \text{duration} \times \text{value} \times \text{change in yield}$$

Assume that an investor has just paid C\$1,000 for a bond priced at 100, denominated in Canadian dollars with a 6% coupon and a term of ten years to maturity. This bond might initially have a duration of 7.66 years. If Canadian interest rates for ten-year borrowings suddenly decline, investors will flock to the bond with a 6% coupon and bid up the price. Suppose that the market rate for ten-year borrowings in Canada drops to 5.9% immediately after the bond is issued. The price change can then be calculated as:

$$7.66 \times \text{C\$1,000} \times (0.060 - 0.059) = \text{C\$7.66}$$

so this bond would now have a market value of C\$1,007.66 and a price of 100.77. Conversely, if Canadian interest rates for ten-year borrowings rise, the value of the bond will decline until the current yield is in line with the market.

As this example illustrates, the prices of long-term bonds can be much more volatile than the prices of short-term bonds because of their longer duration. In the face of the same interest-rate change, the price of a bond with a duration of 12.5 years would have risen by 1.25%, and the price of a bond with a duration of 2.3 years would have risen by 0.23%. This relationship can be visualised using price/yield curves, drawn on a graph with the vertical axis denoting bond prices and the horizontal axis representing interest rates. As Figure 4.1 on the next page shows, a given increase in yield will cause the price of a bond with long duration to fall much more than the price of a bond with shorter duration, and a given decrease in yield will cause its price to rise more. This graphical relationship is known to bond investors as convexity.

Inflation and returns on bonds

Interest rates can be thought of as having two separate components. The first is recompense for inflation, the change in prices that is expected to

The price/yield curve 4.1

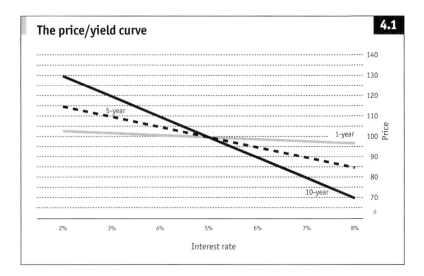

occur during the term of a borrowing. The second is the payment the bond investor exacts for the use of its money after taking inflation into account. The sum of these components is the nominal interest rate. Bond coupons and bond yields are both nominal interest rates.

The payment to the investor beyond expected inflation is the real interest rate. The real interest rate cannot be known precisely, but there are ways to estimate it. For example, the current yield on a bond that is indexed for inflation could be compared with the yield on a bond with the same maturity date not indexed for inflation. The difference between these two rates can be understood as the inflation premium investors demand for buying bonds that are not indexed. If the expected inflation rate increases, the yield on such bonds will have to increase for the investor to receive the same real return, which means that the price of the bond must fall. Thus the bond markets are closely attuned to economic data concerning employment, wage increases, industrial capacity utilisation and commodity prices, all of which may be indicators of future inflation.

Exchange rates and bond prices and returns

Many bond buyers invest internationally. To purchase bonds denominated in foreign currencies, they must convert their home currency into the relevant foreign currency. After eventually selling the bonds, they must convert the foreign-currency proceeds back into their home cur-

Table 4.4 **Bond-market returns, 1995 (%)**

	Canada	France	Germany	Japan	UK	US
Return in local currency	19.30	17.12	16.78	14.14	16.65	18.59
Return in dollars	22.71	27.81	26.49	10.42	15.77	18.59

Source: Merrill Lynch

rency. Their return is thus highly sensitive to exchange-rate movements.

For example, consider a Japanese investor that spent $10,000 to purchase a US bond at a time when ¥1 was worth 0.0083 cents (an exchange rate of ¥120 to $1). The bond would therefore have cost ¥120,000. Assume that by the time the investor wishes to sell the bond, the yen has depreciated against the dollar by 10%, so that ¥1 is now worth 0.0075 cents (an exchange rate of ¥133.33 to $1). Even if the price of the bond is unchanged, the value of the investment would be ¥133,330, a gain of 11.11%.

The effects of currency movements can overwhelm the returns on the bonds themselves. Table 4.4 compares average bond-market returns in local currency and in dollars for 1995, a year in which falling interest rates everywhere led to much higher bond prices. The dollar strengthened against the Japanese yen and the pound sterling but weakened against other currencies, which dramatically affected returns for international investors.

Thus the strengthening of a country's currency can increase the demand for its bonds and raise prices, other things remaining the same. However, other things rarely remain the same. As explained in Chapter 2, the main reason for a change in the exchange rate between two countries is a change in their relative interest rates. Why this occurs will determine the effect on bond prices. In the example above, if the yen is weaker against the dollar because Japanese interest rates have fallen, bond prices in the United States might strengthen. If, however, the yen is weaker against the dollar because US interest rates have risen, bond prices in the United States might fall. In summary, the relationship between exchange-rate changes and bond prices is not always predictable.

The yield curve

The interest rate that lenders require of any borrower will depend on

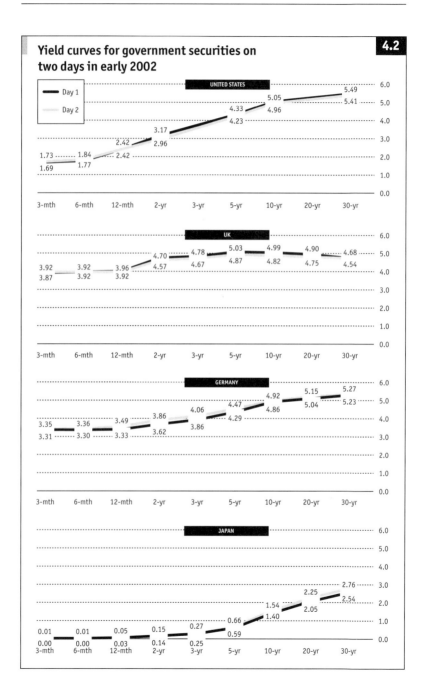

Yield curves for government securities on two days in early 2002

4.2

UNITED STATES

- Day 1
- Day 2

| 3-mth | 6-mth | 12-mth | 2-yr | 3-yr | 5-yr | 10-yr | 20-yr | 30-yr |

Day 1: 1.73 ... 1.84 ... 2.42 ... 2.96 ... 3.17 ... 4.23 ... 4.96 ... 5.05 ... 5.49
Day 2: 1.69 ... 1.77 ... 2.42 ... 2.42 ... 4.33 ... 5.41

UK

3.92 ... 3.92 ... 3.96 ... 4.70 ... 4.78 ... 5.03 ... 4.99 ... 4.90 ... 4.68
3.87 ... 3.92 ... 3.92 ... 4.57 ... 4.67 ... 4.87 ... 4.82 ... 4.75 ... 4.54

| 3-mth | 6-mth | 12-mth | 2-yr | 3-yr | 5-yr | 10-yr | 20-yr | 30-yr |

GERMANY

3.35 ... 3.36 ... 3.49 ... 3.86 ... 4.06 ... 4.47 ... 4.92 ... 5.15 ... 5.27
3.31 ... 3.30 ... 3.33 ... 3.62 ... 3.86 ... 4.29 ... 4.86 ... 5.04 ... 5.23

| 3-mth | 6-mth | 12-mth | 2-yr | 3-yr | 5-yr | 10-yr | 20-yr | 30-yr |

JAPAN

0.01 ... 0.01 ... 0.05 ... 0.15 ... 0.27 ... 0.66 ... 1.54 ... 2.25 ... 2.76
0.00 ... 0.00 ... 0.03 ... 0.14 ... 0.25 ... 0.59 ... 1.40 ... 2.05 ... 2.54

| 3-mth | 6-mth | 12-mth | 2-yr | 3-yr | 5-yr | 10-yr | 20-yr | 30-yr |

the term of the borrowing. The yield curve depicts the various rates at which the same borrower is able to borrow for different periods of time. The most closely watched yield curve in any country is that of the national government, which is the closest approximation to a risk-free yield. Other yield curves, such as the one for corporate borrowers, are best understood in comparison with the risk-free yield.

The yield curve is drawn against two axes, the vertical showing yield (expressed in percentage points) and the horizontal giving the term in years. Most of the time the yield curve is positively sloped, going from the lower left corner of the chart to the upper right. In this case, very short-term borrowings would have the lowest yield, with the yield increasing as the term lengthens. The reasons for this shape are readily understandable, as lenders and investors wish to be compensated for the greater risk that inflation will erode the value of their asset over a longer period.

The precise shape of the yield curve varies slightly from day to day and can change significantly from one month to the next. If long-term interest rates rise relative to short-term interest rates, the curve is said to steepen; if short-term rates rise relative to long-term rates the curve flattens. One way to think about this is to regard the yield curve as a forecast of future short-term interest rates. Bond issuers and investors, of course, always have the option of repeatedly purchasing money-market instruments rather than making long-term commitments, so a steeper yield curve implies that they expect money-market yields to be higher in future than they are now. The yield curve is said to be inverted if short-term interest rates are higher than long-term rates. An inverted yield curve is usually a sign that the central bank is constricting the flow of credit to slow the economy, a step often associated with a lessening of inflation expectations. This can make investors in longer-term instruments willing to accept lower nominal interest rates than are available on shorter-term instruments, giving the curve an inverted shape.

The steepness of the yield curve is not related to the absolute level of interest rates. It is possible for the curve to flatten amid a general rise in interest rates, if short-term rates rise faster than long-term rates. Figure 4.2 gives examples of yield-curve changes for government bonds in the United States, the UK, Germany and Japan on two days in 2002.

In the month between these two days, interest rates in the United States fell at the "long" end of the yield curve, but rose for maturities of less than 12 months. In Germany, rates moved higher all along the curve. In the UK, yields declined for all maturities. In Japan, which had the lowest interest rates ever recorded, rates rose at most points on the yield curve beyond five years, making the curve slightly steeper.

Many investors and traders actively sell bonds of one maturity and buy bonds of another as changes in the yield curve alter relative prices. For example, in October 1992 the interest rate on ten-year US Treasuries was 3.5 percentage points above that on two-year Treasuries. By late 1994 ten-year bonds were yielding less than 0.5 percentage points above two-year bonds. Although the prices of both maturities increased, an investor who had sold two-year Treasuries and used the proceeds to purchase ten-year Treasuries in October 1992 would have profited handsomely by playing the yield curve.

Spreads

In general, investors that buy bonds first make a decision about asset allocation. That is, they determine what proportion of a portfolio they wish to hold in bonds as opposed to cash, equities and other types of assets. Next, they are likely to allocate the bond portfolio broadly among domestic government bonds, domestic corporate bonds, foreign bonds and other categories. Once the asset allocation has been determined, the decision about which particular bonds to purchase within each category is based largely on spreads.

A spread is the difference between the current yields of two bonds. It is usually expressed in basis points, with each basis point equal to one-hundredth of a percentage point. To simplify matters, traders in most countries have adopted a benchmark, usually a particular government bond, against which all other bonds are measured. If two bonds have identical ratings but different spreads to the benchmark, investors may conclude that the bond with the wider spread offers better relative value, because its price will rise relative to the other bond if the spread narrows.

Changes in spreads indicate which risks are currently most worrying to investors. Consider the European government bond market, where the benchmark has been the ten-year Bund issued by the German government. Until the late 1990s there was a substantial spread between Bunds and the bonds issued by governments in Italy, Spain and several other European countries. However, as 12 EU countries moved towards the establishment of a single currency, the euro, on January 1st 1999, the spreads within the euro zone narrowed. Investors that had purchased bonds with wide spreads against the Bund profited as spreads narrowed. Even at a time of rising interest rates, when bond prices generally decline, traders astute enough to foresee changes in spreads can do well. Spreads can also widen or narrow if investors sense a change in the issuer's creditworthiness. If a firm's sales have been weak, investors may think there is a greater likelihood that the firm will be unable to service its debt, and will therefore demand a wider spread before purchasing the bond. Conversely, investors frequently purchase bonds when they expect that the issuer's rating will be upgraded by one of the major credit agencies, as the upgrade will cause the bond's price to rise as its yield moves closer to the benchmark interest rate.

Enhancing security

An issuer frequently takes steps to reduce the risk bondholders must bear in order to sell its bonds at lower interest rate. There are three common ways of doing this:

- **Covenants** are legally binding promises made at the time a bond is issued. A simple covenant might limit the amount of additional debt that the issuer may sell in future, or might require it to keep a certain level of cash at all times. Convenants are meant to protect bondholders not only against default, but also against the possibility that management's future actions will lead ratings agencies to downgrade the bonds, which would reduce the price in the secondary market.
- **Bond insurance** is frequently sought by issuers with unimpressive credit ratings. A bond insurer is a private firm that has obtained a top rating from the main ratings agencies. An issuer pays it a premium to guarantee bondholders that specific bonds will be serviced on time. With such a guarantee, the issuer is able to sell its bonds at a lower interest rate. Bond insurance is a particularly popular enhancement for municipal bonds in the United States, as shown in Figure 4.3 on the next page. Its popularity also has increased in Europe; there were $14 billion of insured bonds issued outside the United States in 2004.
- **Sinking funds** ensure that the issuer arranges to retire some of its debt, on a prearranged schedule, prior to maturity. The issuer can do this either by purchasing the required amount of its bonds in the market at specified times, or by setting aside money in a fund overseen by a trustee, to ensure that there is adequate cash on hand to redeem the bonds at maturity.

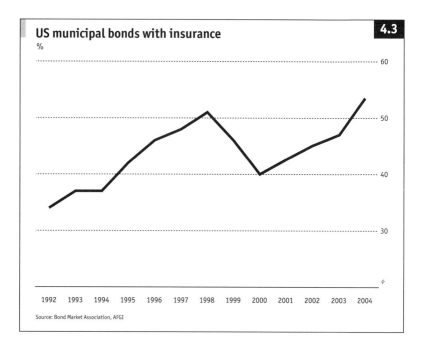

US municipal bonds with insurance

%

Source: Bond Market Association, AFGI

Repurchase agreements

The role of repurchase agreements, or repos, is essential to the smooth functioning of the market.

Repos were discussed in Chapter 3, but to summarise: a repo is a contract in which a seller, usually a securities dealer such as an investment bank, agrees to sell bonds in return for a cash loan, but promises to repurchase the bonds at a specific date and price. For the seller, a repo offers a low-cost way of borrowing money to finance the purchase of more bonds. For the buyer, a repo is a low-risk alternative to keeping cash in the bank, as the securities serve as collateral. A reverse repo is the same operation with the parties switching sides, so that the securities dealer trades money for securities belonging to an investor.

The largest part of the repo market is the overnight market. However, big investors often enter into term repos for longer periods. In such cases, repos can offer an inexpensive way to take a large position ahead of expected changes in bond prices. Suppose, for example, that an investor expects long-term interest rates to fall. It might arrange a reverse repo, selling long-term bonds to a dealer, taking the dealer's loan and buying yet more long-term bonds. If long-term interest rates fall

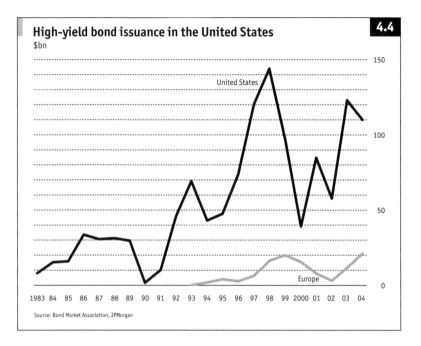

High-yield bond issuance in the United States
$bn

4.4

United States

Europe

1983 84 85 86 87 88 89 90 91 92 93 94 95 96 97 98 99 2000 01 02 03 04

Source: Bond Market Association, JPMorgan

before the repo matures, the investor sells both sets of bonds at a profit, earning far more than if it had simply bought and held bonds. Conversely, however, the investor's loss from this leveraged transaction would be magnified if interest rates move in the opposite way.

High-yield debt – or junk

One of the most important bond-market developments in recent years is the issuance of debt by entities with weak credit ratings. Such bonds are called high-yield debt or below-investment-grade debt. They are better known to the public as junk bonds.

Until the 1980s firms and government agencies rated "below investment grade" were largely shut out of the debt markets. Starting in about 1983, institutional investors in the United States began to allocate a small proportion of their assets to bonds that did not meet normal investment criteria. Early high-yield bonds were frequently used to finance leveraged buy-outs, with the issuers using the borrowed money to buy up all the shares in a firm and operate it as a privately held business. Today they may be used for many different purposes. High-yield markets were slower to develop in Europe and Asia. The European

Central Bank estimates that about 10% of euro-zone corporate bonds are rated below investment grade, compared with 40% in the United States. High-yield bond issuance in the UK and Japan is small, but many firms and governments in emerging economies issue securities that are not rated investment grade and are traded as high-yield bonds. Figure 4.4 on the previous page traces the growth of the high-yield market in the United States and Europe.

Some bonds that carried investment-grade ratings when they were issued now trade as high-yield bonds because the issuer's financial condition has deteriorated. These are known as fallen angels. When the condition of the issuer of a below-investment-grade bond improves significantly, the bond may gain an investment-grade rating. In this case, traders refer to it as a rising star. In 2004, as economic conditions improved, only 23 US companies with $38 billion of outstanding bonds were downgraded to junk status, while 36 issuers with $47 billion of outstanding bonds became rising stars.

Below-investment-grade bonds usually trade at a substantial spread to Treasuries and high-grade corporate bonds. On average, rates on high-yield bonds in the American market are about 400 basis points higher than the rates on Treasuries of similar maturity. But this spread can vary considerably depending on the economy. In December 2000, as the US economy was weakening, the average yield reached 941 basis points above Treasuries. In return for offering higher interest, high-yield bonds carry a much larger risk of default, especially at times of economic stress. In 2001, a recession year, 8% of US high-yield bonds went into default. In 2005, when the US economy was much healthier, the default rate was extremely low.

International markets

The bond markets have long since ceased to be domestic markets. As restrictions on the cross-border flow of capital have been reduced or eliminated, investors have increasingly been able to buy bonds regardless of the national origin of the issuer and the currency of issue. About $1.6 trillion of corporate bonds trade outside the issuer's home country, along with about $1.4 trillion of government debt and $10 trillion issued by financial institutions. Nearly half of the world's most heavily traded securities, US Treasury bonds, are now owned by investors outside the United States, as shown in Figure 4.5.

The issuance of bonds outside the issuer's home country can occur in two different ways:

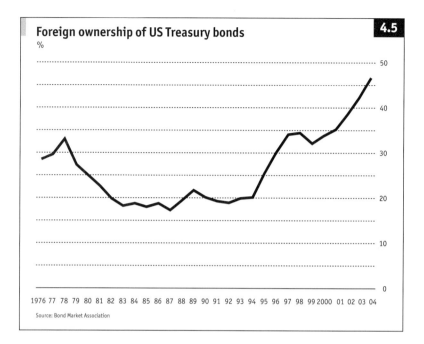

Foreign ownership of US Treasury bonds   **4.5**
%

50

40

30

20

10

0

1976 77 78 79 80 81 82 83 84 85 86 87 88 89 90 91 92 93 94 95 96 97 98 99 2000 01 02 03 04

Source: Bond Market Association

◪ **Foreign bonds** are issued outside the issuer's home country and are denominated in the currency of the country where they are issued. Special names are used to refer to many such issues. Yankee bonds are dollar-denominated securities issued in the United States by non-US issuers. Bonds issued in sterling by issuers from outside the UK are known as bulldog bonds, and the term samurai bonds refers to yen bonds placed by foreign issuers in the Japanese market.

◪ **Eurobonds** are denominated in neither the currency of the issuer's home country nor that of the country of issue, and are generally subject to less regulation. Thus a sterling-denominated bond offered in London by a Japanese firm would be considered a foreign bond, and the same security offered in London but denominated in dollars or Swiss francs would be called a eurobond. (The market for eurobonds is discussed in Chapter 6.)

Why would an issuer choose an international issue rather than a domestic one? First, it may wish to match its borrowing to the income that is intended to pay for that borrowing. A French firm intending to build an electrical generation plant in Turkey, for example, might borrow in Turkish liras rather than in euros because the electricity will be priced and sold in liras. Second, the greater liquidity of the main bond markets, particularly New York and London, means that borrowers from other countries can often obtain lower interest rates than at home, even after taking currency risk into account. This is particularly true for issuers from countries where financial markets are underdeveloped and investors' willingness to purchase local-currency bonds is limited. Third, an international issue is often undertaken to establish the issuer's reputation among international investors, to ease the way for future borrowings or share offerings.

As illustrated in Tables 4.1 on page 59 and 4.2 on page 63, the United States has by far the world's largest domestic bond market, accounting for almost half of all bonds in circulation. International bonds of US issuers equal only one-sixth of the amount outstanding domestically. The picture is very different for many other countries. Germany and the UK have disproportionately large shares of the international bond market, with German issuers having sold more bonds internationally than domestically.

Emerging-market bonds

Until the 1990s, only the most creditworthy of issuers could issue bonds in the international markets. Governments unable to obtain investment-grade ratings on their sovereign debt were restricted to borrowing from banks or from domestic credit markets. Companies in these countries were excluded from the international debt markets as well because, with few exceptions, the ratings agencies impose a sovereign ceiling, meaning that no borrower in a country can be rated as high as its national government. If the sovereign debt of the national government was deemed to be a poor credit risk, the country's corporate debt was automatically treated the same way.

Over the past two decades, however, investors have come to accept the debt of these so-called emerging-market countries as a separate category of investment. The main characteristic of emerging-market debt, apart from a below-investment-grade credit rating, is high price volatility. On average, weekly changes in the price of emerging-market bonds are about four times as great as changes in the price of government and corporate bonds issued in the more developed markets.

Firms and governments in dozens of emerging economies have issued bonds internationally. However, four countries – Brazil,

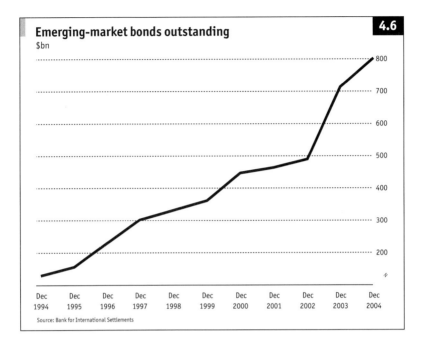

Emerging-market bonds outstanding
$bn

4.6

Dec 1994 · Dec 1995 · Dec 1996 · Dec 1997 · Dec 1998 · Dec 1999 · Dec 2000 · Dec 2001 · Dec 2002 · Dec 2003 · Dec 2004

Source: Bank for International Settlements

Argentina, Mexico and South Korea – account for nearly half of all emerging-market bonds outstanding. Total issuance grew nearly tenfold between 1991 and 1997. It then slowed in the wake of the financial crises in Asia in 1998, as shown in Figure 4.6, before resuming rapid growth early in 2000. Issuance fell to near zero in late 2001 and early 2002, as financial crises in Turkey and Argentina, combined with the global economic slowdown, curbed investor interest. Brazil has more bonds outstanding than any other emerging-market economy, but South Korea – which by some criteria is not an emerging market – had the most issuance in 2004. The euro has displaced the US dollar as the main currency of issuance.

The main cause of the emerging-market bond boom from 1994 to 1997, apart from the general decline in interest rates throughout the world, was exchange-rate policy. The governments of many emerging-market countries either fixed their exchange rates against certain foreign currencies or pegged their exchange rates, allowing them to change in a pre-announced way. As interest rates in the more advanced economies were much lower than those in emerging markets, businesses took advantage of the opportunity to sell international bonds in the expectation that their domestic currency income could easily be exchanged for enough foreign currency to service the bonds. However, when market forces made it impossible for governments in Thailand, South Korea, Indonesia and several other countries to maintain their currency pegs in 1997, the currencies fell sharply. Similar events occurred in Russia in 1998. Many issuers, unable to afford the foreign exchange required to service their bonds, defaulted.

When the markets became more welcoming to emerging-market issues in 1999, corporate bonds were more prominent than they had been previously. Corporate bonds accounted for about 30% of emerging-markets issuance in the first quarter of 2000. However, as the world economy slowed in 2000 and many countries entered recession in 2001, investors shunned both government and corporate bonds from most emerging economies. Net issuance of bonds by companies based in developing countries was nil in 2000 and 2001. When the Argentinian government imposed foreign-exchange controls and then defaulted on its debt in 2001 and 2002, Argentinian companies were unable to service their own debts and were forced into default as well, reminding investors that changes in government policy are always a risk to holders of corporate bonds. Issuance of international bonds by companies in emerging-market economies has not resumed, although some of these companies have made greater use of their domestic bond markets.

Bond indexes

The return on bonds depends greatly upon external forces, particularly interest rates. This makes it difficult to measure investment managers' success on an absolute scale, as even the best managers will earn negative returns (lose money) when interest rates rise. Leading investment banks have therefore constructed bond indexes against which to judge the overall performance of a particular bond portfolio.

Indexes serve to answer several different questions. First, how does the total return on a particular bond, including interest payments as well as changes in market value, compare with the total return on bonds from similar issuers? A large number of indexes track the return on narrow categories of bonds to offer a measuring stick. Second, how well has a particular manager done? A large institutional investor might divide its bond portfolio among many managers, asking them to follow diverse strategies. Comparing them with one another would not reveal how well each has pursued the desired strategy. Comparison with appropriate indexes, however, would show whether it was worthwhile for the investor to pay the manager, or whether a better return could have been obtained simply by tracking the index by purchasing precisely those bonds. Third, do particular bond-investment strategies persistently underperform other strategies? If one index lags another year after year, an investor has reason to wonder whether the mix of bonds tracked by the lagging index is a sensible investment.

Bond indexes come in two basic types:

- **Benchmark.** The simplest, the benchmark index, tracks the performance of a bond issue that is deemed an appropriate benchmark for an entire category of bonds. This type of index is particularly useful for sovereign bonds, as there is only a single sovereign issuer in each country that issues bonds of varying terms. In countries whose governments issue long-term bonds, the benchmark bond is normally an issue with ten years to maturity.
- **Weighted.** The other common type of index measures the total return of an identifiable group of bonds. The index number is set equal to 100 at an arbitrary start date. Such indexes are usually weighted, which means that the importance of any bond in the index is based on the size of the issue compared with the total size of all issues included in the index. The performance of an index depends heavily on which bonds are included, because the spreads of the individual bonds will change in various ways. There are hundreds of weighted indexes. For example, three major Japanese investment banks publish weighted indexes of the Japanese bond market. The Nomura Bond Performance Index includes issues with an investment-grade rating and at least ¥1 billion of bonds outstanding. The Nikko Bond Performance Index has similar selection criteria, but with a starting date of December 1979. The Daiwa Bond Index, in contrast to the other two, includes only issues with at least ¥5 billion outstanding. None of these three indexes can be said to be superior to the others; they simply take slightly different snapshots of the market.

Index shortcomings
Despite their widespread use, weighted bond indexes are problematic for several reasons:

◨ **Inconsistency.** No index can track precisely the same bonds over time, because most bonds eventually mature or are called, and many cease to be actively traded.

◨ **Uncertain pricing.** Calculating changes in a bond index requires a determination of the price change on each bond in the index. Many bonds, however, trade infrequently, so there may be no recent transactions to provide current price information. Even if transactions have occurred, the compiler of the index may not be able to learn the price. The compiler must therefore seek to estimate the price of the bond, rather than relying on actual transactions. As a result, a bond index is inherently far less precise than an index of shares that are traded on a daily basis.

◨ **Disqualification.** A bond may be dropped from an index if it ceases to meet the criteria for inclusion, particularly if it is upgraded or downgraded by ratings agencies. Such an event will force portfolio managers who are tracking the index to sell the bond at the same time as many other money managers are selling the same bond for the same reason, exacerbating its price decline. This occurred, for example, when South Korea lost its AA credit rating in 1997 and managers who were tracking AA-bond indexes were forced to dump South Korean bonds at a loss. In December 2001, Argentina's weighting in the JP Morgan Emerging Market Bond Index Plus (EMBI +) was reduced by half after the government implemented an exchange of bonds that had been included in the index, but that it was no longer able to service.

◨ **Poor diversification.** Some indexes include few issuers, forcing fund managers who are tracking the index to have undiversified portfolios. This was a problem for managers of emerging-market portfolios in 1998: Russia had a heavy weighting in the EMBI + because it had issued large amounts of bonds. The more bonds the Russian government issued, the more bonds portfolio managers needed to buy to track the index, leaving them with large losses when the government suspended payments on many bonds.

Credit default swaps

Corporate-bond investors are making increased use of credit default swaps, a relatively new type of contract that allows investors to express a view on the creditworthiness of a particular company or sector without actually owning the underlying bonds. This innovation has been important in the corporate market, where investors often find that a bond they wish to buy is not available.

A credit default swap is a contract in which two parties agree to exchange the risk that a borrower will default on its bonds or loans. The seller of the swap receives a fee from the buyer. In return, the seller will compensate the buyer if there is a "credit event", such as the borrower failing to pay its obligations on time or filing for bankruptcy, as happened with Delphi Corp in October 2005. Selling protection on a particular "name", such as a company, is thus similar to owning that company's bonds, in that the seller is exposed to the risk of default. Buying protection is analogous to holding a "short" position in a bond – that is, agreeing to sell a bond you do not own, in the expectation that the bond can be repurchased in future at a lower price.

Credit default swaps on a given name are usually priced similarly to that name's bonds, and the price can change frequently as investors reassess the likelihood of a credit event. If no credit event occurs, the seller of protection profits from the premium it received from the buyer. If a credit event does occur, the buyer of protection delivers the defaulted notes or bonds to the seller, and the seller must pay the buyer the full face value of the securities. The precise amount of the seller's loss in that case depends on the value of the bonds after the credit event. Alternatively, the parties can settle the contract for cash at any time.

One virtue of credit default swaps is that investors are able to express views on an issuer even if it has few bonds outstanding. Suppose, for example, that a company announces that its earnings are far below expectations, and investors begin to speculate that it may file for bankruptcy. Credit default swaps allow an unlimited number of investors to position themselves to profit if the company does or does not file; without credit default swaps, only those investors owning the company's bonds or loans could take such positions.

5   Securitisation

TRADITIONALLY, investors have favoured bonds for their safety and predictability. A fixed-rate bond promises guaranteed cash flows: the amount and date of each interest payment are specified when the bond is issued, as are the dates on which the bond may be redeemed. The investor therefore knows precisely how much money it will receive five, ten or 20 years in the future, and the conditions, if any, under which the bond may be called prior to maturity.

An asset-backed security is a type of bond offering no such certainty. The security, in most cases, is not backed by the full faith and credit of a government or a private company. Rather, a creditor, most often a lender, issues securities supported by a stream of income the issuer expects to receive in the future from specific assets. There is no assurance that the income will be received as anticipated. Some of it might not arrive at all. Sometimes the assets will be liquidated earlier than expected, resulting in less interest income than the bondholders assumed they would receive. As a result, future cash flows can only be guessed at rather than known with a high degree of confidence.

In return for accepting this uncertainty, investors in asset-backed securities are able to achieve higher returns than on regular government or corporate bonds. At the same time, the securities are far more readily bought and sold (they have greater liquidity, in market parlance) than the individual assets underlying them, making it easier for investors to get into or out of a particular type of investment. These advantages have made asset-backed securities hugely popular. Perhaps $10 trillion of securities backed by various types of assets are outstanding around the world.

Asset-backed securities are sold either with fixed rates of interest or with floating rates. They can be broadly divided into two categories:

- **Mortgage-backed securities.** These are supported by first mortgages on residential property.
- **Non-mortgage securities.** These can be backed by assets of any other sort.

Mortgage-backed securities accounted for approximately 80% of the asset-backed securities outstanding throughout the world at the end of

Table 5.1 **Asset-backed securitisations in the United States, amounts outstanding excluding mortgages ($bn)**

	Auto loans	Credit-card loans	Home-equity loans	Manufactured-housing loans	Student loans	Equipment leases	Others
1996	71	181	52	115	10	24	52
1998	87	237	124	25	25	41	193
2000	133	306	152	37	41	59	344
2002	222	398	287	45	74	68	450
2004	232	391	454	42	115	71	554

Source: Bond Market Association

2004. Securitisation of other sorts of assets has been growing rapidly. The value of non-mortgage asset-backed securities outstanding was more than $2 trillion at December 2004. Worldwide issuance in 2004, excluding mortgage-backed securities, was $886 billion, according to *Asset-Backed Alert*, an industry publication. Of this amount, $193 billion was issued outside the United States, and $693 in the United States. Table 5.1 shows the size of this market in the United States by type of asset.

The securitisation process

Securitisation is the process by which individual assets, which on their own may be difficult to sell or even to attach a value to, are aggregated into securities that can be sold in the financial markets. The earliest known securitisations occurred in Denmark, where mortgage bonds have served to finance house purchases for many years. Mortgage securities became widely used in the United States in the 1970s. Since then, innovation has led to the securitisation of other sorts of assets, and asset-backed securities have taken root in several countries in Europe and Asia.

The securitisation process begins with the creation of the assets that will later be securitised. This usually occurs in the normal course of business: a mortgage bank extends a mortgage to a homebuyer; a bank gives a customer a credit card; a studio releases a feature film. Under normal circumstances, such an asset is carried on the firm's books, with the money earned by that asset, such as loan payments, to be reported as income in whatever future year it is received.

Securitisation involves transforming, or packaging, such assets into securities that can be sold to third parties. Securitisation is accomplished with the help of an investment bank, which sets up a trust whose sole purpose is to own the assets being securitised. Usually, each trust is created to own a pool composed of a single type of asset, such as $100m of automobile loans. The trust will purchase the assets in the pool from the firm that created them, using money raised by the sale of asset-backed securities to investors. The owners of the securities are entitled to receive whatever income the assets generate, and in most cases to a pro-rata share of the assets themselves. When individual assets owned by the trust are retired – for example, when an individual loan is paid off – the size of the trust diminishes. Eventually, all the assets will be retired, at which point the trust will terminate.

In general, the diversity of the assets underlying an asset-backed security provides safety to investors. According to Standard & Poor's, a rating agency, 18 asset-backed securities defaulted in 2001 – more than had defaulted over the previous 16 years. Six of these defaults were related to the collapse of Enron, a US energy company that entered bankruptcy in late 2001. Defaults in more recent years have been rare.

Recourse to guarantees
In many cases, investors in an asset-backed trust benefit from certain guarantees. Governments frequently guarantee part or all of the payment on residential mortgages to encourage housing construction. The original lender may also guarantee loan payments to induce investors to buy its assets. In this situation, the lender sells the assets to the trust with recourse, meaning that the trust will seek reimbursement from the lender if an individual borrower should fail to pay interest or principal as scheduled.

Why securitise?
The impetus for securitisation lies in the benefits that it brings to firms that choose to securitise their assets. Securitisation may prove attractive for several reasons:

  ▰ It enables a firm to specialise in particular aspects of a complex business in which it might have a special advantage, rather than participating in all areas of the business. Many large financial companies have become successful by taking unorthodox approaches to one specialised task, such as lending to owners of mobile homes or identifying the characteristics of potentially profitable credit-card customers. A firm might have no unusual expertise in other parts of the business, such as managing the assets once they have been created. Selling off the assets through securitisation allows the firm to focus on what it does best, where it can add the greatest value.

◪ Selling assets allows issuers to change their risk profile. Among the risks facing a recording artist, for example, is the possibility that changing tastes will result in fewer sales of his or her albums. By securitising certain recordings, the artist can receive a specified amount of revenue immediately. The artist might lose the opportunity to reap huge profits from a release that turns out to be a hit, but also sheds the risk that he or she will fall from popular favour and experience declining sales. If the artist so desires, it may even be possible to structure the transaction so that, should a record sell more than a specified number of copies, he or she receives a portion of the windfall profit.

◪ Issuers may wish to reduce their need for capital. Take the case of a bank that is required by regulators to maintain capital according to the size and type of its assets. When the bank extends a loan, the loan's market value appears as an asset on its balance sheet, and the bank must then set aside the appropriate amount of capital to cover potential declines in the value of that asset. The institution may find that having much of its capital tied up in this way limits opportunities to use that capital for purposes that may generate better returns for shareholders, such as financing new investment or acquiring other firms. Securitising the assets allows the bank to remove them in whole or in part from its balance sheet, thereby freeing up capital for other uses. The bank will no longer receive the interest payments on the loans, but it also has shed the risk that the loans will not be serviced in a timely manner. It can either return the unneeded capital to shareholders or use it to build up parts of the business, such as the origination of loans that are to be securitised, which may enable it to earn better returns for shareholders.

◪ The sale of securitised assets creates publicly available prices. Some types of assets, such as property or rights to recordings, are complicated to trade and, because they are unique, can be difficult to value. Asset-backed securities are usually much easier to trade than the underlying assets themselves. If securities

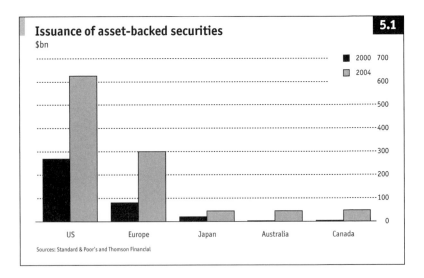

Issuance of asset-backed securities
$bn

5.1

Sources: Standard & Poor's and Thomson Financial

backed by office-building mortgages are selling for half the price they were two years ago, investors, regulators and managers can then have a reasonable idea of what a lender's portfolio of commercial mortgages might be worth even when those specific assets have not been securitised.

Market development

Until recently, securitisation was a huge business in the United States and almost non-existent elsewhere. Several factors encouraged its development. First, the regulatory climate was generally favourable to innovation. The government imposed few obstacles on the growth of the business and, particularly in the area of residential mortgages, even encouraged it. Second, the American legal system did not stand in the way. In countries such as Japan and Italy, by contrast, laws intended to protect the rights of borrowers have until recently inhibited the securitisation of assets, as it has been uncertain whether a trust would have clear title to any assets it might purchase from an issuer. A third influence has been the willingness of investors to perform the complicated mathematical analysis required to determine the value of asset-backed securities. In some countries, investors who were accustomed mainly to buying and holding bonds and equities were not used to such sophisticated analysis, and were slow to accept asset-backed products.

This situation has begun to change quite rapidly. Although about three-quarters of all asset-backed securities are still issued in the United States, securitisation has become popular in Europe and is starting to catch on in Asia (see Figure 5.1). This geographic distribution is likely to change significantly. Japan began to permit securitisation in 1993 as a means of allowing troubled banks to dispose of assets, such as property held as collateral for debtors who have defaulted. An estimated ¥4 trillion ($40 billion) of securitised instruments was issued in 2003. Taiwan passed a law to encourage securitisation in June 2003, and securities worth over NT$50 billion ($1.7 billion) were issued in 2004. Indian issuers sold Rs308 billion ($7 billion) of securitised instruments in the year to March 2005. Other emerging-country governments are also eager to promote development of markets for asset-backed securities, although legal uncertainties continue to stand in the way.

Mortgage-backed securities

Mortgages are by far the most important source of asset-backed securities. Such securities give investors the right to interest payments from a large number of mortgage loans, which are bundled together into securities. Most mortgage-backed securities are based on residential mortgages, but there is also a significant market in commercial mortgage-backed securities (CMBS). These are usually based on pooled loans of a single type, such as mortgages on hotels or office buildings.

Fannie Mae led the way

Although the Danes are credited with first developing the idea of issuing mortgage bonds, the most important step in the creation of the modern market for asset-backed securities was the establishment of the Federal National Mortgage Association (FNMA) in 1938. This company, known as Fannie Mae and originally a government agency, was established to create a secondary market in mortgages. The primary mortgage market involved the decision by a private company, known as the originator, to lend to a home buyer. When it purchased such a loan from the originator in the secondary market, Fannie Mae made it possible for the originator to make yet more loans, providing a substantial impetus to the housing market. With Fannie Mae as a model, private-sector entities began to purchase individual mortgages in secondary-market transactions as early as 1949, and US government regulators formally permitted thrift institutions to buy and sell mortgages in 1957.

From its earliest days, Fannie Mae took steps that were essential to the growth of the secondary market. It established standard procedures to be used in originating the mortgages it would buy, including methods of valuing property, rules for assessing individual borrowers' creditworthiness, and rules relating mortgage eligibility to income. It also set rules to govern servicing, the collection of interest and principal payments from borrowers, which most often was handled by the originator. Such standards eventually smoothed the development of mortgage-backed securities: although each mortgage backing a particular security would be different in detail, investors could be assured that every individual mortgage complied with the same general standards.

Pass-through certificates

Initially, Fannie Mae used government money to purchase mortgages from the lenders that had originated them, with the interest payments on the mortgages serving to repay the government. Then, in the 1960s, investment bankers hit upon an idea for tapping private investment by turning mortgages into securities, rather than buying and selling individual mortgages. These new securities were called pass-through certificates, so named because the principal and interest due monthly from the mortgagors of the loans backing the security would be passed directly to the investors. Pass-throughs, first issued in 1970, were the first modern asset-backed securities.

CMBS

Many different types of mortgages are securitised. As well as a lively market for single-family mortgage securities, there is substantial issuance of commercial mortgage-backed securities, known as CMBS. These may be based on mortgages for apartment buildings, housing for the elderly, retail developments, warehouses, hotels, office buildings and other sorts of structures. CMBS were first issued by Resolution Trust Corporation, a US government agency established to dispose of the assets of failed thrift institutions in the early 1990s. Discovering that it could dispose of these loans far more quickly by securitising them than by selling them off one by one, Resolution Trust Corporation issued nearly $18 billion of securities before ceasing operations in 1998.

Following in its footsteps, investment banks now routinely securitise commercial mortgages, primarily for sale to life insurance companies. Total CMBS issuance in 2004 was approximately $94 billion in the United States, $25 billion in Europe and about $8 billion in Asia.

Table 5.2 **Fannie Mae securities ($bn)**

Calendar year	Amount issued	Amount outstanding
1990	97	300
1992	194	445
1994	130	530
1996	150	651
1998	326	835
2000	212	1,058
2002	723	1,538
2004	527	1,846

Source: Bond Market Association

REMICs

Another important step in the development of securitisation came in 1986, when the US Congress amended the tax laws to provide for Real Estate Mortgage Investment Conduits, known as REMICS. REMICS are a legal device to ensure that the income produced by a mortgage-backed security is taxable to the investors who have purchased the securities, but not to the trust that nominally owns the underlying mortgages and collects the payments from individual mortgagors. Many mortgage-backed securities in the United States are now issued through REMICS.

US agency securities

Several entities sponsored by the US government are authorised to promote secondary markets for mortgage-backed securities. Collectively, the securities they issue are known as agency securities. The market for US agency securities has burgeoned into one of the biggest financial markets of any kind. By 2005 average daily trading volume in agency securities exceeded $250 billion, having increased eightfold in ten years. In general, agency securities are called after the agency that issued them, and each agency's securities have slightly different characteristics.

Fannie Maes

Fannie Maes are issued by the former Federal National Mortgage Association, which is now a shareholder-owned company using Fannie Mae as its corporate name. Each Fannie Mae security is backed by loans made in different parts of the country, enabling investors to reduce the

Table 5.3 **Ginnie Mae activity ($bn)**

Calendar year	Securities issued	Amount outstanding
1990	64	404
1992	82	420
1994	111	451
1996	101	506
1998	150	537
2000	103	612
2002	172	538
2004	127	442

Source: Bond Market Association

risk that economic woes in a particular region will cause a dispropor-tionate number of the securities in a particular pool to go into default. The interest rates on the individual loans in a fixed-rate mortgage pool may vary within a range of 2.5 percentage points. Based on these indi-vidual interest rates, Fannie Mae issues each security bearing a specific rate of interest, and guarantees that investors will receive timely pay-ment of principal and interest each month, even if individual borrowers fail to pay. The company makes its money from the difference between the rates individuals pay to borrow and the lower interest rates paid to investors in pass-throughs, plus various fees. The amount of outstanding Fannie Maes exceeds $1.8 trillion (see Table 5.2 on the previous page).

Ginnie Maes

Ginnie Maes are securities issued by private lenders, mainly mortgage bankers, under the auspices of the Government National Mortgage Association, a US government corporation. The GNMA (hence the name Ginnie Mae) was split off from Fannie Mae in 1968, and is intended to promote home ownership among families of modest means. Each indi-vidual mortgage in a Ginnie Mae pool is guaranteed by some US gov-ernment agency, such as the Veterans Administration, which guarantees mortgages for former members of the US armed forces. The lender groups the mortgages to form a pool of loans having similar payment characteristics and maturities, and then receives Ginnie Mae permission to issue securities based on these mortgages. The lender is responsible for collecting interest and principal from individual borrowers and

Table 5.4 **FHLMC securities ($bn)**

	Amount issued	Amount outstanding
1990	74	321
1992	179	409
1994	117	461
1996	120	554
1998	251	647
2000	167	822
2002	547	1,082
2004	365	1,209

Source: Bond Market Association

sending monthly payments to the holders of the securities it has issued, but the full faith and credit of the US government guarantee that investors will receive all principal and interest payments due. Ginnie Maes worth over $400 billion are now in the hands of investors (see Table 5.3).

Freddie Macs

Freddie Macs are issued by the Federal Home Loan Mortgage Corporation (FHLMC), a private-sector corporation established under government charter. Like Fannie Mae and Ginnie Mae, Freddie Mac operates only in the secondary market and does not lend money directly to individual borrowers. The corporation is obliged by government regulation to devote a share of its mortgage financing to low-income and moderate-income families. Its securities are similar to those issued by Fannie Mae, with which it competes, and do not constitute obligations of the US government. Table 5.4 shows the growth of its lending.

Farmer Macs

Farmer Macs are pass-throughs of mortgages on farms and rural homes. The Federal Agricultural Mortgage Credit Corporation (FAMCC), a shareholder-owned company established by the US government, securitises both agricultural mortgages and loans guaranteed by the US Department of Agriculture, some of which are not mortgages. The company guarantees interest and principal payments to the purchasers of its securities, and its guarantee is backed by a $1.5 billion

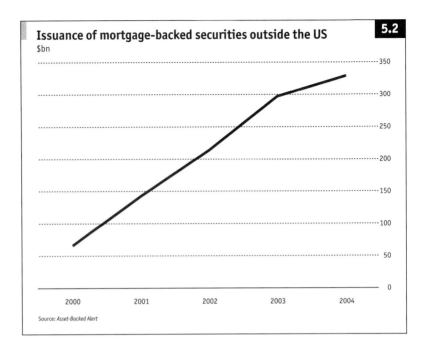

Issuance of mortgage-backed securities outside the US
$bn

5.2

Source: Asset-Backed Alert

line of credit from the US Treasury. The volume of Farmer Mac securities is much smaller than that of the other government-sponsored participants in the US secondary mortgage market.

Mortgage securities outside the United States

A total of $329 billion of mortgage securities was issued outside the United States in 2004, nearly five times the $66 billion issued in 2000 (see Figure 5.2). Here are examples of how markets for mortgage-backed securities have developed in a number of countries outside the United States.

Canada

NHA MBS are mortgage-backed securities issued under the National Housing Act by Canada Mortgage and Housing Corporation, an agency of the Canadian government. The corporation purchases and securitises mortgages issued by authorised private-sector lenders in Canada. Its pass-through securities are backed by single-family mortgages, mortgages on multi-family buildings, mortgages on social housing, or a combination of the three. Interest and principal payments are guaranteed by the corporation, and thus by the Canadian government. The corporation had C$73 billion (US$58 billion) of mortgage-backed securities outstanding at December 2004.

Denmark

Denmark has over $150 billion of mortgage-backed securities outstanding, an extremely large amount for a small country. Danish mortgage securities are backed by fixed-rate residential mortgages with terms of 10–30 years, although, as in the United States, individual borrowers are free to pay off a mortgage before its maturity date without penalty. Unlike US mortgage-backed securities, those in Denmark combine commercial and residential properties, and investors typically receive interest payments quarterly rather than monthly. The underlying mortgages remain on the balance sheet of the mortgage bank that originated them, and are not sold to a trust.

Germany

Pfandbriefe are securities issued by certain mortgage banks or state banks in Europe. *Pfandbriefe* were a German creation, but Spanish and French financial institutions also are major issuers. There are two basic varieties: *Hypothekenpfandbriefe*, which account for 27% of outstanding *Pfandbriefe* and are backed by residential mortgages meeting standards established by the German government; and *Oeffentliche Pfandbriefe*, which are backed by public-sector debt from Germany or other European countries.

Pfandbriefe differ from other asset-backed securities in that they are issued directly by banks, rather than through special-purpose vehicles, and the assets remain on the banks' balance sheets. Also *Pfandbriefe*, unlike other asset-backed securities, are not backed by a fixed pool of assets. The issuing bank can add to the asset pool from time to time and is legally responsible if the assets fail to generate enough income to pay the bond holders. For these reasons, investors in *Pfandbriefe*, unlike investors in most other types of asset-backed securities, must pay close attention to the financial strength of the bank issuing the securities, as it is the ultimate guarantor of payment. Most German mortgages are not securitised through *Pfandbriefe*, as only mortgages not exceeding 60% of the value of the property are eligible. *Pfandbriefe* issuance hit a record €325 billion in 1999, but fell to €209 billion in 2004. Germany accounted for 70% of total issuance, Spain for 18% and France for 9%.

The UK

The first mortgage-backed security in the UK was a £50m issue for National Home Loans in 1987. A total of £1 billion of mortgage-backed securities was issued that year in the UK, and the market has grown steadily since. Expansion has been retarded by the unique characteristics of the British residential mortgage market. A high proportion of mortgages have floating rates that adjust frequently; long-term fixed-rate mortgages are uncommon; and borrowers are able to increase the amount of an outstanding mortgage or to change lenders at little cost. These characteristics make many British mortgages unsuitable for packaging into long-term securities. Nonetheless, British issuance of mortgage-backed securities reached £77 billion in 2004.

Other parts of Europe

Elsewhere in Europe, issuance of mortgage-backed securities has been quite modest, although the creation of the euro is encouraging mortgage securitisation. Issuance in the euro zone in 2004 was €59 billion ($71 billion), mainly in Spain and the Netherlands. Strictly private-sector transactions account for almost all of this amount, as there is no European equivalent of Fannie Mae or Ginnie Mae.

Japan

In Japan, development of mortgage-backed securities was hindered by laws allowing mortgagors to object to the resale of their mortgages. The first attempt to issue a mortgage-backed security failed in 1998. However, several issues were completed successfully in 2000, and issuance in 2004 exceeded ¥1 trillion ($9 billion).

China

The People's Bank of China, the central bank, authorised the issuance of mortgage-backed securities in April 2000. However, there was no issuance until 2005.

Non-mortgage securities

As investors became accustomed to purchasing mortgage-backed securities, financial-market participants naturally began considering the possibilities of other types of asset-backed securities. The most avid participants in this process are banks, which have been able to make use of securitisation to find a new role as intermediaries between borrowers and investors rather than as the ultimate providers of the borrowed funds. Many non-bank lenders have also turned to securitisation to fund their activities, particularly as securitisation allows them to grow far more rapidly than they could if they had to raise capital to support a large portfolio of loans.

Credit-card securities

These were until recently the largest single category of non-mortgage asset-backed securities in both the United States and Europe. Many large banks have securitised part or all of their credit-card portfolios in order to put their capital to more profitable uses. Approximately $370 billion of credit-card securities, typically offering floating interest rates, were outstanding in the United States in 2005, along with several billion dollars in Europe, mainly in the UK.

Home equity loans

Securities backed by home equity loans, often guaranteed by second liens (which offer security only after the borrower's debt to holders of the first mortgage has been satisfied), have flourished in the United States. These became popular after tax-law changes removed preferences for other types of consumer borrowing. Some $476 billion of home-equity asset-backed securities was outstanding in mid-2005, accounting for one-quarter of the American ABS market.

Automotive loans

Often securitised by the finance arms of auto manufacturers, automotive loans are well established in the asset-backed market. Some $226 billion of auto-loan securities were outstanding in the United States in 2005, and far smaller amounts in Canada and Europe. There are also substantial amounts of securities backed by loans on agricultural and construction equipment. Unlike most credit-card and home equity securities, asset-backed securities based on auto loans typically have fixed interest rates.

Manufactured-housing securities

Introduced in the early 1990s, manufactured-housing securities had been considered high-risk loans unsuited for securitisation, as borrowers often have modest incomes, lending procedures were not uniform, and the homes themselves were not considered likely to appreciate in value from year to year. However, once non-bank lenders began to offer and securitise manufactured-housing loans, high interest rates

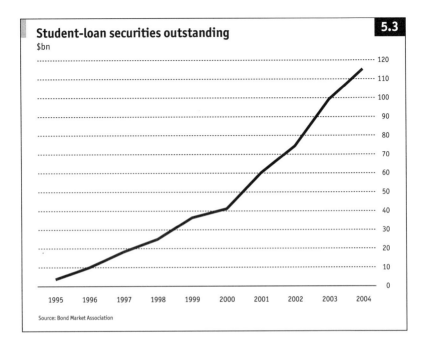

Student-loan securities outstanding
$bn

5.3

Source: Bond Market Association

made them attractive to investors. Some $12 billion of securities backed by manufactured housing were sold in the United States in 1999. Many of the loans went into default as economic growth slowed and unemployment rose in 2000 and 2001, when issuance fell to only $2 billion. Few new securities of this type have been issued, and outstandings have declined as borrowers have repaid their loans.

Student loans

Student loans have been securitised only since June 1993. Most student-loan securitisation is conducted by the Student Loan Marketing Association (SLMA), a shareholder-owned company established by the US government. The company, known as Sallie Mae, purchases student loans in the secondary market and packages them for sale as securities. Figure 5.3 shows the amount outstanding, which accounted for 7% of all US asset-backed securities by 2005.

CDOs

Collateralised debt obligations, created in the early 1990s, have become a major part of the asset-backed market. CDOs are securities representing ownership of corporate loans. Unlike the other types of assets most frequently securitised, the loans underlying CDOs are not standardised, and an investor may find it difficult to predict how they will perform. Some CDOs may also be based in part on bonds, other asset-backed securities, or credit default swaps (explained in Chapter 4). Some CDOs involve a large amount of leverage, which has caused financial regulators to express concern about potential losses should the assets not perform as expected. An estimated $287 billion of CDOs was outstanding in the US in mid-2005. CDOs account for 15% of asset-backed securities.

Assorted others

Novel types of asset-backed securities are frequently offered for sale. Small-business loans have successfully been securitised by several banks, even though they constitute a fairly heterogeneous asset. Film distribution companies, such as The Walt Disney Co, have successfully securitised the anticipated revenue from groups of films, and in 1998 a singer, David Bowie, securitised future revenue from recordings that had already been issued. Securities backed by anticipated ticket revenue have been used to build sports stadiums in several American cities. Unlike loan securitisations, however, sports and entertainment securitisations are usually one-of-a-kind deals and do not account for a large proportion of the market. They pose some significant risks not present in other types of securitisation, as the value of the securities depends heavily on the ability and willingness of particular entertainers or athletes to promote their product in future.

Asset-backed commercial paper

The assets that support medium-term and long-term securities can also be used to back commercial paper, a security with a maturity of less than 270 days. Fully supported paper has repayment guaranteed by a source other than the underlying assets, such as a surety bond or a letter of credit, and repayment of partially supported asset-backed paper depends primarily on the cash flow from the pool of assets. The paper is issued by a trust or other special-purpose vehicle, which uses the proceeds to purchase assets such as receivables. The trust may purchase these assets from a single firm or from several different firms.

Asset-backed commercial paper was created to meet investor demand for high-quality commercial paper in the face of limited corporate issuance. In effect, by repackaging long-term obligations, investment banks are able to market securities with the desired term. About $850 billion of such paper was in circulation in the United States at the end of 2005.

Structured finance

The basics of asset-backed securities are reasonably simple: the issuer pools the assets that are to underlie the securities, and then issues securities giving the owners the right to income from those assets. But matters can get far more complicated. A significant portion of the asset-backed market consists of structured securities: securities designed to allow the investor to accept a greater or smaller amount of risk in return for a greater or smaller expected return. The best-known structured securities are collateralised mortgage obligations, or CMOs, but there are many non-mortgage variants as well.

To create structured securities, the issuer divides the securities backed by a pool into sections, called tranches or classes, with different characteristics. One CMO created from a mortgage-backed security, for example, might consist of all principal and interest payments received during the first three years. A second tranche might consist of payments received in years 4–7, and so on. Non-mortgage securities can be structured in a similar way. Usually, 3–5 separate securities are created from each pool of assets. The highest-risk tranches often are marketed to individual investors, who may be enticed by the high yields without fully understanding the risks involved.

In many cases, issuers and their investment bankers design asset-backed securities to meet the needs of particular investors with regard to the timing of income, regulatory restrictions on investments, or tax considerations. One widely used technique is to create STRIPS, securities which treat the interest-bearing component of the security separately from the repayment of principal. These components behave very differently from one another. Interest-only STRIPS, for example, will lose value when interest rates fall, as more borrowers will pay their loans early and thus pay less interest than anticipated, even as the corresponding principal-only STRIPS gain in value as their owners receive principal payments sooner than expected. Of equal concern to investors, however, may be the fact that the interest received by the owners of interest-only STRIPS may, in some countries, be taxed at a higher rate than the capital gains earned by the owners of the principal-only STRIPS.

The optionality factor

This structuring creates a way to attach an explicit price to the optionality that is inherent in most asset-backed securities. The optionality stems from the fact that in most cases the borrower of a loan that has been securitised has the right to repay early, and in some cases may have the right to extend the loan rather than repaying as scheduled. The shortest-term tranche, usually called the A tranche, is least likely to be affected by repayments and is therefore the most stable among the structured securities. The next segment, the B tranche, could be expected to be more volatile, and investors will require a higher interest rate to purchase it. The most volatile tranche of a structured security is the support tranche, which is entitled to principal and interest payments in the most distant time period and therefore, by design, is the tranche that absorbs most of the prepayment and extension risk. For CMOs, the support tranche is referred to as the planned amortisation class, or the Z tranche. This tranche offers high returns when interest rates are stable. When rates rise or fall significantly, however, individuals may be more inclined to repay their loans or to extend payment, and the value of the Z tranche can fluctuate widely. For this reason, it is sometimes referred to in the market as "toxic waste".

US agency securities make up the biggest part of the CMO market.

Pricing

The price of a fixed-rate asset-backed security is usually expressed as an interest-rate yield compared with the yield of an appropriate benchmark, most often government bonds of similar maturity. Floating-rate asset-backed securities are usually priced from a widely used floating interest rate, such as the London Inter-Bank Offer Rate (LIBOR). The difference between the yield of an asset-backed security and that of its benchmark varies greatly and depends upon many factors:

■ **Credit risk.** When an economy is strong, borrowers are expected to have little difficulty meeting their obligations and the premium required by investors in asset-backed securities will be small. If the economy is seen to be slowing or in recession, however, investors in asset-backed securities will demand wider spreads to compensate for the risk that individual borrowers will encounter financial distress and default on their loans. This spread-widening was clearly in evidence in August 1998, for example, after economic troubles in East Asia and Russia's moratorium on some

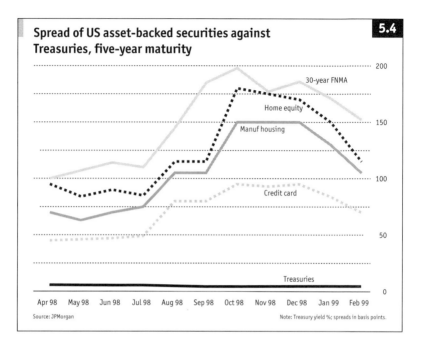

5.4

Spread of US asset-backed securities against Treasuries, five-year maturity

30-year FNMA

Home equity

Manuf housing

Credit card

Treasuries

Apr 98 May 98 Jun 98 Jul 98 Aug 98 Sep 98 Oct 98 Nov 98 Dec 98 Jan 99 Feb 99

Source: JPMorgan

Note: Treasury yield %; spreads in basis points.

bond payments caused many investors to anticipate an economic slowdown. As these worries receded, early in 1999, spreads again narrowed, as shown in Figure 5.4.

◪ **Rating.** Credit-rating agencies evaluate asset-backed securities with methods similar to those used for corporate securities. In particular, they closely scrutinise the financial strength of any firm or government agency that purports to guarantee payment of interest and/or principal if the securities fail to perform as expected. Higher-rated asset-backed securities can be expected to trade much closer to their benchmarks than lower-rated securities.

◪ **Asset characteristics.** Two pools of credit-card loans or fixed-rate mortgages may appear similar, yet have very different characteristics. Investors quantify and study the characteristics of the assets, such as the weighted average maturity, the weighted average age of the underlying loans and the delinquency rate, in order to compare the expected cash flows of different pools.

◪ **Prepayment risk.** One of the greatest risks faced by investors in asset-backed securities is that individual borrowers may pay part or all of the principal of their loans ahead of schedule. This occurs most often at a time of declining interest rates, and can force the owners of securities to reinvest the prepaid funds at a lower rate of interest than they had expected to receive. Also, some tranches of structured securities may lose a large part of their value if prepayments are greater than expected. Large investors in asset-backed securities have developed elaborate mathematical models to estimate prepayment rates, but these models are often subject to significant error.

◪ **Extension risk.** This is the reverse of prepayment risk. If market interest rates rise, the average term of the loans in a pool may be higher than expected as borrowers avoid prepayment, causing investors in the securities to be stuck with a comparatively low-yielding asset for longer than they anticipated. Extension risk, like prepayment risk, is difficult to model accurately.

◪ **Underwriting risk.** Some of the banks that originate asset-backed securities are known to be scrupulous in making the underlying loans. These securities will generally have lower yields than similar securities issued by banks that are thought to be less careful about underwriting loans.

◪ **Servicing risk.** Servicing is the collection of principal and interest payments from individual borrowers. The servicer receives a fee for collecting each payment and passes the remainder of the payment to the trustee to be paid out to the investors. Some servicers are far more successful than others at collecting timely payments and dealing with borrowers who are in default. The quality of the servicer will be reflected in the price of each security.

Buying asset-backed securities

Their comparatively high yield makes asset-backed securities attractive investments. Most types of asset-backed securities, including mortgage-backed securities, are sold in small denominations and can be purchased from brokerage firms. Some securities, notably *Pfandbriefe*, are traded on stock exchanges. However, because the value of an individual asset-backed security may be dramatically altered by prepayments or other factors that are difficult to project, owning a single security can be risky for an unsophisticated investor. For this reason, individuals may be better off investing in a fund that owns many asset-backed securities than purchasing the securities directly.

Measuring performance

On average, mortgage-backed and asset-backed securities produce substantially higher returns than government or corporate bonds of similar maturity and asset quality. However, the returns on asset-backed securities are often far more volatile than those of other types of fixed-income securities, and some types of asset-backed securities may be far more volatile than others. Investing in individual asset-backed securities requires considerable quantitative skill. Investors can obtain highly detailed information about the individual loans in each security, as well as the characteristics of the borrowers and the rate at which the loans are being repaid. The extent to which repayment rates, late payments and defaults differ from expectations can greatly affect the value of the securities.

Several investment banks publish indexes of the performance of asset-backed securities. The performance of these indexes can readily be compared with the performance of corporate-bond indexes. Many US agency mortgage securities are owned by mutual funds that hold only this type of security, and the annual rates of return of these funds are widely published in newspapers.

Tracking the performance of more esoteric varieties of asset-backed securities can be difficult. Because of their unique characteristics, these securities often trade in comparatively illiquid markets, and this makes it difficult to attach a meaningful value to them.

6 International fixed-income markets

M OST FINANCIAL-MARKET ACTIVITY takes place wholly within the boundaries of a single country and is denominated in that country's currency. A large and growing share, however, now crosses national boundaries, as individuals move capital into currencies that seem to offer greater returns, and as borrowers search the globe for money at the lowest price.

This international market for money can be divided into two segments. In some cases investors and borrowers will arrange transactions in a country other than their own, using that country's currency. In other cases, a transaction will be arranged in a currency other than that of the country where it occurs. Until recently, the former were known simply as foreign transactions, and the latter were referred to as Euromarket transactions. The distinction between the two has blurred, however, as this chapter will explain.

A brief history of the Euromarkets

The idea of using the money of one country to transact business in another is not a new one. Such offshore dealings have gone on for centuries, often with the aims of avoiding taxes, regulation or confiscation. The name Euromarket was first applied to the acceptance of offshore deposits in 1957, at the height of the cold war, when Moscow Narodny Bank decided to transfer its dollar deposits out of the United States to foreclose the possibility that the US government would confiscate Soviet assets. The Russians had their dollars transferred from New York to a French bank that had the cable address EUROBANK, and soon all dollars deposited in European banks took the name Eurodollars.

Market surge

These dollars helped create a new financial market as a result of the Bretton Woods system of fixed exchange rates, around which the economy of the non-communist world was organised after the second world war. This system still had aspects of a gold standard: if a country had a balance-of-payments deficit, it would settle the imbalance by paying gold to its creditor countries. In theory, the loss of that gold would lead the country's central bank to contract the money supply, which would slow the economy, which would in turn reduce demand for imports and thus bring the balance of payments back into balance. By the late 1950s, however, the United States seemed to be running a persistent balance-of-payments deficit, and government officials grew concerned that the country's gold stocks were running low. One cause of the problem was thought to be that foreigners were issuing too many securities in the United States and then exchanging the proceeds for foreign currency to use in their home countries. This worsened the US payments imbalance, putting yet more pressure on gold reserves. The US government responded with a set of policies, of which the centrepiece was the interest equalisation tax, recommended by President John Kennedy in July 1963 and enacted in August 1964. By claiming 15% of the interest received by Americans on stocks and bonds issued by Europeans (securities from Canada, Japan and less-developed countries were exempt), the tax was intended to reduce capital outflows and thus staunch the loss of gold.

Back in business

The tax accomplished its immediate objective, as the so-called Yankee bond market, in which foreigners sold dollar-denominated bonds in the United States, quickly dried up. The financing needs that had given rise to Yankee bonds remained, however, and European financial markets were still in sufficient disarray from the war that they could not raise large amounts of capital. Investment bankers quickly hit upon the idea of selling dollar-denominated bonds in London, where, as long as they were not sold to American residents, the securities would be unaffected by the US tax.

The first Eurobond, a $15m offering by Autostrade, an Italian motorway company, was issued in 1963. In 1964, 76 separate eurobond issues raised almost $1.2 billion, and the Eurobond market was firmly established. When the Interest Equalisation Tax was extended to bank loans in 1965, banks moved much of their dollar-based international lending to London as well. As British banking regulations did not apply to foreign banks lending in foreign currencies, banks from around the world flocked to set up offices in London. By the time the Interest Equalisation Tax was removed in 1974, the Euromarket was a prominent part of the international financial scene.

The international bond market today

The international market is neither an exchange nor a particular group

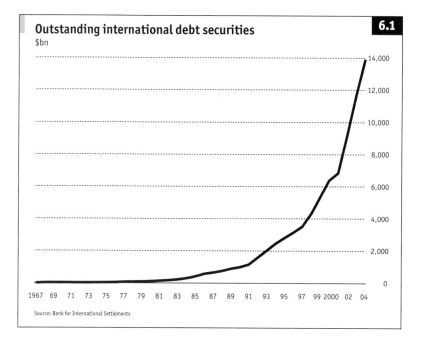

Outstanding international debt securities
$bn

6.1

Source: Bank for International Settlements

of products. Rather, the term refers to a decentralised system in which currencies held outside their home countries are reloaned without being converted to another currency. Most Euromarket dealings take the form of bank loans to customers and short-term loans from one bank to another. The securities markets, however, account for a large and rapidly growing share of international activity. The size of the market, expressed in terms of securities outstanding, is shown in Figure 6.1.

By comparison, there are approximately $36 trillion of debt securities of all types outstanding in domestic financial markets. The international markets, with about $14 trillion of debt securities outstanding, thus constitute 28% of the total worldwide market for debt securities.

As Figure 6.2 on the next page illustrates, international securities are playing an increasingly important role in the global securities markets. The international markets are also growing more rapidly than domestic markets. The precise number of securities traded is unknown, but it is thought to be well over 100,000.

As with domestic debt instruments, international instruments come in three main varieties: bonds, medium-term notes and short-term

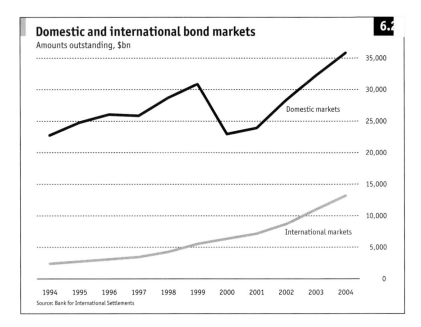

Domestic and international bond markets
Amounts outstanding, $bn

6.2

35,000
30,000
Domestic markets
25,000
20,000
15,000
10,000
International markets
5,000
0

1994 1995 1996 1997 1998 1999 2000 2001 2002 2003 2004
Source: Bank for International Settlements

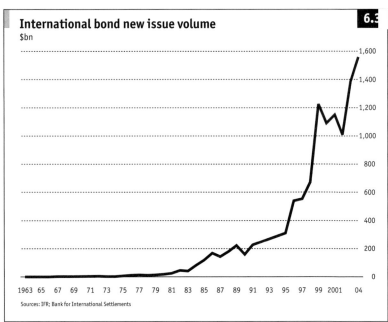

International bond new issue volume
$bn

6.3

1,600
1,400
1,200
1,000
800
600
400
200
0

1963 65 67 69 71 73 75 77 79 81 83 85 87 89 91 93 95 97 99 2001 04
Sources: IFR; Bank for International Settlements

Table 6.1 **Net international bond and note issues, by currency ($bn)**

	1995	1998	2000	2002	2004
Euro	...	...	406.0	495.0	924.0
US dollar	74.1	404.3	554.1	436.0	380.0
D-mark	55.1	69.1	...	...	...
Pound sterling	10.1	55.3	91.9	52.0	134.0
French franc	5.2	27.1	...	...	...
Australian dollar	14.3	-4.5	-1.0	9.0	30.0
Yen	108.4	-24.7	11.2	-18.0	27.0
Canadian dollar	-2.1	-7.8	-2.6	4.0	26.0
Swiss franc	4.4	7.0	3.5	8.0	13.0
Hong Kong dollar	4.0	6.9	4.9	7.0	7.0

Source: Bank for International Settlements

commercial paper. The issuance of new bonds and notes has been increasing rapidly, as shown in Figure 6.3.

Although these instruments are sometimes referred to as Eurodollar paper, the term is a misnomer. The US dollar is only one of the currencies used in the Euromarket. It is equally possible to issue securities denominated in yen (Euroyen), Swiss francs, New Zealand dollars (Eurokiwis) and any other freely convertible currency. Historically, the US dollar and the yen have been the main currencies of issuance, with the D-mark a distant third. When the single European currency, the euro, was created at the start of 1999, it quickly became the most important vehicle for issuance of international securities, as shown in Table 6.1. (It should be noted that the Euromarket and the market for euro-denominated securities are by no means the same thing; euro-denominated securities issued in a country that has adopted the euro as its currency are domestic instruments, not international ones.)

A borrower's decision to issue bonds in a particular currency does not mean that the borrower requires that currency to finance investments. The larger and more sophisticated borrowers tapping the international market for financing will borrow in whichever currency offers the most attractive interest rates at a given time and then, through the foreign-exchange markets, obtain the desired currency. The large share of issuance occurring in US dollars in most years therefore reflects favourable dollar interest rates and the large pool of investors preferring

Table 6.2 **Net issuance of international money-market instruments ($bn)**

	1995	1998	1999	2000	2002	2004
Commercial paper	4.7	22.2	49.1	55.2	23.7	40.4
Other short-term paper	12.7	−12.4	86.4	97.0	−22.8	20.9

Source: Bank for International Settlements

to purchase dollar-denominated securities, rather than the issuers' need for dollars.

Money-market instruments

As well as bonds, which have maturities of up to 30 years, and medium-term notes, with maturities of 1–5 years, short-term instruments are also traded in the international markets. Commercial paper, sometimes referred to as euro-commercial paper, is debt with a maturity of less than 270 days, issued by corporate borrowers. There is also a lively international market in other short-term paper, sometimes called short-term euronotes. These are mainly tradable bank deposits, similar to certificates of deposit, and government securities maturing within one year. As Table 6.2 shows, demand for international money-market instruments, modest until recently, exploded in 1999 with the adoption of the single European currency, then fell as low long-term rates made issuance of long-dated bonds more attractive.

Historically, the majority of international money-market instruments have been traded in US dollars, with yen, Swiss francs, pounds sterling, D-marks and Hong Kong dollars also being used significantly. Since 2002, however, the euro has vied with the dollar as the main currency of issuance.

In comparison with domestic money markets, trading in international money-market instruments remains small. In 2004, for example, some $498 billion in commercial paper and $178 billion of other short-term securities were issued in domestic markets around the world. This was ten times the net issuance of commercial paper in the international markets. In some years, the amount of other short-term securities outstanding in international markets actually declines.

The issuers

As many aspects of the international markets are unregulated, there are

Table 6.3 **International debt securities outstanding, by nationality of issuer ($bn)**

	1994	1998	2000	2002	2004
US	210	839	1,762	2,714	3,354
Germany	189	501	913	1,446	2,332
UK	213	366	563	782	1,403
France	185	264	314	517	930
Netherlands	81	183	293	433	690
Italy	85	114	209	371	683

Source: Bank for International Settlements

no restrictions as to who may issue bonds. However, investors generally require that issuers obtain ratings from credit-rating agencies, just as they do with most domestic issues of bonds and commercial paper. There is a considerable market in bonds that are rated below investment grade. This is a significant attraction for companies in countries where there is no domestic market for below-investment-grade bonds.

Entities based in the United States normally make up the most important group of issuers. In 2004, however, the UK was the largest country of issuance, as extremely low US interest rates encouraged US companies to fund themselves in the domestic market. However, companies and governments in many different countries turn to the international markets for financing. The biggest issuers of international debt securities include the Republic of Italy, the World Bank, leading banks and telecommunications companies, the governments of Denmark and Sweden, and the European Investment Bank, an arm of the European Union. Table 6.3 lists the countries whose corporations and governments are the largest borrowers in the international markets.

During the 1990s many borrowers in emerging economies entered the international debt markets for the first time. Previously, both firms and governments in less advanced economies had raised capital mainly through bank borrowings, which typically have higher interest rates and shorter terms than bonds. After years of inflation, stabilisation programmes and other economic reforms made countries such as Mexico and Argentina more attractive to foreign investors, and relaxation of financial regulations has permitted firms in these countries to sell bonds abroad more readily. Typically, corporations from emerging-market countries succeed in selling bonds internationally only after the national

Table 6.4 **Emerging market issuers of debt securities, amount outstanding ($bn)**

	1996	1998	2000	2002	2004
Argentina	29.9	54.4	71.7	85.4	93.2
Brazil	28.8	41.5	56.1	70.1	73.1
South Korea	43.9	53.1	49.7	54.6	66.9
Mexico	43.3	53.6	65.8	65.7	59.2
Hong Kong	25.9	31.6	31.6	41.7	49.4
Philippines	7.1	10.6	15.6	20.2	25.0
Malaysia	10.1	12.7	15.3	23.4	23.4
Russia	1.3	20.4	17.7	20.8	23.4
Hungary	13.5	12.4	10.3	10.3	16.5
Venezuela	3.4	10.9	11.0	12.5	15.5
China	13.9	17.6	17.5	17.2	14.7
Thailand	12.5	14.4	14.2	10.9	9.7
Indonesia	10.8	17.4	11.0	9.2	4.4

Source: Bank for International Settlements

government has obtained ratings from credit-rating agencies and completed a sovereign bond issue. Both government and corporate issuers in these countries typically break into the market with bonds maturing in as little as two or three years, but they are able to issue securities with longer maturities as they become better known to investors.

The growth of emerging-market issuance has been erratic owing to the financial and exchange-rate crises that have afflicted major borrowers. In 1994, for example, issuers from emerging countries sold $32.5 billion of debt in the international markets, but issuance fell to $22 billion the following year, after Mexico was forced to devalue its peso in December 1994. Some $72 billion was sold during 1997, but in 1998, as exchange-rate problems ravaged Thailand, South Korea, Russia and several other countries and threatened to spill over into Latin America, emerging-market debt issuance fell to $24.3 billion. The prices of these securities are often quite volatile as well, offering extremely attractive returns for investors at some points and declining sharply at other times. In early 2002, after Argentina effectively defaulted on its bonds and devalued its currency, Argentinian government bonds were selling for as little as one-quarter of their face value. Table 6.4 lists the biggest emerging market borrowers, by nationality.

Financial institutions are by far the largest borrowers in the international bond markets, accounting for about 70% of all debt securities outstanding. Corporate issuers rank a distant second, accounting for about one-eighth of the debt traded in international markets. The role of government and state agency issuers has diminished markedly. These proportions vary greatly from country to country. Public-sector issuers, for example, account for the majority of the outstanding international debt securities issued by entities in Argentina, Greece and Turkey. At the other extreme, private-sector borrowers account for the lion's share of the bonds and short-term paper sold internationally by entities from Hong Kong, India, Switzerland and the United States.

Types of instruments

The variety of instruments traded in the international markets is similar to that available in the domestic markets of countries with advanced financial systems:

- **Fixed-rate bonds.** These are the most widely traded instrument, accounting for approximately three-quarters of all bonds and notes outstanding in the Euromarket. In recent years there have been some extremely large fixed-rate issues, with one corporate eurobond issue in 2001 reaching $14 billion.
- **Floating-rate bonds.** Almost all issued by financial institutions, these accounted for 26% of the total amount of bonds outstanding at December 2004.
- **Equity-linked bonds.** These constitute less than 5% of the paper traded in the Euromarket. Almost all of them are convertible, meaning they can be exchanged for the issuer's shares at a predetermined time and price. Equity-linked bonds are issued almost exclusively by non-financial corporations.

The swaps market

Neither the type nor the currency of an international bond issue provides a clear indication of the obligations the borrower has taken on. This is because the international bond markets are tightly linked to the swaps market. Swaps are derivative instruments that permit the user to exchange one set of payment obligations for another. Often, an issuer will sell bonds of whatever type and currency offers the most attractive interest rate at the time of issue and simultaneously enter a swap so that it can make payments in the form desired.

Table 6.5 **Notional value of interest-rate swaps and forwards ($trn)**

Maturity	1998	2000	2002	2004
0–1 year	16.1	21.7	33.2	52.5
1–5 years	17.2	21.2	33.9	65.5
Over 5 years	8.8	12.3	20.8	42.2

Source: Bank for International Settlements

Swaps can make financial reports misleading. For example, an industrial firm that entered the international markets to issue £100m of fixed-rate ten-year bonds with a 6% coupon might be assumed to face a £6m annual interest payment, when in reality it swapped the payments for floating-rate US dollar payments, the size of which will depend upon US interest rates. If US interest rates were to rise suddenly, the firm could thus find itself in financial distress even though it has no dollar-denominated borrowings.

The most common transactions are fixed-for-floating swaps in the same currency. In such deals, the issuer exchanges payment obligations with a counterparty, usually a bank. An issuer of fixed-rate bonds would exchange its fixed payment obligation for the obligation to pay a floating interest rate on a similar amount of principal. Conversely, an issuer of floating-rate bonds might trade its payment obligation for a fixed-rate payment. The desirability of such a transaction depends on swap spreads, the premiums banks demand for agreeing to take on fixed-rate payments (which are usually higher but stable) and to cede floating-rate payments (which are usually lower but variable). There is a lively market in swaps, and market participants can easily obtain current swap spreads from financial information providers.

In the case of long-term bonds, swaps lasting until the bonds' maturity may be difficult to obtain in the market. In such a case, an issuer might arrange a fixed-for-floating swap for five or ten years, after which it would reassume the obligation to make fixed payments or, perhaps, arrange another swap transaction. Table 6.5 shows the growth of the market for interest-rate swaps of different maturities. The figures, in trillions of dollars, represent the face value of obligations being swapped, not the much smaller amounts that individual participants have at risk as interest rates change.

The volume of new interest-rate swaps is obviously much larger than the volume of new international bond issues, as most swaps are related to domestic bond issues or other types of obligations. The swaps market was almost entirely a telephone market up to 2002, but an electronic swaps trading system sponsored by major banks began in 2002.

Global bonds

A global bond is an issue that is marketed simultaneously in the international markets and in the domestic market of the currency of issue. The first global bond, a $1.5 billion issue by the World Bank in 1989, was sold simultaneously as a domestic security in the United States and as an international security in the Euromarket, with the issuer dedicating separate portions, or tranches, to each market. Until 1999, the number of global issues was quite small, as a large issue is needed to make the procedure worthwhile. However, a general increase in investor demand for large (and hence more liquid) issues has resulted in several huge global issues. The biggest so far, a $16.4 billion issue by France Telecom in March 2001, included bonds denominated in dollars, euros and sterling, with maturities ranging from two to 30 years.

Bond issuance

The method for issuing securities in the international markets is significantly different from that in most domestic markets. The requirement for registration or regulatory approval depends on where the issue will occur and whether the issuer wishes the bonds to trade on an exchange after the issue. In general, disclosures about the issuer's financial condition and other matters may be substantially less than would accompany a domestic issue in many countries of the European Union, Canada, or the United States.

Most international bond issues are sold by a syndicate or selling group of investment dealers formed for the purpose. The principal investment bank, the syndicate manager, determines the price at which the issue will be sold and allocates the bonds to the other dealers in the syndicate. Syndicate members handle the bonds on a fixed-price re-offer basis, meaning that they agree to sell the bonds to customers only at the established price as long as the bonds are still in syndicate. Once the issue is sold, the syndicate breaks and the bonds can trade in the secondary market at prices determined by demand and supply.

In certain cases, the issuer and its lead bank will agree on a bought deal. This means that one bank or a syndicate purchases the entire issue and seeks to resell it in the market, taking the risk that it will lose money if it is unable to sell the bonds for more than it has paid the issuer. In other cases, the bonds will be sold on a best efforts basis, reverting to the issuer in the event that the members of the syndicate are unable to sell them.

Trading

The market for international bonds is largely an over-the-counter market. Although more than 16,000 international bond issues are listed on the Luxembourg Stock Exchange, and bonds are traded on other bourses as well, primarily in London, most dealing occurs over the telephone rather than at exchanges. Several banks are attempting to create electronic trading systems, but these remain in their infancy.

The lack of market information has contributed to illiquidity, which is perhaps the most severe problem confronting the international markets. Many international bonds disappear into investors' portfolios and are then held to maturity, which keeps trading volume rather small. For example, the Luxembourg Stock Exchange handled fewer than 7,000 bond trades in 2004, or less than one trade for every three listed bonds.

Trading in international bonds is also restricted by national regulations. Some countries allow dealers to sell bonds only to large, sophisticated investors, known in legal terminology as qualified institutional buyers, called QIBS (pronounced quibs). The American authorities prohibit the sale of international bonds to American residents for 40 days after issue, and require that such bonds be seasoned by being sold first to other investors before Americans may buy them.

Towards international standards

As it is difficult for national regulators to set rules for markets that operate all over the world, the leading dealers created the International Capital Markets Association (ICMA) to establish standard practices. Based in Switzerland, the ICMA is now recognised as a self-regulatory organisation by the British authorities, and all major dealers adhere to its rules. Among other things, the ICMA has established procedures for clearing transactions, including a reporting system so firms can identify and reconcile errors that may have occurred in writing down the name and quantity of a security that has been bought or sold. The ICMA has also agreed on settlement procedures, so that for all international bond trades among its members, money and securities change hands on the third business day after the transaction.

Table 6.6 **International bond prices**

	Red date	Coupon	S&P rating	Bid price	Bid yield	Day's chge yield	Mth's chge yield	Spread v. govt. bonds
US $								
EIB	1.09	5.25	AAA	89.8364	6.72	0.07	0.47	0.72
ABN Amro	6.07	7.125	AA–	98.6712	7.35	0.16	0.63	1.39
Canadian $								
Bayer L-Bk	8.04	9.50	AAA	114.6927	6.07	0.09	0.20	0.10
Toronto M	5.04	8.5	AA+	109.8195	6.12	0.08	0.27	0.15
Swiss francs								
EIB	1.08	3.75	AAA	99.4726	3.82	0.02	0.49	1.08
Brit Colum	2.02	3.25	AA–	102.207	2.38	0.02	0.52	0.36
Australian $								
S. Aust Gov	6.03	7.75	AA–	104.2365	6.51	0.08	0.09	0.79
GMAC Aust	5.01	9.00	n/a	104.3628	6.47	0.03	–0.14	1.32

Obtaining price information

There is no central source for price and volume information concerning the international markets. Most issues trade infrequently, if at all. In any case, most transactions are conducted between a customer and a bond dealer, which has no obligation to inform the public about the details of any transaction. Thus the reported price of a bond may be imputed from the prices of other, similar bonds, rather than the price at which a transaction actually occurred.

Nonetheless, financial information services do seek to report the prices of international bonds, and price tables appear in some newspapers. Table 6.6, drawn from the *Financial Times*, lists bonds denominated in four different currencies. Following the maturity date, the bond coupon and the rating assigned by Standard & Poor's, a ratings agency, the table provides bid prices (prices at which investors or dealers have offered to purchase the bonds) in relation to the initial offering price of 100. The bid yield column calculates the yield the bonds would offer if purchased at the bid price, thus giving an indication of what investors consider to be an appropriate interest rate for bonds of that currency, maturity and credit quality. The next two columns give the change in the yield over the past day and the past month. The last column provides the spread between the yield on the given bond and the yield on a bond of the same maturity issued by the national government whose currency is being used. This number offers the purest measure of credit risk, as it represents the premium investors demand for holding a bond other than a government bond.

In Table 6.6 it can be seen that bonds issued by the European Investment Bank in US dollars, maturing in 2009, are yielding 6.72%, but the same institution's bonds in Swiss francs, maturing in 2008, are yielding only 3.82%. An investor considering a purchase, however, would surely note the fact that the US dollar bonds yield only 0.72 percentage points more than US Treasury securities, whereas the Swiss franc bonds yield 1.08 percentage points more than Swiss government bonds. The investor might therefore decide that the lower-yielding Swiss franc bonds offer better value, relative to other securities available in the market.

Looking ahead

The international bond market developed largely as a response to taxation and regulation in domestic bond markets. It allowed issuers to borrow money in the currency of their choice without being bound by the regulations of the country whose currency they used. Because the bonds were issued in bearer form, without being registered in the buyer's name, they allowed investors to protect their anonymity and, in some cases, avoid taxation.

Over the years, however, many of the distinctive features of the international market have been eroded. As national governments have liberalised their rules for issuing and trading securities and eased restrictions on cross-border capital flows, the advantages of Euromarket issues have ceased to loom large. Efforts to impose a withholding tax on bond interest received by individual investors within the European Union could eliminate much of the tax advantage of issuing abroad. Global bond issues and the creation of cross-border issues within the EU have blurred the distinction between Eurobonds and other international bond issues. Some securities traditionally considered to be domestic, such as *Pfandbrief* mortgage bonds issued in Germany, are now promoted heavily to foreign investors and are considered international instruments.

These changes have blurred the difference between Eurobonds and foreign bonds. The term international bonds is now applied to both, and the Euromarkets label has largely been made redundant. But although the Euromarkets may have faded into history, the international bond markets are flourishing and are likely to grow rapidly.

7 Equity markets

"IT IS USUALLY AGREED that casinos should, in the public interest, be inaccessible and expensive. And perhaps the same is true of Stock Exchanges." So wrote a British economist, John Maynard Keynes, in 1935. Keynes's jibe is not entirely misplaced; more than a few punters approach the stockmarkets in the same spirit as the racetrack or the roulette wheel. Yet for all their shortcomings, as Keynes himself acknowledged, stockmarkets offer one singular advantage: they are the best way to bring people with money to invest together with people who can put that investment to productive use.

The origins of equities

Equity, quite simply, means ownership. Equities, therefore, are shares that represent part ownership of a business enterprise. The idea of share ownership goes back to medieval times. It became widespread during the Renaissance, when groups of merchants joined to finance trading expeditions and early bankers took part ownership of businesses to ensure repayment of loans. These early shareholder-owned enterprises, however, were usually temporary ventures established for a limited purpose, such as financing a single voyage by a ship, and were dissolved once their purpose was accomplished.

The first shareholder-owned business may have been the Dutch East India Company, which was founded by Dutch merchants in 1602 and issued negotiable share certificates that were readily traded in Amsterdam until the company failed almost two centuries later. By the late 17th century, traders in London coffee houses earned their living dealing in the shares of joint-stock companies. But it was not until the industrial revolution made it necessary to raise large amounts of capital to build factories and canals that share trading become widespread. Today, the capitalisation of the world's stockmarkets exceeds $36 trillion. Table 7.1 on the next page gives the total stockmarket capitalisation – the value of all shares listed – in several countries; Table 7.2 on page 131 shows the value of share turnover in various countries.

Raising capital

Raising capital remains the main function of equity markets. But the equity markets are not the only way for firms to raise capital. Before

Table 7.1 **Equity market capitalisation, September 2005**

Country	Market capitalisation ($bn)
US	16,693
Japan	3,954
UK	3,036
Euronext	2,607
Canada	1,479
Germany	1,198
Spain	1,048
Hong Kong	982
Switzerland	881
Australia	821
Italy	778
OMX	775
South Korea	600
India	513
Taiwan	435

a Includes former Amsterdam, Brussels and Paris stock exchanges.
b Includes Copenhagen, Helsinki, Stockholm, Tallina, Riga and Vilnius stock exchanges.
Source: World Federation of Exchanges

turning to the markets to obtain financing, firms undertake a detailed analysis of alternative methods of meeting their requirements.

Loans

Loans are the main type of financing available to firms that have not issued securities. Lenders such as banks are accustomed to analysing the business plans and financial condition of small firms, and often lend to companies that would have difficulty raising funds in the financial markets. Bank loans, however, are expensive, and banks can lend only a limited amount to a single borrower. Firms which are able to do so often prefer to diversify their borrowing by selling bonds, securities that entitle the holder to payment of interest and repayment of principal at predetermined times. Bonds (discussed in Chapter 4) have the disadvantage of imposing a fixed repayment obligation, which may be difficult to meet if the firm's revenue is weak. Some firms can meet part of their financing needs by securitisation (discussed in Chapter 5), the sale of

Table 7.2 **The value of share turnover, $bn**

	2000	2004
US	32,994	20,976
UK	4,559	5,169
Japan	2,640	3,352
Euronext[a]	4,911	2,472
Germany	2,120	1,541
Spain	1,581	1,203
Italy	1,987	969
Switzerland	638	791
Taiwan	986	719
Canada	647	651
Australia	226	524
China	...	517
South Korea	381	488
Sweden	387	463
Hong Kong	377	439

a Comprises Amsterdam, Brussels and Paris Exchanges.
Source: World Federation of Exchanges

securities backed by assets that will generate income in the future. But some firms lack the sorts of assets that are readily packaged into securities, and others may be too small to make securitisation worthwhile. In many countries, markets for securitised assets have yet to develop.

Equity

Equity, unlike all of these other forms of financing, represents the owners' investment in the firm. Bankers and bond investors will be more generous if the firm has substantial equity capital, because this ensures that the borrowers, the firm's owners, have put their own money at risk. The disadvantages of issuing equity are that the firm's profit must be divided among the shareholders and that managers and directors must give primary consideration to investors' interest in improved short-term earnings rather than pursuing strategies that show less immediate promise.

Balancing act

Because each type of financing has advantages and disadvantages, a firm typically raises capital in several different ways. Firms carefully manage the relationship between their borrowing and their equity, known as the debt-to-equity ratio or gearing. There is no ideal debt-to-equity ratio. In general, a ratio below about 0.5 indicates that the firm has borrowed little and may not be taking maximum advantage of its shareholders' capital. Such a firm is said to be underleveraged. Gearing enables the firm to earn a greater amount of profit for each share of equity. Firms may also find it wise to increase their gearing if there are tax advantages to borrowing or if long-term interest rates are low. But if the debt-to-equity ratio is excessive, the firm is said to be highly geared or overleveraged. It is more vulnerable to financial distress, as it must continue to service its borrowings even if sales and profits are weak.

Venture capital

Another way of financing a business is with venture capital. Venture capitalists invest in new or young firms in return for equity in the firm. They are not lenders, but are equity investors at a stage at which the firm's shares do not yet trade on public markets. Unlike most equity investors, venture capitalists typically play an active role in selecting management and overseeing strategy. They normally seek to sell their shares within a few years, usually by taking the firm public and selling their shares on the public equity markets. Venture capital is a well-established form of financing in the United States and the UK. Growth in Continental Europe has been more modest.

Types of equity

There are various different types of equity, each having its own characteristics.

Common stock or ordinary shares

Common stock, as it is known in the United States, or ordinary shares, according to British terminology, is the most important form of equity investment. An owner of common stock is part owner of the enterprise and is entitled to vote on certain important matters, including the selection of directors. Common stock holders benefit most from improvement in the firm's business prospects. But they have a claim on the firm's income and assets only after all creditors and all preferred stock holders receive payment. Some firms have more than one class of common stock, in which case the stock of one class may be entitled to greater voting rights, or to larger dividends, than stock of another class. This is often the case with family-owned firms which sell stock to the public in a way that enables the family to maintain control through its ownership of stock with superior voting rights.

Preferred stock

Also called preference shares, preferred stock is more akin to bonds than to common stock. Like bonds, preferred stock offers specified payments on specified dates. Preferred stock appeals to issuers because the dividend remains constant for as long as the stock is outstanding, which may be in perpetuity. Some investors favour preferred stock over bonds because the periodic payments are formally considered dividends rather than interest payments, and may therefore offer tax advantages. The issuer is obliged to pay dividends to preferred stock holders before paying dividends to common shareholders. If the preferred stock is cumulative, unpaid dividends may accrue until preferred stock holders have received full payment. In the case of non-cumulative preferred stock, preferred stock holders may be able to impose significant restrictions on the firm in the event of a missed dividend.

Convertible preferred stock

This may be converted into common stock under certain conditions, usually at a predetermined price or within a predetermined time period. Conversion is always at the owner's option and cannot be required by the issuer. Convertible preferred stock is similar to convertible bonds (see Chapter 4).

Warrants

Warrants offer the holder the opportunity to purchase a firm's common stock during a specified time period in future, at a predetermined price, known as the exercise price or strike price. The tangible value of a warrant is the market price of the stock less the strike price. If the tangible value when the warrants are exercisable is zero or less the warrants have no value, as the stock can be acquired more cheaply in the open market. A firm may sell warrants directly, but more often they are incorporated into other securities, such as preferred stock or bonds. Warrants are created and sold by the firm that issues the underlying stock. In a rights offering, warrants are allotted to existing stock holders in proportion to their current holdings. If all shareholders subscribe to the offering the firm's total

Table 7.3 **Initial public offerings**

	US		UK	
Year	Number	Value $bn	Number	Value £bn
1995	676	37.3	89	5.1
1996	932	59.2	197	12.9
1997	664	74.0	139	15.3
1998	433	52.4	71	5.7
1999	556	93.7	79	5.0
2000	443	99.9	240	7.9
2001	101	43.1	83	7.1
2002	109	41.1	62	2.9
2003	152	47.6	53	3.3
2004	310	72.4	210	4.2

Source: Bloomberg

capital will increase, but each stock holder's proportionate ownership will not change. The stock holder is free not to subscribe to the offering or to pass the rights to others. In the UK, a stock holder chooses not to subscribe by filing a letter of renunciation with the issuer.

Issuing shares

Few businesses begin with freely traded shares. Most are initially owned by an individual, a small group of investors (such as partners or venture capitalists) or an established firm which has created a new subsidiary. In most countries, a firm may not sell shares to the public until it has been in operation for a specified period. Some countries bar firms from selling shares until their business is profitable, a requirement that can make it difficult for young firms to raise capital.

Flotation

Flotation, also known as an initial public offering (IPO), is the process by which a firm sells its shares to the public. This may occur for a number of reasons. The firm may require additional capital to take advantage of new opportunities. Some of the firm's original investors, such as venture capitalists, may want it to buy them out so they can put their money to work elsewhere. The firm may also wish to use shares to compensate employees, and a public share listing makes this easier as the value of the shares is freely established in the marketplace. The flotation need not involve all or even the majority of the firm's shares. Table 7.3 shows that the annual value of IPOs in the United States grew sevenfold during the 1990s before collapsing in 2001. The value of IPOs in the UK, although much smaller, has been less volatile. Canada, Australia, China and Japan have had larger numbers of initial offerings since 2003, but there have been few IPOs in Europe.

Some of the biggest flotations in recent years have involved the privatisation of government-owned enterprises, such as Deutsche Telekom in Germany and YPF, a petroleum company, in Argentina. Such large firms are often floated in a series of share issues rather than all at once, because of uncertainty about demand for the shares. According to the OECD, privatisations raised $435 billion between 1996 and 2001, much of which was financed by issuance of shares. Another source of large flotations is the spin-off of parts of existing firms. In such a case, the parent firm bundles certain assets, debt obligations and businesses into the new entity, which initially has the same shareholders as the parent. Among the largest spin-offs in recent years were the 2002 sale of Citigroup's Travelers Insurance subsidiary for $3.9 billion and the May 2004 sale of a 30% stake in Genworth Financial, a company controlled by America's General Electric, for $3.5 billion. A third source of large flotations has been decisions by the managers of established companies with privately traded shares to allow limited public ownership, as in the case of UPS, a US package-delivery company.

Private offering

Rather than selling its shares to the public, a firm may raise equity through a private offering. Only sophisticated investors, such as money-management firms and wealthy individuals, are normally allowed to purchase shares in a private offering, as disclosures about the risks involved are fewer than in a public offering. Shares purchased in a private offering are common equity and are therefore entitled to vote on corporate matters and to receive a dividend, but they usually cannot be resold in the public markets for a specified period of time.

Secondary offering

A secondary offering occurs when a firm whose shares are already traded publicly sells additional shares to the public – called a follow-on offering in the UK – or when one or more investors holding a large proportion of a firm's shares offers those shares for sale to the public. Firms

Table 7.4 **Secondary public offerings in US markets**

Year	Number	Value $bn
1995	589	55.8
1996	726	75.5
1997	674	121.4
1998	405	64.9
1999	397	95.3
2000	386	129.1
2001	408	82.9
2002	395	71.4
2003	488	67.1
2004	576	85.9

Source: Bloomberg

that already have publicly traded shares may float additional shares to increase their total capital. If this leaves existing shareholders owning smaller proportions of the firm than they owned previously, it is said to dilute their holdings. If the secondary offering involves shares owned by investors, the proceeds of a secondary offering go to the investors whose shares are sold, not to the issuer. Table 7.4 provides data on the extent of secondary offerings in US markets.

The flotation process

Before issuing shares to the public, a firm must engage accountants to prepare several years of financial statements according to the Generally Accepted Accounting Principles, or GAAP, of the country where it wishes to issue. In many countries, the offering must be registered with the securities regulator before it can be marketed to the public. The regulator does not judge whether the shares represent a sound investment, but only whether the firm has complied with the legal requirements for securities issuance. The firm incorporates the mandatory financial reports into a document known as the listing particulars or prospectus, which is intended to provide prospective investors with detailed information about the firm's past performance and future prospects. In the United States, a prospectus circulated before completion of the registration period is called a red herring, as its front page bears a red border to highlight the fact that the regulator has not yet approved the issuance of the shares.

Different approaches to selling the shares

The sale of the shares to investors is normally handled by an investment bank or issuing house. Investment banks do this in three different ways. In the case of good-quality issuers, the investment banker usually serves as the underwriter. An underwriter commits its own capital to purchase the shares from the issuer and resell them to the public. It uses its knowledge of the market to decide, subject to the issuer's approval, how many shares to issue and what price to charge. This is critical: if the price is set too high, the underwriter may be stuck with unsold shares, but if the price is set too low, the issuer will realise less money than it could have. In some cases, the underwriter may sell the shares by tender, simply asking potential investors to bid for shares. If it is unhappy with the price its shares will bring, the issuer can postpone or withdraw the flotation, or find a private buyer rather than selling to the general public.

Another method of flotation is for an investment bank to distribute the shares on a best-efforts basis. In such a case, the investment bank is not underwriting the shares and has no risk if they fail to sell; rather, it is simply committing to use its best efforts to sell the shares on behalf of the issuer. Any unsold shares will be returned to the issuer. Investors are usually suspicious of a best-efforts flotation as it implies that the investment bank did not have a sufficiently high opinion of the issuer to be willing to underwrite the shares.

The third type of flotation is an all-or-none offering. This is a best-efforts offering undertaken on the condition that all shares are sold at the offer price. If some shares remain unsold, the entire offering is cancelled.

Firms in the UK may float shares with an offer for sale. This requires establishing a price at which the shares are to be sold, printing the entire prospectus in newspapers and soliciting applications to purchase shares directly from the public. Regulations make direct flotation difficult in many countries.

The number of initial public offerings was much higher in the late 1990s than in previous years. This is partly because of the explosion of interest in fields where new firms are prominent, such as computer networking and internet commerce. Also many countries have changed their regulations to make flotation easier. It is now common for firms that have never reported a profit to sell shares to the public, a practice that was unusual before the mid-1990s. By 2000, however, it became evident that many of these new firms were unlikely ever to make a profit, and some of them failed. Investors grew reluctant to buy new issues, and the number of IPOs declined sharply. IPO activity was slack in 2001–03, as firms were reluctant to issue shares at a time of weak stock prices, but IPOs regained popularity in 2004–05.

Investing in IPOs

Investors often compete intensely for shares in new flotations, which can cause the prices of shares to rise sharply in the first few hours or days after issuance. After this initial rise, however, evidence from the United States indicates that most new issues subsequently trade for some period below the price at which they were initially offered, so an investor can buy them more cheaply than at the time of flotation. Some never regain the prices they reached in the first few days of trading. For this reason, many experts consider it unwise for unsophisticated investors to buy newly floated shares.

US authorities have investigated alleged improprieties by investment banks in connection with IPOs. The investigations have led to claims that some banks gave favoured clients an opportunity to buy new issues at the offer price and then to profit by reselling to less sophisticated investors in the ensuing price run-up. Employees at some investment banks also have been accused of unduly promoting IPOs in which they personally stood to profit by obtaining shares at the offer price and then reselling them at a mark-up. Some investors nonetheless consider IPOs to be attractive investments, as in some cases the shares reach a level of many times the offer price.

Share repurchases

Just as firms may issue new shares, they may also undertake to acquire their own shares from willing sellers, a process known as a repurchase or a buy-back. A repurchase may be undertaken for several reasons:

- A firm may wish to repurchase all of its own shares and become a privately owned corporation.
- A partial share repurchase is often used to boost a sagging share price, particularly because it signals to the market that the company's own managers, who presumably know its prospects best, consider the shares undervalued.
- A repurchase gives the firm a way to return excess capital to

shareholders. Many countries give favourable tax treatment to gains from the sale of securities, known as capital gains. In such a case, taxable shareholders will benefit if capital is returned via a share repurchase rather than through a dividend.

◪ Some firms repurchase shares for the purpose of using them in employee compensation programmes.
◪ Some repurchase offers are aimed at investors who own only a small number of shares in order to reduce the expense of dealing with shareholders.

The attractiveness of repurchase programmes depends heavily on tax considerations. They are infrequently used in countries, notably Germany, which treat the proceeds as regular income rather than as a capital gain.

The issuer holds any repurchased shares as treasury stock. Treasury stock is not entitled to a vote on corporate matters and does not receive a dividend. However, the firm is free to resell treasury stock or to use it for employee compensation without further shareholder approval. A shareholder's ownership of the company would be diluted if treasury stock were to be returned to public ownership in future.

Factors affecting share prices

Theoretically, the value of a share of stock should be precisely equal to the net present value of the proportion of the company's future profits represented by the share. In other words, estimate how much profit the company is likely to earn each year in the future, use an appropriate discount to determine how much each future year's earnings are worth today then divide the sum of all future years' discounted earnings by the number of common shares outstanding. The result should be the current share price.

This tautological definition, unfortunately, is of little practical use in deciding whether the current price of a share represents a fair value. The actual price at which a given share may be purchased or sold in the market depends both on factors specifically related to the firm and on general market factors. These two types of factors include the following, covered in no particular order of importance.

Earnings

A firm's earnings are the difference between the revenue it claims to have generated during a given period and the expenses it has incurred,

Table 7.5 **Dividend yields**

Country	Sample began	Average dividend (%)	Lowest annual dividend (%)	Date of lowest dividend
Belgium	1961	4.0	1.3	1999
Canada	1956	3.3	1.1	2000
France	1964	4.0	1.6	2000
Germany	1973	2.7	1.1	2000
Italy	1981	2.8	1.0	1981
Japan	1953	1.3	0.4	1990
Netherlands	1973	4.6	1.7	2000
Switzerland	1973	2.3	0.9	1998
UK	1963	4.7	2.1	2000
US	1947	3.6	1.1	1999

Source: Bank for International Settlements

as reported on its financial statements. Earnings depend partly on factors internal to the firm, such as management and product quality. But they are also strongly affected by external factors, such as demographic trends, changes in the rate of economic growth and exchange-rate movements that may affect the firm's foreign business. Earnings are not always a good measure of a firm's health, because the firm can "manage" earnings by controlling the timing of receipts and expenditures and by choosing among alternative methods of accounting. Analysts often prefer to focus on earnings before interest, taxes, depreciation and amortisation (EBITDA), a measure that is generally felt to give a better picture of core business operations.

Cash flow
The difference between the income received in a given year (as distinct from the income credited to sales made in that year, which may not actually have been received) and cash outlays is called cash flow. It indicates whether the business generates enough cash to meet current expenses. A strongly positive cash flow helps the share price; a negative cash flow often indicates a troubled firm.

Dividends

A dividend is a payment made to shareholders. In most countries, the markets prefer shares that pay significant dividends, because the dividend provides some return even if the share price does not appreciate. Some pension funds and other institutional investors are allowed to own only shares that pay dividends. The relevant figure is the dividend yield, which is simply the annual dividend per common share divided by the current price per share. An increase in the dividend usually boosts the share price. There are exceptions, however, particularly if the firm's cash flow is insufficient to pay the dividend. Young, fast-growing companies often pay little or no dividend, as they wish to use their available cash to take advantage of growth opportunities.

Historically, dividend yields have varied greatly from country to country and from time to time, as shown in Table 7.5.

The large differences among countries are the result of a number of factors, such as tax laws that encourage or discourage dividend payments and the power of shareholders to demand higher dividends from corporate management. In 1999 and 2000, in an environment of rising share prices, low inflation and generally declining interest rates, dividend yields in all the main industrial economies fell to levels that were extremely low by historical standards. Dividend yields around the world generally rose as profits recovered from cyclical lows after 2000.

The dividend is paid to all owners of record on a specified date. To receive a dividend, the investor must possess the shares on the dividend date, which means that it must have purchased them far enough in advance (usually two to three days) for the share transfer to be completed before the dividend is paid. A stock is said to go ex-dividend as soon as the deadline for buying the shares in time to receive the dividend has passed. The price of the shares normally falls by roughly the amount of the dividend once the stock has gone ex-dividend.

As well as cash dividends, firms may issue stock dividends to shareholders. A stock dividend, also known as a capitalisation issue, transfers some of the company's cash reserves to shareholders by giving them additional shares.

Asset value

The firm may own assets, such as property, mineral reserves or shares in other firms, the value of which increases or decreases owing to market forces. Changes in their value may be reflected in the share price.

Analysts' recommendations

Many stockbrokerage firms employ securities analysts, whose job is to issue recommendations as to which shares offer the best opportunity at a given point in time. There are two basic methods of analysis. Fundamental analysis examines a firm's business strategy, the competitive environment and other real-world factors to develop estimates of earnings per share for several years into the future. Technical analysis seeks to draw conclusions about future price trends by examining past relationships between different variables and past movements in the price of a stock.

Analysts' recommendations are frequently criticised for lack of objectivity, as some stockbrokerage firms are also engaged in underwriting shares and have an incentive to recommend a company's shares in order to win its underwriting business. In some cases, analysts may also have made personal investments in the shares they recommend. Nonetheless, the announcement that an analyst has upgraded or downgraded a particular share or increased or decreased an earnings estimate can have a significant impact on the price.

Inclusion in an index

Many institutional investors seek to build portfolios that mimic the behaviour of a stock-price index. Inclusion in an index is usually positive for a share's price, because investors will wish to own whichever shares the index includes.

Interest rates

Increased interest rates generally depress share prices. A given share dividend will be less attractive when less risky investments, such as bank deposits and money-market instruments (see Chapter 3), are offering higher returns. Also higher interest rates often presage slower economic growth, which may slow the growth of a firm's profits. However, investors usually view inflation as dangerous to asset values, so higher interest rates may have a positive effect on share prices if they are judged necessary to keep inflation in check.

Bond returns

Investors compare the relative returns available from investing in shares and in bonds. If bond prices have fallen, shares may become less attractive as investors find better value in the bond market.

General economic news

New information about the inflation rate, the rate of economic growth, employment, consumer spending and other economic variables can have a significant impact on share prices in general. A given piece of economic news can also have important effects on different sectors within the overall market. For example, a decline in outstanding credit-card balances may hurt the prices of bank shares, because it may mean that credit-card borrowers will be paying less interest, but the implication that consumers' capacity for new credit-card spending is now larger may help the prices of retailers' shares.

Fads

At times investors may take an otherwise inexplicable liking to certain categories of shares. In such a case, shares in the favoured sectors often do well regardless of individual firms' earnings reports or cash flow. In many countries, for example, technology shares became hugely popular in the late 1990s. According to the IMF, technology shares accounted for 22.9% of German stockmarket capitalisation in 1999, compared with 3.5% in 1990; in India the weight of technology shares rose from 0.2% to 19.9% over the same period.

Stock splits

A firm may undertake a stock split to increase investor interest in its shares. The firm may believe that the price of an individual share is so high that it deters investors, or it may simply hope that investors associate a split with good performance. The firm determines the ratio of new shares to old. In a two-for-one split, for example, a shareholder will own two shares for each share previously owned, and the post-split value of each share will be half the value of a share before the split. A reverse stock split reduces the number of shares outstanding by issuing one new share for a given number of old shares. Neither a split nor a reverse split changes the proportionate ownership of each investor or the firm's total capitalisation.

Market efficiency

The shares of highly capitalised firms are traded frequently, and their prices often move from minute to minute. The path these movements follow is known to economists as a random walk. This means that current or past share prices are of no help in predicting future prices, so the fact that a share's price has risen (or fallen) does not mean that its next movement is likely to be up (or down).

Many price changes have no identifiable cause, and simply reflect the desires of two investors at a particular moment. But there are also price changes that can be attributed to the arrival of new information in the market. For example, a press release announcing that an aircraft manufacturer has won a big order will boost its shares, but the higher price may not last as investors examine the customer's finances and conclude that it may not be able to afford the planes. The efficient market hypothesis contends that investors cannot make money trading on news reports and other public information, because the information is reflected in share prices as soon as it is known.

A stronger form of the efficient market hypothesis holds that share prices already incorporate all relevant information, whether public or non-public. If this were true, there would be no value in studying a company or an industry before deciding whether to buy shares. The evidence for this assertion, however, is weak. Although the markets do act quickly on information, there are many anomalies, situations in which an astute investor is able to profit from identifying factors that are not yet reflected in a share's price.

Key numbers

Investors have a great deal of information to use in deciding which shares to buy. Some of this is derived from sources external to the firm, such as government economic statistics and news reports. Essential information can also be gleaned from each firm's financial reports and from trading in the market. Financial reports may be prepared by an auditing firm or may be unaudited. Accounting rules differ from country to country, so companies' reports may not be strictly comparable. Furthermore, the way in which income and outlays are treated in financial reports is often a matter of judgment, and disputes over the accuracy of reports are common.

Price/earnings ratio

The price/earnings ratio may be the best-known number used to assess equities. This ratio, also known as the multiple, is obtained by dividing the current share price by reported earnings per share. It offers an easy way to identify firms whose shares seem underpriced or overpriced relative to the market. Unfortunately, the term price/earnings ratio is ambiguous. Newspaper stock tables typically divide the share price by the most recent 12 months' earnings. However, it is also possible to construct a price/earnings ratio using the most recent quarterly earnings

Table 7.6 **Price/earnings ratios**

Country	Sample began	Average P/E	Peak P/E	Peak date
Belgium	1961	13	29	1973
Canada	1956	20	255[a]	1994
France	1973	12	30	1973
Germany	1973	13	27	2000
Italy	1986	18	36	2000
Japan	1981	39	85	2000
Netherlands	1973	12	32	2000
Switzerland	1973	13	30	1998
UK	1970	13	28	2000
US	1957	16	41	2002

a Firms had low earnings owing to write-offs.
Source: Bank for International Settlements

multiplied by four, half-year earnings multiplied by two, projected earnings for the current fiscal year, or estimated earnings for the year ahead.

Individual firms' share prices, and therefore their price/earnings ratios, fluctuate greatly. Some firms, notably those in fashionable sectors, are able to sustain high share prices with no earnings at all because investors anticipate that they will be very profitable in future. In early 2000, the price/earnings ratio of technology shares listed on Asian stockmarkets exceeded 130, three times the ratio for shares of other types of companies. There are important national differences in price/earnings ratios, as illustrated in Table 7.6.

Some investment strategies rely heavily on price/earnings ratios. Value investing, for example, involves identifying equities whose price/earnings ratios are lower than they have been in recent times, in the expectation that the ratio will revert to its trend, that is, the price will rise.

Beta
Beta is a measure of a share's price volatility, relative to the average volatility of the national stockmarket. A share with a beta of 1.0 will, on average, move in tandem with the market average; a share with a beta of 1.5 can be expected to rise (or fall) 1.5% when the market rises (or falls) 1%. A share with a negative beta moves, on average, in the opposite direction from the market.

A high positive beta signifies a risky share that can be expected to outperform the market in good times but fall more than the market in bad times. The shares of many small firms, so-called small-cap stocks, carry high betas. A stock with a positive beta of less than 1.0 is a conservative investment; it is safer in a falling market, but offers less potential for appreciation when the market is rising. Shares with negative beta are for contrarians who want stocks that are likely to rise as the market falls. The betas of widely traded shares can be found in many investment periodicals and in research reports issued by stockbrokerage firms.

Return on equity

Return on common equity seeks to measure how well management has put shareholders' capital to use. Firms usually report their return on equity in their annual financial statements. It is computed by the following formula:

$$\frac{\text{Net income} - \text{preferred dividends}}{\text{Value of common equity} - \text{most intangible assets} + \text{deferred tax liability}}$$

Return on equity is a useful tool for comparing the performance of the firms within an industry. In general, investors prefer firms with higher returns on equity, but the figure can be deceptive. A firm can improve its return on equity by borrowing to increase net income (the numerator) without issuing more equity (the denominator). Such leverage, however, makes earnings more variable from year to year, as the debt must be serviced even if sales are poor. A higher return on common equity is usually associated with more volatile earnings.

Return on capital

Return on capital is the broadest gauge of a firm's profitability. It is not always reported in financial statements, but must be calculated according to one of several formulas. One is:

$$\frac{\text{Net income} + \text{minority interest} + (\text{interest paid} - \text{tax deduction})}{\text{Tangible assets} - \text{bills payable within one year}}$$

Although the actual calculation of a firm's return on capital can be complicated, the result can be used to compare the performance of firms in different industries or to look at the performance of a single firm over a period in which, because of share issues or repurchases, its capital structure may have changed significantly.

Value added

A concept developed in the 1990s and marketed by consulting firms under various trade names, value added measures how much the firm's management has increased the value of shareholders' investment. This recognises that common equity is not a free resource, because shareholders are forgoing other opportunities in order to invest in the firm. Value added offers a method for ranking firms' performance after taking their true cost of capital into account. The ranking may be quite different from one based on return to equity or return to capital.

Measuring return

Investors often measure the performance of equities by computing the total return over a given period, such as a year. Total return can be computed by the following formula:

$$\frac{(\text{Price at end of period} - \text{price at start}) + \text{dividends paid} + \text{accrued interest on dividends}}{\text{Price at start of period}}$$

For example, assume a share is traded for $10 at the start of the year and $12 at the end of the year. A dividend of $1 is paid after six months and another dividend of $1 is paid at year's end. The relevant interest rate is 8% per year. The investor's return for the full year includes:

Share price appreciation	$2.00
Dividends	$2.00
Interest on first dividend ($1 x 0.08/2, reflecting interest for six months at an 8% annual rate)	$0.04
Interest on second dividend (none during period)	$0.00
Total gain during period	$4.04
Total return ($4.04/$10 starting price)	40.4%

This return, it should be noted, cannot actually be obtained by the investor. The share price appreciation can be realised only by selling the

Table 7.7 **Share prices**

52-week									
High	Low	Name	Div	PE	Sales100s	High	Low	Last	Change
25.15	18.00	Baldor	0.48	32	679	22.00	20.87	20.87	−1.11
64.00	26.00	BearSt	0.60b	12	6,867	46.90	45.15	45.65	−2.00
25.95	24.80	BearS pfY	1.88		238	25.25	25.15	25.20	...
64.95	42.90	BeckCoult	0.64	43	2,015	50.65	49.50	49.50	+0.75
39.25	29.96	BectDck s	0.39f	20	7,920	36.31	35.90	36.01	−0.34

Source: New York Stock Exchange

shares, which will incur a commission charge that reduces the investor's profit.

Confusingly, the share with the higher total return is not always the better investment. In many countries taxes on dividends are due immediately, but taxes on capital gains from securities are deferred until the securities are sold and then imposed at lower rates as well. A total return derived mainly from share price appreciation may therefore be worth more to an investor than a total return derived mainly from dividends. Also, the simple calculation of total return makes no allowance for risk. With all other things remaining the same, an investor would expect to obtain a greater total return on a share with a high beta than on a share with a low beta, in recompense for the greater risk the investor bears.

Obtaining share price information

Major newspapers in most countries print detailed tables of share performance on a daily basis. These tables are typically organised by exchange, so to locate the information on a particular stock it is necessary to know which exchange the shares trade on. Most newspapers do not have space to report on all publicly traded shares, and typically limit their reports to shares with market capitalisation or average daily trading volume above a specified level. The precise organisation of share price reports differs from one newspaper to another.

An example of a typical share price table from the United States is shown in Table 7.7. It cites five different equities issued by four different firms, which are listed in abbreviated form in the column headed "Name". As well as identifying the issuing companies, this column contains other information about some of the shares. Two different issues by Bear, Stearns & Co are listed, the first being common stock and the second, marked "pf Y", being one of several issues of Bear, Stearns preferred shares; the other preferred shares are not shown. The last firm listed, Becton Dickinson, has the letter "s" to the right of its name, indicating that its shares have split. The two columns to the left, which report the highest and lowest prices paid for each share over the past year, will have been adjusted to take account of stock splits. If, for example, Becton Dickinson's shares had split two-for-one, the actual high for the past year would have been 78.50, but that figure was halved by the table's compiler to 39.25 to take account of the fact that there are now twice as many shares outstanding.

The first share in the table, Baldor, stands out prominently from the others. It is underlined because its trading volume on this day was high, with more than 1% of its shares changing hands. As shown in the column headed "Sales 100s", some 67,900 shares of Baldor were traded. Interestingly, however, this heavy trading had little impact on the share price. The closing price of the firm's shares was 20.87, the same as the previous day's closing price. This was the stock's lowest price on the day.

Two columns of particular interest to investors are immediately to the right of the firms' names. The column headed "Div" lists the dividend paid on the shares over the past year. The dividend for the Bear, Stearns common shares has the letter "b" attached, indicating that the firm also paid a stock dividend, distributing additional shares to each of its shareholders; the "f" attached to the Becton Dickinson dividend indicates that the firm has increased its annual dividend rate. The meaning of these letters must be obtained from the footnotes to the table. Lastly, the column headed "PE" is the price/earnings ratio determined by using each company's reported earnings per share over the previous 12-month reporting period. Baldor has a high price-to-earnings ratio and Bear, Stearns has a much lower one. No figure is reported for the preferred shares, as these have no claim on the firm's earnings once the obligatory dividend has been paid.

This information summarises the previous day's trading. Information on a particular share's performance during the trading day is available from many electronic sources, including stock brokerages and information service providers. This may include additional data, such as charts of the share's minute-by-minute price movements and calculations of the share's price volatility, which are not normally available in newspaper tables.

The over-the-counter market

The vast majority of publicly available equities are seldom bought or sold and are of no interest to institutional investors. Such shares are usually traded over the counter (OTC). In the United States, which has far more publicly traded companies than any other country, an estimated 25,000 firms trade over the counter, about three times as many as trade on organised exchanges. (In the United States, trading on the NASDAQ stockmarket is often referred to as over-the-counter trading, but this convention is outdated.)

OTC trading requires a brokerage firm to match a prospective buyer and a prospective seller at a price acceptable to both. Alternatively, the brokerage firm may purchase shares for its own account or sell shares that it has been holding. A trade may be difficult to arrange owing to a lack of sellers or investors, and the price at which the transaction is completed may be very different from the last price at which those shares were traded hours or even days before. Firms whose shares trade over the counter normally have few shareholders and little equity outstanding. If a firm wishes to raise larger amounts of capital in the equity market and to appeal to a broader shareholder base, it will seek to list its shares on a stock exchange.

Stock exchanges

Stock exchanges provide a more organised way to trade shares. They are generally superior to the OTC market for several reasons. First, they bring many investors together, offering greater liquidity and thus making it possible to obtain better prices. Second, the exchange is able to obtain and publish the prices at which trades have occurred or are being offered, giving investors an important source of information not available on the OTC market. Third, the exchanges have rules and procedures to ensure that parties live up to their commitments. All well-known companies whose shares are traded publicly list their shares on exchanges. Exchanges set requirements for listing, and very small firms or firms whose shares seldom trade will not qualify. The exchanges with the greatest number of new listings in recent years are listed in Table 7.8.

The first stock exchange was established in Antwerp, then part of the Netherlands, in 1631. The London Stock Exchange opened in 1773, and the Philadelphia Stock Exchange, the first in the New World, began trading in 1790. By the middle of the 19th century, with industry hungry for capital, almost every major city had its own bourse. The UK alone had 20 different stock exchanges. This was necessary because most listed

Table 7.8 **New listings in major markets**

Exchange	1998	2000	2002	2004
London	202	399	201	423
Toronto	116	116	106	346
Australian Stock Exchange	63	175	89	186
NASDAQ	487	605	121	170
Tokyo	57	206	94	153
New York Stock Exchange	202	122	151	152
Mexico	3	2	121	110
Hong Kong	32	90	117	70
Euronext[a]	287	108	18	32
Deutsche Börse	67	153	6	6

a Includes Amsterdam, Paris and Brussels exchanges.
Source: World Federation of Exchanges

firms were unknown outside their home region and so preferred to list their shares locally, and most investors were individuals who preferred to buy the shares of firms that they knew.

Many of these exchanges disappeared as capital markets became national and then international. Now most countries (the United States being the main exception) have a single dominant stock exchange. It is increasingly common for companies to list their shares on foreign exchanges as well as domestically, giving them access to a wider array of investors. International equity issues (shares issued outside the issuing company's home country) were rare at the beginning of the 1990s, but they increased substantially between 1996 and 2000 before the steep stockmarket declines of 2001 discouraged issuance (see Table 7.9 on the next page). The number of new listings rose along with share prices in 2004.

The biggest exchanges

The overwhelming majority of the world's equity trading takes place on just four exchanges: the New York Stock Exchange; the NASDAQ stockmarkets (formerly known as the National Association of Securities Dealers Automated Quotation System); the Tokyo Stock Exchange; and the London Stock Exchange. The New York Stock Exchange is by far the largest as measured by market capitalisation, listing domestic shares

Table 7.9 **International equity issues, by nationality of issuer ($bn)**

	1996	1998	2000	2002	2004
All countries	82.4	125.9	316.7	103.0	214.1
France	7.4	17.3	17.3	11.4	25.2
Germany	8.7	7.5	40.4	5.4	21.2
UK	8.4	14.9	31.6	14.8	20.5
China	...	1.1	21.3	5.4	18.0
Italy	4.5	7.6	5.6	2.8	12.7
Japan	0.8	10.0	8.8	2.5	7.3
Spain	1.7	7.5	8.3	3.6	6.2
Netherlands	7.2	7.6	25.8	6.6	6.0
South Korea	1.2	0.5	1.0	1.6	5.4
Switzerland	0.1	6.0	8.3	10.1	4.2
US	8.1	17.8	70.5	1.2	1.9

Source: Bank for International Settlements

whose total value exceeded $12.9 trillion at mid-2005. NASDAQ had a market capitalisation of about $3.4 trillion, well below its peak of over $5 trillion in early 2000. The Tokyo Stock Exchange, which lost its status as the world's largest with the dramatic decline in Japanese share prices, rebounded to become the world's second largest with a capitalisation of $3.4 trillion. The London Stock Exchange, the world's fourth-largest equity exchange by market capitalisation, listed shares worth $2.7 trillion at mid-2005.

Some smaller exchanges, notably Frankfurt, Madrid and Euronext, which combines the Amsterdam, Brussels and Paris bourses, grew rapidly in market capitalisation in the late 1990s, as newly privatised banks, telecommunications companies and airlines listed their shares. Some exchanges have sought to tap new markets by setting up small-company bourses, such as the Alternative Investment Market in London and the Neuer Markt in Frankfurt, in imitation of the NASDAQ stock-market. However, many of these exchanges struggled with the dearth of new listings after share prices fell worldwide in 2000, and some of them were closed down.

The economic importance of stockmarkets varies greatly from country to country. Although the United States has by far the largest market for equities, stockmarket capitalisation represents a larger proportion of

Table 7.10 **Stockmarkets' economic importance**

	Market capitalisation as % of GDP, end 2003
Switzerland	227.6
Singapore	190.3
South Africa	183.1
Malaysia	156.0
Luxembourg	142.0
UK	138.8
US	130.6
Finland	106.2
Sweden	98.1
Japan	68.8

Source: World Federation of Exchanges

GDP in several other countries, as shown in Table 7.10. Investors' trading propensity varies greatly from country to country as well.

Despite the worldwide enthusiasm for share ownership, not all stock exchanges are prospering. The number of exchanges worldwide nearly trebled during the 1990s, as many emerging countries adopted laws to encourage share trading. At the same time, consolidation in the financial industry left a comparatively small number of brokerage firms dominating equity trading worldwide. These firms are now actively seeking to reduce costs by concentrating trading in the largest financial centres. This trend has been assisted by economic and monetary union within the European Union, which has meant that share prices in 12 countries are quoted in euros, so that a Finnish or Italian company can list its shares as easily in Paris or Frankfurt as in Helsinki or Milan. Investors, as well as share issuers, have an incentive to trade in the market where a given stock trades most actively, because greater liquidity makes it easier to complete a transaction quickly and at a good price. Smaller, less liquid exchanges in countries such as Argentina and Portugal have seen a significant portion of their business move to other countries, and the major exchanges have been forced to compete with one another to dominate trading in the most active shares.

These pressures are dramatically reshaping stock exchanges. At the beginning of the 1990s almost all stockmarkets were mutual ventures, owned co-operatively by individuals or firms who made money by

Table 7.11 **Stock exchange demutualisations**

Exchange	Year
Stockholm Stock Exchange	1993
Helsinki Stock Exchange	1995
Copenhagen Stock Exchange	1996
Amsterdam Exchanges	1997
Borsa Italiana	1997
Australian Stock Exchange	1998
Iceland Stock Exchange	1999
Athens Stock Exchange	1999
Stock Exchange of Singapore	1999
Toronto Stock Exchange	1999
London Stock Exchange	2000
NASDAQ Stock Exchange	2000
Tokyo Stock Exchange	2001
Philippine Stock Exchange	2002
Budapest Stock Exchange	2002
New York Stock Exchange	2006[a]

a Pending regulatory approval.
Sources: Ian Domowitz and Benn Steil, "Automation, Trading Costs, and the Structure of the Securities Trading Industry", *Brookings-Wharton Papers in Financial Services*, 1999; news reports

trading there. The owners generally had little incentive to support modernisation of the exchange, as more efficient trading could result in lower profits for themselves. Starting in 1993, however, a number of smaller exchanges demutualised and became profit-making corporations, often issuing publicly traded shares themselves. With shareholders demanding profits, and with profitability heavily dependent upon trading volume, these exchanges now have strong incentives to reduce costs and offer new products and services. By May 2000, when Japanese law was amended to allow exchanges to be joint-stock companies, all of the world's main stock exchanges had either demutualised or at least begun the process of demutualisation, with the notable exception of the New York Stock Exchange (see Table 7.11). That exchange, the world's largest, announced in 2005 that it would sell shares to the public in conjunction with its planned merger with the electronic Archipelago exchange, scheduled for 2006.

Competitive pressures have forced many exchanges to merge or close their doors, and much more of this is likely. Exchanges operating on a small scale face disadvantages that are almost insurmountable. The high cost of new technology has forced even big exchanges to seek partners. In May 2000 Deutsche Börse, in Frankfurt, announced a merger with the London Stock Exchange to form iX, a single exchange that would trade shares in both London and Frankfurt; among other cost savings, the merger would have allowed both exchanges to use the same computer systems to handle trading and record-keeping. Although that merger was called off, the announcement led the stockmarkets in Paris, Brussels and Amsterdam to form Euronext, a single pan-European exchange. The Lisbon and Oporto exchanges, among the smallest in Europe, voted to merge with Euronext in December 2001. Many smaller European stock exchanges may affiliate with one or another of these larger exchanges. In Japan, the Osaka Stock Exchange joined with America's NASDAQ exchange to open the NASDAQ Japan Market in June 2000, to help Osaka compete with the much larger Tokyo Stock Exchange. Both NASDAQ and the New York Stock Exchange have acquired upstart electronic exchanges in an effort to move more trading through their systems.

Although these stock-exchange mergers and joint ventures generate headlines, the growth or disappearance of a particular exchange has little economic consequence. The fact that most exchanges are identified with a particular city does not imply that they are a significant source of tax revenue or employment at that location. For example, computers allow a large proportion of the business done on exchanges based in Stockholm and Frankfurt to be undertaken by people physically located in London. The exchanges have become little more than businesses competing with one another, seeking to capture the fees from share trading, and national well-being does not ride on their success or failure.

International listings

Until the late 1990s almost every firm listed its shares exclusively on a stock exchange in its home country. Investors, particularly pension funds and insurance companies whose liabilities were entirely in their home country, preferred to own assets denominated in that same currency and generally avoided investing abroad. In any case, national differences in accounting rules made it hard for investors to compare firms based in different countries.

International listings became much more common in the 1990s, as

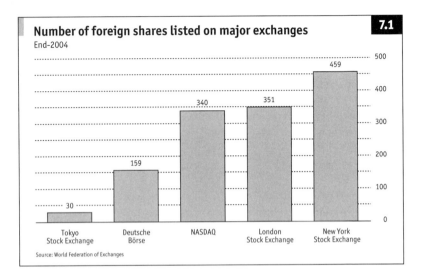

Number of foreign shares listed on major exchanges   **7.1**
End-2004

Source: World Federation of Exchanges

share issuers sought to tap capital markets around the world. Many multinational firms listed their shares on major exchanges in North America and Europe. The number of international listings fell sharply in the early 2000s, as issuers sought to avoid the costs of complying with regulations in various countries and of restating financial reports according to diverse national norms. Sophisticated investors, such as pension funds, increasingly are willing to buy shares in any market and do not require a listing in the local market. London is the most important location for international share trading. Figure 7.1 shows the number of foreign listings at the biggest stock exchanges.

Depositary receipts

A firm may not wish to list its shares internationally for various legal and financial reasons. Depositary receipts offer a means for firms to tap foreign capital markets without directly listing their shares abroad. The best-known securities of this sort are American Depositary Receipts, or ADRS, which are traded in the United States, and Global Depositary Receipts, or GDRS, which trade mainly in London. Latin American companies account for a large share of trading in ADRS, and the GDRS of Indian companies are the biggest source of GDR trading in London.

These securities come in two varieties. A sponsored ADR or GDR is set up at the behest of the share issuer, which deposits the desired number of its own shares with a bank in the country where the receipts are to be traded. The receipts themselves are technically securities issued by the bank, giving the holder a claim on the earnings and price appreciation of the shares the bank holds. An unsponsored ADR or GDR is set up on the initiative of an outside party, such as an investment bank, rather than of the firm that has issued the shares. Both sponsored and unsponsored depositary receipts trade on stock exchanges. The main difference between them is that owners of unsponsored receipts may have more difficulty obtaining financial reports and other information from the share issuer, because the issuer has not sought to issue the receipts.

At July 2005, the ADRs of 299 firms were trading on the New York Stock Exchange and a further 117 on NASDAQ. Some 118 firms had listed GDRs on the London Stock Exchange.

Emerging markets

During the 1990s there was rapid growth in equity markets in many Latin American, Asian, African and east European countries, which are collectively known as emerging markets. There is no precise definition of this term, but it is generally applied to countries where per head incomes are lower than in Japan, Australia, the United States, Canada and western Europe, and where open capital markets are a recent development. In previous decades, many emerging-market countries had extremely high inflation rates and were ruled by governments with a deep suspicion of capital markets. The reversal of both of these trends led to a fourfold increase in emerging-market equity issues, from $5.6 billion in 1991 to $22.8 billion in 1997, before the onset of financial crises in Asia caused issuance to slow. Much of this growth occurred in Asian countries where equity markets were negligible or non-existent before 1990, notably India and China. Issuance reached a record $44 billion in 2000, fell to less than one-quarter of that amount in 2001, and then climbed back above $30 billion in 2004, not counting the robust share issuance in South Korea and Singapore.

Emerging-market share prices are generally more volatile than those in more developed markets. This is because of both the comparatively small capitalisation of the markets and strong investor sensitivity to potential political or economic changes. This volatility is particularly pronounced for foreign investors, because even if a particular emerging-market share rises in local currency terms, exchange-rate movements may lead to a loss in terms of the investor's currency. Figure 7.2 on the next page illustrates the volatility of stockmarkets in emerging economies.

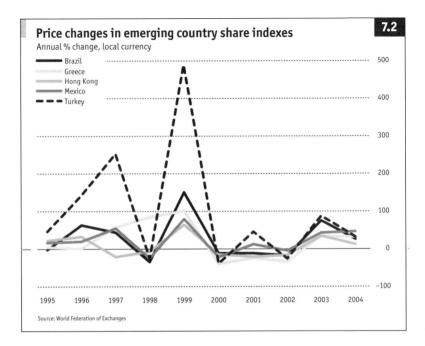

Price changes in emerging country share indexes　　**7.2**

Annual % change, local currency

- Brazil
- Greece
- Hong Kong
- Mexico
- Turkey

500
400
300
200
100
0
-100

1995　1996　1997　1998　1999　2000　2001　2002　2003　2004

Source: World Federation of Exchanges

Trading shares

A share trade begins when an investor contacts a stockbrokerage firm to place an order to buy or sell stock. There are many different types of orders, which give the broker varying amounts of discretion. The most basic is a market order or an at best instruction, which instructs the broker to buy or sell the desired number of shares at the best price presently available in the market. A limit order requires the broker to complete the transaction only at the specified price or better, with the risk that the order will never be executed because the specified price is not reached. A stop order instructs the broker to buy or sell the shares once a specified price is reached, although the actual transaction price can be above or below the specified level.

Investors may also qualify their orders in various ways. A day order is good on only one particular day and is cancelled if it is not executed. A good-till-cancelled order, also known as an open order, remains active until it is either filled or cancelled. A fill-or-kill order requires the broker-age firm to buy or sell all the shares immediately or else to cancel the entire order, and an immediate or cancel order, known as an execute or eliminate order in the UK, tells the broker to buy or sell as many shares

Table 7.12 **Exchanges adopting automated auction trading in shares**

Exchange	Year
Athens Stock Exchange	1997
Australian Stock Exchange	1997
London Stock Exchange	1997
Osaka Securities Exchange	1998
Toronto Stock Exchange	1998
Pacific Stock Exchange	1999
Tokyo Stock Exchange	1999
Irish Stock Exchange	2000

Sources: Domowitz and Steil; exchange reports

as possible immediately and to cancel the remainder of the order.

After verifying the investor's order, the brokerage firm passes it to its brokers at the appropriate stock exchange. In some cases, a given equity may trade on several exchanges. A broker working in its client's best interest will undertake the trade wherever it can obtain the best price.

How stock exchanges work

There are vast differences in the ways that stock exchanges function.

The traditional model for a stock exchange is known as an auction market, in which shares for purchase or sale are offered to brokers on a trading floor. An auction market uses specialised brokers, known as specialists or marketmakers, who are required to ensure orderly trading in the particular shares for which they are responsible. A brokerage firm sends each buy or sell order to its floor broker, who communicates it to the specialist. Each specialist maintains a book listing the bid price for each pending offer to buy the share and the asked price or offer price for each offer to sell. Floor brokers of other firms may accept the highest bid price or the lowest offer price to complete the trade. If there is a lack of bids or an imbalance between buy and sell orders that keeps a particular share from trading, the specialists must buy or sell shares in order to keep the market functioning smoothly.

This sort of auction market used to be the norm. But in the past few years computerisation has permitted the development of electronic auction markets as well. All major stock exchanges now operate primarily through electronic auctions, with the sole exception of the New York Stock Exchange.

Electronic auction markets function in one of three different ways. Some offer a continuous or order-driven auction, in which the highest prices being bid and lowest prices being offered are continuously updated by computers, which automatically match buy and sell orders. Call auction markets execute trades at predetermined times rather than continously, to assure adequate liquidity in particular shares. Dealer markets, such as America's NASDAQ, have substantial human involvement. On NASDAQ, marketmakers post the prices at which they are prepared to buy and sell shares on brokers' screens, and brokers choose among the competing marketmakers to handle the desired trade. Other exchanges use hybrid systems, with the way in which a transaction is handled depending upon the size and liquidity of the particular stock.

Screen-based auction markets have been gaining ground because they offer lower costs per share traded. These savings are possible because they require fewer staff and less costly floor space. Several new electronic exchanges have been created in the expectation that a lower trading cost per share will attract business. NASDAQ and the New York Stock Exchange both agreed to purchase competing electronic exchanges in 2005.

Traditional auction markets with human brokers retain certain advantages. They are generally better for large buy or sell orders, because a broker can break a million-share order into pieces and try to transact each piece quietly without moving the market price, whereas a million-share order posted on a computerised system will cause the price to rise or fall. If the electronic system does not have marketmakers, as is sometimes the case, a buy or sell order for an unpopular stock may not find a match; this cannot occur in a market where a marketmaker is available to arrange a trade. Nevertheless, as electronic share auction systems have become more sophisticated, they have forced drastic change upon exchanges with a high-cost human infrastructure. Most exchanges have abandoned floor trading altogether because of the cost.

Competition in trading

The precise way in which trading is organised greatly affects the cost of buying equities. Until the mid-1970s most stock exchanges allowed their members, the brokerage firms, to charge fixed commissions for each share bought or sold. Commissions were deregulated in the United States in 1975 and in the UK in 1979. This opened the way for discount brokerages, which offer share trading by telephone and use the resultant cost savings to charge lower commissions. Since 1996 internet brokerages have handled individual transactions by personal computer at even lower cost. The fall in commissions to as little as a few US cents per share has permitted individuals to attempt new trading strategies, aiming to take advantage of tiny changes in a share's price, that would not be feasible with higher commissions. One of these is day trading, which involves the purchase of shares with the intention to resell quickly and reap a tiny profit.

The fact that an investor communicates electronically with a stockbroker, however, has no bearing on the way the share trade occurs. This is generally up to the broker, which has considerable discretion in arranging the trade and, in the case of a stock traded on more than one exchange, in deciding where the trade will be transacted.

Where trades are routed through marketmakers, investors may face a large gap, or spread, between the price at which the marketmaker offers to buy shares and the price at which it is willing to sell them. In 1997 the US government alleged that the members of NASDAQ conspired to maintain wide spreads. Spreads subsequently narrowed, and the presence of day traders, individuals who trade "inside" a marketmaker's spread by buying for more than the posted bid price and selling for less than the posted offer price in order to eke out a small profit, has caused them to narrow further. In January 1998 the average NASDAQ spread was 0.55% of the share price. By 2000 this had fallen to 0.32%, and by 2005 it averaged approximately 0.1%. The average spread on the New York Stock Exchange was similar.

There has also been concern about payment for order flow, a practice in which a marketmaker rebates part of its spread to stockbrokerage firms that bring it business, as these payments may induce stockbrokers not to make a trade in the way most beneficial to the customer. As spreads narrow, payment for order flow is less attractive to marketmakers, as they have less opportunity to profit from the transaction.

A further source of price competition has come with the growth of private electronic stock exchanges. Several such electronic communications networks, or ECNs, are used by large investors to trade shares without going through traditional exchanges. These systems consist of computers that comb electronic sources for buy and sell offers. ECNs do not buy or sell shares, but serve as conduits. The Securities and Exchange Commission first authorised ECNs to operate as stock exchanges in 1998. Two of the largest ECNs, Instinet and Archipelago, were targeted for purchase by NASDAQ and the New York Stock Exchange, respectively, in 2005.

Some ECNs are catering for individual investors, and others are focusing on large institutional trades. Their presence is squeezing the profitability of marketmakers, as the ECNs often permit narrower spreads. Certain ECNs, however, attempt mainly to match the buy and sell orders they have received – a process known as internalisation – and may offer pricing inferior to that available on the stock exchanges. Like payment for order flow, ECNs are an artefact of regulation, and their role will diminish if US regulators require that all customer orders on all exchanges be displayed together, to ensure that customers receive the best price available at a particular time.

Institutional trading

Individual investors' stockmarkets trades almost always involve a small number of shares of a single security. Institutional investors, however, have different requirements, and their trades may be handled differently.

- **Block trades** involve offers to buy or sell large amounts of stock, usually 10,000 shares or more. On a floor-based exchange, block trades are often handled off the floor by brokers who must assemble enough buyers or sellers to complete the transaction, but who must act quickly and discretely to prevent word of the impending deal from moving prices in the market. Block trades are more difficult to complete on screen-based exchanges, because posting an investor's intentions on members' screens would immediately change the price. In such a case, the trade is typically broken into smaller transactions conducted over a period of time, and the broker seeks to disguise the magnitude of the intended purchase or sale. Block trades account for about half of the trading volume on the New York Stock Exchange and about one-quarter of the volume on NASDAQ.
- **Basket trades** allow investors to trade shares in several different companies as part of a single transaction. This type of trading, which is confined to a few big exchanges, is popular among investors that are attempting to mimic a particular index, and who therefore want to buy or sell some shares of each stock in the index at the same time.
- **Program trades** are initiated by computers which have been programmed to identify share prices that are out of line with

the prices of futures or options on those same shares. The program trader may then buy shares and sell options, or vice versa, in some combination in order to profit from what may be a tiny anomaly in prices. Program trades accounted for more than half of all trading on the New York Stock Exchange in 2005.

◪ **Short sales** are transactions in which an investor (a short seller) borrows shares for a specified period and then sells them at the current market price, in the expectation that the price will be lower when it must buy shares to repay the lender. The short seller loses money if the share price does not fall as expected. In some countries, information about short positions must be reported and published. This can be important information for investors, because the existence of large short positions in a particular share means that short sellers will be needing to buy those shares in the market so they can repay the brokers from whom they have borrowed.

Clearing and settlement

An important function of stock exchanges is to ensure that trades are completed precisely as the parties have agreed. This involves two separate functions, clearing and settlement.

When brokers have executed a trade on an exchange, they report the details to the exchange. The exchange's clearing house reconciles the reports of all brokers involved to make sure that all parties are in agreement as to the price and the number of shares traded. Settlement then involves the transfer of the shares and money. Formerly, most exchanges operated their own clearing and settlement systems. As the cost of clearing and settlement is a significant part of the total cost of trading, however, exchanges have been under pressure to combine their systems or to engage third parties able to handle these functions more efficiently.

Settlement must occur within a time limit established by regulators. In the more advanced economies trades are settled within three days, and US, Canadian and European exchanges are seeking to make the settlement time even shorter. In less active markets, particularly in poorer countries, settlement can take a week or more. Lengthy settlement times deter investors, because they increase the chance that a transaction will not be completed and also make it difficult to resell shares quickly.

Investing on margin

Investors often purchase shares with borrowed money. Stockbrokerage firms make such loans, known as margin loans, accepting the purchased shares as collateral. Margin lending is regulated by national banking authorities, who generally insist that credit be extended for only a portion of the value of the shares purchased. An investor's initial margin is the amount of cash that must be deposited with the broker to acquire shares with a margin loan. Margin investors must also maintain a specified maintenance margin. The maintenance margin requires the owner to maintain a certain amount of equity, which is the current market value of the shares less the amount of the margin loan. If the market value of the shares falls, the amount of the investor's equity will decline. If the amount falls below an agreed level, the lender may issue a margin call, requiring the investor to deposit additional cash. If the investor fails to meet the margin call, the lender may sell the shares and apply the proceeds against the outstanding debt. The amount of margin debt outstanding varies greatly over time. Margin borrowing is generally considered a sign of investor optimism, as margin investors can lose heavily if share prices fall.

Measuring market performance

Private information providers and exchanges have developed many gauges to track the performance of equity markets. Two types of performance are particularly important to investors: those related to price, and those related to risk.

Price measures

There are two basic types of price measures:

- **Averages**, such as the Dow Jones Industrial, Utility and Transportation Averages on the New York Stock Exchange, track the value of a specific group of shares, with adjustments for the capitalisation of each company in the average and for the inclusion of new companies to replace those that have merged or gone bankrupt.
- **Indexes**, such as the *Financial Times* Stock Exchange (FTSE) 100-stock index in London, relate the current value of the shares in the index to the value during some base period, also adjusting for the deletion of some shares and the inclusion of others.

No index or average can offer a perfect picture of the market, because the shares tracked represent a non-random sample of all shares listed and each measure tracks a different set of shares. There is no single answer to a question such as: How did the Frankfurt stockmarket do in the early 1990s? The Commerzbank Index was at 1,701.2 on the last day of 1990 and 2,358.9 on the last day of 1995, a gain of 38.7%. The DAX Performance Index ended 1990 at 1,398.2 and was at 2,253.88 five years later, a gain of 61.2%. This difference reflects the composition of the indexes. The Commerzbank Index includes 78 shares that account for about 70% of Frankfurt share trading. The DAX tracks 30 stocks that account for about 61% of trading.

Several new indexes, such as the Dow Jones Euro Stoxx 50 and the Euro-Stars index of 29 euro-zone stocks, are competing to become the investment benchmark for Europe. Matters are even more confusing in New York, where three separate indexes – the Standard & Poor's 500 Stock Index, the New York Stock Exchange Composite Index and the Dow Jones Industrial Average (DJIA) – all tell different stories about price trends. According to the S&P 500, New York stocks rose 9% in 2004. The NYSE Composite rose 12.6%, and the DJIA, which is composed of 30 stocks, rose just 3.2%.

There are several reasons for these differences. First, there is no statistically sound way to create an index which is truly representative of the market; each index comprises different shares, and its performance depends upon the shares included. Second, all indexes are vulnerable to selection bias. When a firm whose shares are in the index merges, becomes a privately held firm or enters bankruptcy proceedings, the sponsor of the index has great flexibility to pick a replacement. There is an incentive to select a firm whose shares are popular and widely followed, because a strong performance by that share will, in turn, stimulate interest in the index.

A third reason is the growing popularity of index or tracker funds, which seek to mimic the performance of a particular index. The manager of a tracker fund does not select particular shares, but maintains a portfolio of the same shares as are in the index being tracked, in the same proportion. The S&P 500 is a particularly popular index for trackers, increasing the demand for the shares it includes; the other two main New York Stock Exchange indexes are not as widely used by fund managers.

As well as these general market indexes there are thousands of indexes developed to measure various aspects of equity trading, from bank shares listed on a particular market to emerging-market stockmarkets as a

Table 7.14 **Performance of stockmarket indexes (annual percentage return, without reinvested dividends)**

Index	Country	1996	1998	2000	2002	2004
FTSE 100	UK	11.63	14.55	−10.20	−24.48	7.54
S&P/TSX Composite	Canada	25.74	−3.19	6.20	−13.97	12.48
CAC 40	France	23.71	31.47	−0.01	−33.75	7.40
DAX	Germany	27.40	18.52	−20.70	−43.94	7.34
S&P/MIB	Italy	11.07	45.18	2.48	−27.26	14.98
Nikkei 225	Japan	2.55	−9.28	−27.20	−18.63	7.61
AEX	Netherlands	33.56	29.85	−5.04	−36.32	3.09
SMI	Switzerland	19.54	14.29	7.47	−27.84	3.74
NASDAQ	US	22.71	39.63	39.30	−31.53	8.59
S&P 500	US	20.26	26.67	−10.14	−23.37	8.99

group. Table 7.14 on the next page shows the annual performance of some of the major indexes in recent years.

Risk measures

The risk of investing in a particular stockmarket is measured by its volatility. This term has a precise statistical meaning when applied to stockmarkets: a market's volatility is the annualised standard deviation of daily percentage changes in a selected stock price index. A market's volatility varies from time to time. The volatility of all major markets soared during the big stock price drops of October 1997 and September 1998. But some markets seem persistently less volatile than others. London has been the least volatile of the world's main markets in recent years, and the Italian exchange has been among the most volatile.

8 Commodities and futures markets

MANAGING RISK is one of the essential functions of financial markets. One of the biggest of these risks is time. The completion of any business transaction requires time, but if prices change during this period a potentially profitable deal may turn out to be a costly mistake. The purpose of futures markets is to help protect against the risks inherent in a world where prices change constantly.

The mechanism used to obtain this protection is a futures contract, an agreement to buy or sell an asset in the future at a certain price. Futures contracts come in two basic forms. This chapter deals with the standardised contracts that are traded on futures exchanges. Forward contracts, which are not standardised and are traded privately rather than on exchanges, are discussed in Chapter 9, as are options and other derivative contracts that are used, as futures contracts are, to manage risk.

Futures markets were an outgrowth of commodities markets, which allow a person to acquire or sell physical stocks of minerals, grains and other long-lasting products. Commodities markets have existed for millennia. They have served the important function of setting prices for commodities, and have offered a means for those who produce a commodity to trade it for other sorts of goods. Commodities markets, however, cannot help the investor whose store of commodities loses value as the price declines, or the potential user who watches the price of a commodity rise before it can obtain a needed supply. Futures markets were developed to play this role.

The origin of futures trading is lost in history. It is known that in Renaissance times the merchants who financed trading voyages sometimes arranged to sell wares that they expected to receive but did not yet have in hand. By the late 1500s, fish dealers in Holland were buying and selling herring that had yet to be caught, and the sale of other commodities on a to-arrive basis soon followed. At a time when communications were poor and transport was unreliable, these markets allowed manufacturers to lock in the price of their raw material and assured ship owners a profit on their cargoes. The leap from one-off deals to standardised contracts came in 1865, when the Chicago Board of Trade began trading futures contracts in grain.

The characteristics of commodities

Commodities are physical goods, but not all physical goods are commodities. Commodities have certain characteristics that make it feasible to trade them in markets:

- They can be stored for long periods, or in some cases for unlimited periods.
- Their value depends heavily on measurable physical attributes and on the physical location of the commodities.
- Commodities with the same physical attributes and the same physical location are fungible. If a buyer has contracted to purchase petroleum of a certain density and sulphur content or wheat of a certain type and moisture content, it need not be concerned about which well pumped the oil or which farmer raised the wheat.

Most participants in the markets for physical commodities are producers, users, or firms that have established themselves as intermediaries between producers and users. Few investors are interested in physical commodities strictly as a financial investment, because it is usually much less costly to purchase and hold futures contracts than to purchase and store the commodities themselves.

Why trade futures?

Futures contracts, unlike bonds and shares, do not represent long-term investments with income potential. On the contrary, a futures contract pays no interest or dividends, and the money tied up in it is money that cannot be invested to receive interest. All futures-market investors operate from one of two fundamental motives.

Hedging

This involves the use of futures or other financial instruments to offset specific risks. In April, before planting his soyabeans, an Iowan farmer might sell September futures contracts, which commit him to supply soyabeans at the agreed price after harvest. The farmer, who must sell his product in the physical commodities market after harvest, thus uses futures to hedge the risk that the price of a tonne of soyabeans will decline between April and September. Conversely, a processor who hopes to purchase soyabeans in September may buy soyabean futures contracts in April to protect itself against the risk that the price of the physical commodity, raw soyabeans, might rise over the summer. Typically, hedgers have made a decision to take on certain types of risks and to avoid others. For example, a French oil company might determine not to trade petroleum futures, as its shareholders have deliberately chosen to take oil-related risks by investing in the firm, but it might buy euro futures to prevent a fluctuating dollar from affecting the profit it reports in euros.

Speculation

This involves trading with the intention of profiting from changes in the prices of futures contracts, rather than from a desire to hedge specific risks. Although speculation is often derided as an unproductive activity, it is essential to the smooth functioning of the market. By buying and selling contracts with great frequency, speculators vastly increase liquidity: the supply of money in the markets. Without the liquidity that speculators provide, the futures markets would be less attractive to hedgers because it would be more difficult to buy and sell contracts at favourable prices. Firms that use futures for hedging may also be active as speculators. In many markets a prominent role is also played by floor traders or locals, individuals trading for themselves on a full-time basis.

Futures contracts

A futures contract represents a deal between two investors who may not be known to each other and are unaware of one another's motives. A futures contract is a derivative, because its price and terms are derived from an underlying asset, sometimes known as the underlying. (Other types of derivatives are discussed in Chapter 9.) A new contract may be created any time two investors desire to create one. Although there is a limit to the amount of copper that can be mined in a given year, there is no limit to the number of copper futures contracts that can be traded.

Types of contracts

Futures contracts can be divided into two basic categories:

- **Commodity futures** were once based exclusively upon bulk commodities, known as physicals. Recently, however, the rising demand for ways to manage risks has led to trading of non-physical contracts as well.
- **Financial futures** contracts were first traded only in 1972. Despite initial controversy over their desirability, they have become

popular as a result of the abandonment of fixed exchange rates in the major industrial countries in the 1970s and the deregulation of interest rates in subsequent years. Trading volume in financial futures now exceeds trading volume in commodity futures by a wide margin.

How futures are traded

To buy or sell futures contracts, an investor must deal with a registered broker, also known as a futures commission merchant. Many futures commission merchants are owned by large banks or securities companies that are active in other financial markets as well. The futures commission merchant maintains staff and computer systems to trade on the exchanges of which it is a member.

The customer's order gives the futures commission merchant specific directions. A market order, also referred to as an at-the-market order, is to be executed immediately, whatever the conditions in the market. A limit order is to be executed only at a specified price. A market-if-touched order is to be executed as soon as the market has reached a specified price, but the actual trade may be at a higher or lower price. An all-or-none order must be filled in its entirety or not at all. A fill-or-kill order must be filled immediately in its entirety or the order is cancelled.

In every trade the two parties take opposite positions. The buyer of the contract, who agrees to receive the commodities specified, is said to be in a long position. The French oil firm mentioned above under "Hedging", for example, would be long euros if it has agreed to receive euros at the expiry of its contract. The seller of a contract is said to be in a short position. It may not own the commodities it has agreed to deliver, but it is obliged to have them or to pay their value in cash at the expiry of the contract.

Once a trade has been completed, the participants are both obligated to the exchange rather than to each other. Either party separately may terminate its contract at any point by arranging an offset, without affecting the other party's position. If the Iowan soyabean farmer mentioned above decides in July to end his September delivery obligation, he would buy (at the price current in July) the same number of September contracts that he previously sold, and the two sets of contracts would cancel each other out. This is often referred to as liquidation of the initial contracts. If the price of the contracts purchased in July is greater than the price at which the farmer originally sold the contracts in April, he will have lost money on his futures transactions; if the price in July is less, he will have made money. Note, however, that as a hedger the farmer is concerned not about futures-market profits but about the amount he will receive for his crop. If he sells his soybeans for a good price, he is likely to regard any loss in the futures market as a sort of insurance premium that bought him protection if soybean prices had fallen.

Contract terms

A futures contract contains the specifications of the transaction. The specifications of all contracts in a given commodity on a given exchange are identical, apart from the expiration dates. This standardisation is an important feature of futures markets as it makes contracts interchangeable, freeing traders and investors from the need to worry about unusual provisions. The specifications cover the following:

- ◪ **Contract size.** This specifies how much of the asset must be delivered under one contract. Size for commodity futures is usually specified by weight or quantity. One cocoa contract traded on the Coffee, Sugar and Cocoa Exchange in New York, for example, involves the obligation to sell or buy 10 tonnes of cocoa. For financial futures, the value of the underlying asset is specified in monetary terms. The buyer of one contract on British pounds on the Chicago Mercantile Exchange is contracting to purchase £62,500.
- ◪ **Quality.** Contracts for commodity futures specify the physical quality of the product the seller has promised to supply. They often use industry-standard product grades. The arabica coffee contract on the Bolsa de Mercadorias & Futuros in São Paulo requires evenly coloured or greenish Brazilian-grown coffee of type six or better, with a maximum of 8% wormy or bored beans, packed in new jute bags of 60kg each. Some contracts allow the seller to substitute substandard product at a reduced price. Quality standards are not relevant for most financial futures contracts, such as currencies.
- ◪ **Delivery date.** Every contract is available with a choice of delivery dates: the dates on which the parties are obliged to complete the terms of the contract. Contracts are typically identified by month, with delivery on a specified day or days of the month. Trading in a contract ceases on or before the delivery date. The Brent Crude oil futures traded on the International

Table 8.1 **The leading futures exchanges**

Exchange	Abbreviation	No. of futures contracts traded (m)		
		1998	2001	2004
Chicago Mercantile Exchange, US	CME	184	316	787
Eurex, Germany/Switzerland	Eurex	145	503	684
Chicago Board of Trade, US	CBOT	217	210	489
Euronext[a]	Euronext	210	203	307
Mexican Derivatives Exchange	MexDer	...	18	204
Bolsa de Mercadorias & Futuros, Brazil	BM&F	66	94	170
New York Mercantile Exchange, US	NYMEX	80	85	133
Tokyo Commodity Exchange, Japan	TOCOM	44	56	75
London Metal Exchange	LME	51	56	67
Korea Exchange	KOFEX	21	42	65

a Figures represent trading on French futures exchange owned by Euronext, formerly known as MATIF and on the former London International Financial Futures Exchange.
Sources: Exchange reports; World Federation of Exchanges

Petroleum Exchange in London, for example, have monthly delivery dates over the next year, quarterly dates for the following 12 months and half-yearly dates for the year after that. Brent trading for a given delivery month ceases on the business day immediately preceding the 15th day before the first day of the delivery month.

◼ **Price limits.** To facilitate smooth trading, each contract specifies the smallest allowable price movement, known as a tick or a point. The tick size of the Chicago Board of Trade's Northern Spring Wheat contract is $1/4$ cent per American bushel (2.84 hectolitres); as one contract covers 5,000 bushels, the price of a contract therefore changes in increments of $12.50 (5,000 × $0.0025). Many contracts also specify daily limits for price changes to avoid large day-to-day price swings. Chicago spring wheat futures may not rise or fall by more than 20 cents per bushel on any day.

◼ **Position limits.** The exchange imposes a limit on the number of contracts a speculator may hold for a particular delivery month and a particular commodity. The purpose of position limits is to

Table 8.2 **Leading futures contracts**

	No. traded (m)		
	1998	2001	2004
3-month Eurodollar, CME	110	184	298
Euro-Bund, Eurex	90	178	240
TIIE 28, MexDer	...	17	206
US 10-year Treasury, CBOT	33	58	196
Mini S&P 500, CME	5	39	167
Euro-Bobl, Eurex	32	100	159
3-month Euribor, Euronext	...	91	158
Euro-Schatz, Eurex	10	93	123
DJ Euro Stoxx 50, Eurex	...	38	122
US 5-year Treasury, CBOT	18	31	105

Source: Exchange reports

prevent a speculator from cornering the market by owning a large proportion of open contracts and thus being able to manipulate the price. Position limits do not usually apply to investors who can prove to the exchange that they are hedgers.

◢ **Settlement.** Most futures transactions do not lead to the actual delivery of the underlying products. However, the contract specifies when and where delivery must be made and may provide for the alternative of cash settlement, in which the parties fulfil their obligations by making or receiving cash payments rather than exchanging goods.

Futures exchanges

Futures trading takes place on organised exchanges. There are about 35 significant exchanges around the world and many smaller ones. Some exchanges that trade futures also trade shares, and most futures exchanges now deal in options. Although many exchanges are co-operatives owned by their members, a growing number are organised as profit-making corporations owned by shareholders, some of whom may not be members. The most important futures exchanges are listed in Table 8.1 and the most widely traded futures contracts in Table 8.2.

There is intense competition among exchanges to develop new contracts and to cut costs to make existing contracts more attractive.

All futures trades are subject to brokerage commissions, taxes and fees levied by the exchange itself. Since many trading strategies aim to exploit small price differences among contracts, even a minor change in the cost structure can have a significant effect on the volume of trading.

The most notable example of head-to-head competition occurred in 1997, when the former Deutsche Terminbörse, in Germany, cut trading costs in a successful effort to capture trading in German government bond futures (Bunds) from the London International Financial Futures Exchange (LIFFE), now part of the Euronext exchange. Bund trading in London fell from 45m contracts in 1997 to none in 1999, while Bund trading in Germany, now handled by the combined German/Swiss exchange Eurex, rose from 16m contracts in 1996 to 144m contracts in 1999 and 184m in 2001.

Such direct competition is exceptional. It is rare that two exchanges offer precisely the same contract, as investors generally gravitate towards the market with more liquidity and the other withers. Competition more often involves contracts that are similar but not identical. One example occurred in 1998, when the Chicago Board of Trade inaugurated a contract based on the Dow Jones Industrial Average of US equities to compete with the highly successful contract on the Standard & Poor's 500 stock index traded on the rival Chicago Mercantile Exchange. However, technology may facilitate direct competition among exchanges. In June 2000 US regulators agreed to allow seven foreign exchanges to offer computerised trading to customers in the United States. One of these was Eurex, a joint venture of the Swiss and German stock exchanges, which began trading futures on US Treasury bonds in competition with the Chicago Board of Trade.

An exchange may discontinue trading in an established contract if there is insufficient interest. For example, the advent of the single European currency on January 1st 1999 meant the end of contracts on 12 countries' currencies and interest rates and their replacement by far fewer contracts on euro exchange and interest rates. In 1997 the French notional bond contract, traded on the MATIF in Paris, was the fifth most active futures contract in the world, with nearly 34m contracts being traded. By 1999, with many other euro-denominated interest-rate futures available, only 6m notional bond futures were traded. Changes in user industries may cause a contract to disappear; the Tokyo Commodity Exchange's cotton yarn futures were discontinued in 2000, after annual volume fell from 2.3m in 1992 to a few thousand contracts in

1999. Many newly introduced contracts are subsequently withdrawn if investor interest proves weak.

Merger pressures

Competitive pressures and the high costs of new technology are driving many exchanges to collaborate or even to merge. In 1990 Japan was home to 16 commodity exchanges, from the Maebashi Dried Cocoon Exchange to the Tokyo Commodity Exchange. Now there are only ten. As a result of mergers in 1991 and again in 1997, Brazil's futures exchange has become one of the world's largest. The Chinese government forced many exchanges to merge or close, reducing the number of futures markets from 40 in 1993 to three in 1999. The Singapore International Monetary Exchange and the Chicago Mercantile Exchange allow certain contracts to be traded on either exchange, and the Tokyo Grain Exchange is collaborating with the much newer Dalian Commodity Exchange in China. The Commodity Exchange, in New York, merged into the New York Mercantile Exchange in 1994, creating the largest exchange devoted exclusively to commodity futures; and the New York Cotton Exchange and the Coffee, Sugar and Cocoa Exchange combined to form the New York Board of Trade in June 1998.

LIFFE and the former Portuguese futures exchange both merged with Euronext in 2002, allowing investors to trade electronically on exchanges in five different countries using the same electronic system. This sort of arrangement has the potential to lower costs for market participants, particularly by reducing the total amount of cash deposits, or margin, required to support their trading (see page 194).

Such alliances and mergers are often intensely controversial. Traditionally, the exchanges have been co-operatives owned by the people who trade there. Traders often fear for their livelihoods if the contracts they handle are traded on other exchanges or with electronic systems, and in many cases they have opposed both technical innovations and co-operation with other exchanges. In 1999 members of the International Petroleum Exchange in London rebuffed merger proposals from the New York Mercantile Exchange for just such reasons, but continuing economic and technological pressures led them to agree a sale to Intercontinental Exchange, a US-based company, in 2001. Many leading futures exchanges, including the CME, Nymex, CBOT and LIFFE, undertook demutualisation in 2000 in order to achieve a shareholder-owned status that allows for faster decision-making. Each exchange initially limited share ownership to its members. LIFFE's shareholder members subsequently voted to merge with Euronext. The CME sold shares to the public in 2002. NYMEX reached an agreement to sell a 10% equity stake to an outside shareholder in September 2005, and the CBOT had an initial public offering in October 2005.

In the United States, regulators have approved the creation of several new, all-electronic exchanges since 2000. One of these, eSpeed, has a large share of trading in government bond futures. The Intercontinental Exchange trades energy futures electronically. Many of the upstart exchanges, however, have failed to gain enough trading volume to challenge the long-established exchanges.

Trading

There are three main methods of trading futures contracts:

- **Continuous-auction or open-outcry trading** is conducted by floor brokers or pit brokers on the floor of the exchange. The brokers stand in a certain area of the floor or in a trading pit or ring, an enclosed area with steps or risers so that each floor broker can see and be seen by all the others in the pit. The futures commission merchant has a clerk outside each pit, who receives customers' orders by telephone. The clerk relays the orders to the firm's floor brokers with hand signals, electronic messages or on slips of paper carried into the pit by runners. The floor broker then announces the buy or sell offer in the pit, and other brokers respond with shouts or hand signals until a price is agreed. This is the form of futures trading most familiar to the public. Until recently, most of the world's main futures exchanges used open-outcry trading for at least some of their contracts. However, exchanges such as Euronext and Eurex have eliminated all open-outcry trading, and much of the trading in financial futures at the Chicago Mercantile Exchange and the Chicago Board of Trade is conducted through electronic systems rather than by open outcry. Canada's Winnipeg Commodity Exchange, which trades futures contracts on barley and canola (rapeseed), abandoned open-outcry trading in 2004. Conversely, the New York Mercantile Exchange opened a trading floor in London in 2005 after the International Petroleum Exchange ceased floor trading.
- **Single-price auction trading**, also known as session trading, is used especially in Japan. An exchange official opens each session of trading in a given contract by posting a provisional price for

the nearest delivery month. Members then put in their buy and sell orders at that price. If sell orders outnumber buy orders, the price is lowered to attract more buy orders; if buy orders outnumber sell orders, the price is raised a fraction. When the number of buy orders is equal to the number of sell orders the price is fixed. All contracts for that delivery month are executed at the fixed price during the session. The process is repeated to set the price for the next-nearest delivery month, and so on. There are four to six sessions for each commodity each trading day.

- **Electronic trading** is conducted over a computer system rather than on a trading floor. Exchange members have exclusive access to the system; others allow non-members to submit buy and sell offers anonymously by computer. In either case, market participants need not be physically located in the same city, or country, as the exchange. Various systems use differing rules to match buy offers with sell offers, to post transaction prices and to inform all market participants of pending buy and sell offers. The details of these rules make a great difference to the way trading occurs and directly affect the ability of market participants to assure themselves of the best possible price.

In general, electronic systems transact contracts at much lower cost than trading pits. Yet some exchanges resisted the introduction of electronic trading. This was partly because of some members' self-interest: electronic systems reduce or eliminate the need for floor brokers, clerks and other personnel. Another reason is that open-outcry trading, in which a floor broker gains a feel for the market by observing other brokers, is generally superior to electronic trading for contracts that are less heavily traded and for the execution of complex trading strategies. However, the competitive pressures among exchanges have become so strong that exchanges have been forced to adopt electronic trading in order to attract investors who demand the lowest possible trading cost.

Electronic systems have opened the way for after-hours trading. This is a recent innovation that allows customers to trade after trading on the exchange floor has stopped for the day. Prices in after-hours trading may not be as favourable as during the trading day because there is less liquidity, but investors are able to respond to late news without waiting for the following day's trading. Electronic trading of some of the most popular contracts is available 24 hours a day.

How prices are set

The method for establishing the price of a contract is set in the contract specifications. These state which currency the price is quoted in and the unit for which the price is quoted. Prices for agricultural futures traded in the United States are normally quoted in cents and, for some contracts, in fractions of a cent. Prices in most other countries and for US financial futures contracts are quoted in decimals rather than fractions.

The quoted price

The quoted price is not the price of a contract but of the specified unit. It must be multiplied by the number of units per contract to determine the price of one contract. Consider the International Petroleum Exchange's Brent Crude contract, which is priced in US dollars even though it trades in London. The quoted price is for a single barrel of oil (42 American gallons, or 159 litres). One contract provides for the future purchase or sale of 1,000 barrels of oil. If a given month's Brent Crude contract is trading at $45.00, one contract costs 1,000 × $45.00, or $45,000. A 10-cent drop in the posted price means a decrease of $100 (1,000 × $0.10) in the value of a contract.

Price movements

Prices in the markets change constantly in response to supply and demand, which are affected mainly by news from outside, although in a highly selective way. A fall in New York share prices will be felt immediately in the Chicago Mercantile Exchange pit where futures on the Standard & Poor's 500 stock index are traded, but may not be noticed in the nearby cattle futures pits. Investors in commodity futures pay close attention to information that could affect the price of the underlying commodity. For example, orange juice futures will soar on reports of frost that could damage the orange crop in Brazil, and copper futures will be sensitive to statistics on construction activity. Investors in financial futures are concerned more with economic data that might signal interest-rate changes.

Limits on price movements

For some contracts, the contract specifications limit the amount that the price may rise or fall in a given day. A limit move means that the contract has fluctuated as much as allowed on that day. A contract that has risen the maximum allowable amount is said to be limit up. One that has fallen the permissible maximum is limit down. A locked market has reached its price limit, and trading may proceed only at current prices or prices closer to the previous day's settlement price.

The spot price

The reference price for any futures contract is the spot price, the amount required to go out and purchase those items today. The difference between the spot price of an asset and the price of a futures contract for the nearest delivery month is the basis or the swap rate. As a contract approaches its delivery date its price normally converges with the spot price. The reasoning is intuitive. If the price of Japanese yen to be delivered 30 days from now is far above the spot price, a buyer could purchase yen now in the spot market and put them in the bank for 30 days rather than buying a futures contract.

Term factor

Most of the time the price of a contract rises as the delivery month becomes more distant. This reflects both the greater risk of big price changes over the life of a longer-term contract and the fact that the buyer of that contract has money tied up for a longer period. If this price relationship exists, with each delivery date for a particular contract having a higher price than the previous delivery date, the market is called a normal market, or is said to be in contango. If near-term contracts cost more than more distant contracts, the market is said to be inverted or in backwardation.

Obtaining price information

The current price of a futures contract is simply the most recent price at which a contract was exchanged. Active traders and investors can subscribe to private information services. In some cases, the information services are able to station reporters on the exchange floor to report on transaction prices; in other cases, the exchange supplies the services with the information. But as prices for heavily traded contracts change constantly, exchange members have an advantage. Only they have the latest information about trades and orders, gained either by being on the trading floor or by monitoring the computer trading system.

Commodity futures markets

There are four main categories of commodity futures: agricultural products, metals, energy and transport.

Table 8.3 **Leading agricultural commodities contracts, 2004**

Contract	Exchange	No. traded (m)
No. 1 soyabeans	Dalian Commodity Exchange	57.3
Soya meal	Dalian Commodity Exchange	24.7
Corn	Chicago Board of Trade	24.0
Soyabeans	Chicago Board of Trade	18.8
Hard white winter wheat	Zhengzhou Commodity Exchange	11.6
Non-GMO soyabeans	Tokyo Grain Exchange	10.0
Sugar No. 11	New York Board of Trade	9.8
Rubber	Shanghai Futures Exchange	9.7
Strong gluten wheat	Zhengzhou Commodity Exchange	9.7
Soyabean meal	Chicago Board of Trade	8.6

Source: Exchange reports

Agricultural futures

Cereals were the first products on which futures contracts were traded. Now hundreds of different contracts are traded on raw and processed grains and oils, live and slaughtered animals, sugar, orange juice, coffee and inedible agricultural products such as lumber, rubber and cotton. Table 8.3 lists the agricultural contracts with the largest volume in 2004.

Until recently, global volume in agricultural futures trading was dominated by the Chicago Board of Trade, which was the first exchange to trade agricultural futures. Since the early 2000s, however, Chinese exchanges have emerged as centres for trading grains, soya products, and industrial commodities. Agricultural futures trading has not consolidated at a few exchanges in the same way as trading in most other types of futures. The survival of many contracts on many exchanges is a result of two characteristics specific to farm products. First, many crops have a large number of varieties, creating demand for several separate contracts for each generic commodity. Although soyabean futures were already heavily traded at the Chicago Board of Trade and the Tokyo Grain Exchange, the latter opened a separate contract in 2000 to meet demand for non-genetically modified soya. Second, agricultural products are processed in many locations, making it useful to have contracts with different delivery points. Thus wheat growers and users can choose among 15 different futures contracts (see Table 8.4).

Similarly, sugar futures trade on Euronext in Europe, the Tokyo Grain

Table 8.4 **Wheat futures contracts**

Exchange	Contract traded	Delivery point
Bolsa de Comercio de Rosario	Wheat	Rosario, Santa Fe
Chicago Board of Trade	Northern spring wheat	Chicago, St Louis, Toledo
Euronext	Milling wheat	Rouen
Kansas City Board of Trade	Hard red winter wheat	Kansas City, Hutchinson
Euronext	Feed wheat	UK
Mercado a Termino de Buenos Aires	Hard bread wheat	Buenos Aires, Rosario, Quequen, Ingeniero White
Mid-America Commodities Exchange	Wheat	Chicago
Minneapolis Grain Exchange	Durum wheat	Minneapolis area
Minneapolis Grain Exchange	Hard red spring wheat	Minneapolis, Duluth
Minneapolis Grain Exchange	Soft white wheat	Columbia River District
South African Futures Exchange	Bread milling wheat	South Africa
Sydney Futures Exchange	Australian standard white wheat	Newcastle
Winnipeg Commodities Exchange	No. 3 Canada western red spring wheat	Thunder Bay
Zhengzhou Commodity Exchange	Hard white winter wheat	Eastern China
Zhengzhou Commodity Exchange	Strong gluten wheat	Eastern China

Source: Exchange reports

Exchange in Japan, the New York Board of Trade in the United States and the Bolsa de Mercadorias & Futuros in Brazil, and coffee futures are traded in London, New York, Tokyo and São Paulo. In each case, the contracts are not precise substitutes for one another, and most farmers and food processors will have a preference for the particular contract that best allows them to hedge their specific risks.

The specificity of agricultural futures has left room for specialised contracts on smaller exchanges. Thus the Euronext bread-wheat contract, which began trading in 1998, aims to exploit demand for a

Table 8.5 **Leading metals contracts**

			No. traded (m)	
Contract	Exchange	1998	2001	2004
Aluminium	London Metal Exchange	20.1	25.4	29.3
Copper	London Metal Exchange	16.0	17.6	18.2
Gold	Tokyo Commodity Exchange	9.4	9.8	18.0
Gold	New York Mercantile Exchange	9.0	6.8	15.0
Platinum	Tokyo Commodity Exchange	10.8	16.2	13.9
Zinc	London Metal Exchange	5.7	7.5	10.2
Silver	New York Mercantile Exchange	4.1	2.6	5.0
Copper	Shanghai Futures Exchange	...	1.8	4.2
Lead	London Metal Exchange	...	3.2	3.8
Nickel	London Metal Exchange	4.7	5.1	3.2

Source: Exchange reports

delivery point in Continental Europe and changes in EU agricultural policies that may lead to greater price instability within Europe. The Warenterminbörse Hannover, in Germany, was established in 1998 with contracts on pork, of which Germany is Europe's largest producer and consumer, and on potatoes. The Commodity and Monetary Exchange of Malaysia, in Kuala Lumpur, has built a successful agricultural futures business on palm oil, a single commodity traded on no other exchange.

Metals futures

Precious metals, such as gold, and industrial metals, such as copper, have been traded in futures markets since the middle of the 19th century. Metals prices can be extremely volatile. Mining companies and industrial users normally maintain large stocks of metals, and futures markets provide a means to hedge the risk that the value of these stocks will fall. Industrial users can also employ futures to stabilise the prices of key raw materials.

Trading in gold futures is quite different from trading in other metals. Although some investors in gold futures mine gold or use it in manufacturing, most gold futures trading is related to gold's traditional role as a store of value in times of inflation. Hence gold is among the most heavily traded of all metals. However, not all gold trading occurs on

Table 8.6 **Leading energy contracts**

			No. traded (m)	
Contract	*Exchange*	*1998*	*2001*	*2004*
Light Sweet Crude	New York Mercantile Exchange	30.5	37.5	52.9
Brent Crude	International Petroleum Exchange	13.6	18.3	25.4
Gasoline	Tokyo Commodity Exchange	...	16.4	24.0
Natural gas	New York Mercantile Exchange	16.0	16.5	17.4
Kerosene	Tokyo Commodity Exchange	...	8.3	13.0
Heating oil	New York Mercantile Exchange	8.9	9.3	12.9
Unleaded gasoline	New York Mercantile Exchange	7.4	9.3	12.8
Gas oil	International Petroleum Exchange	5.0	7.2	9.4

Source: Exchange reports

futures markets, as many speculators trade shares of gold-mining companies as an alternative to futures contracts.

Unlike users of agricultural products, users of metals are not concerned with local variations in quality. Although there are quality differences among ores, metals have been extracted from ore and processed to specific standards before they are traded in financial markets. As a result, metals users throughout the world employ a comparatively small number of contracts, and there is almost no local trading of metals futures. The London Metal Exchange, the Tokyo Commodity Exchange and the New York Mercantile Exchange account for almost all futures trading in metals, but the relatively new Shanghai Futures Exchange has established several metals contracts. China's rapid industrial growth has given the Shanghai exchange an important role in determining the world price of copper. Table 8.5 lists the most widely traded contracts.

Energy futures

Trading in energy-related futures products dates back to the oil crises of the 1970s and, in the United States, to the regulation-induced natural gas shortages of the same period. Futures contracts on petroleum and petroleum derivatives are extremely popular. The amount of oil traded daily in futures markets far outstrips actual world demand for petroleum. There are also contracts based on the spread, or difference, between the prices of different petroleum products. After hurricanes damaged US refineries and production facilities in August and September 2005, energy futures contracts played an important role in helping the markets adjust to extremely high oil and natural gas prices.

Natural gas futures have become well-established in North America, with the New York Mercantile Exchange offering three separate contracts for delivery points in the United States and Canada. Because each contract is tied to the capacity of pipelines serving a specific location, the contracts are of little use to gas users in other countries. Many more natural gas contracts are likely to be created on various exchanges to meet local demands. The most widely traded energy futures contracts are listed in Table 8.6 on the previous page.

The arrival of price competition in wholesale electric markets has led to the creation of futures contracts on electricity. The volume of trading in individual contracts is small, because each is tied to the price of power delivered to a specific location. The Sydney Futures Exchange in Australia, for example, trades separate contracts on electricity delivered to the states of New South Wales and Victoria. The first contract on electricity in the UK began trading on the International Petroleum Exchange in 2000. It is likely that exchanges will offer many other electricity contracts to serve particular markets. Electricity deregulation also stimulated development of the first coal futures contract, which began trading in 1999.

One interesting innovation in commodity futures trading is environmental futures. A programme in the United States created tradable allowances for the emission of sulphur dioxide starting in 1995, each allowance giving the owner the right to emit 1 American ton (907kg) of sulphur dioxide during or after the specified year. The allowances are auctioned annually at the Chicago Board of Trade and are traded privately after auction. This system encourages firms to reduce emissions in the least costly way, and to use the allowances for pollution sources that would be most costly to mitigate. The main purchasers are electric utilities and oil refiners. Some governments want to establish similar tradable permits for other categories of air emissions, particularly carbon dioxide, a gas implicated in global warming, which is emitted mainly in the burning of fossil fuels. After the European Union imposed caps on industries' emissions of carbon dioxide and other so-called greenhouse gases, the International Petroleum Exchange began trading futures in the price of carbon-dioxide emission rights in April 2005. Within three months it was trading more than 500 contracts per day.

Commodity-related futures
As the delivered price of physicals depends greatly upon the cost of

Table 8.7 **Reading a commodity futures price table**

Orange Juice (NYBOT)
15,000lb – cents/lb

Month	Open	High	Low	Settle	Change	Lifetime high	Lifetime low	Open interest
Mar 06	100.50	100.50	99.35	99.95	–0.50	127.95	96.10	17,978
May 06	100.65	100.80	99.75	100.50	–0.15	130.00	96.50	4,105
Jul 06	101.20	101.20	100.25	100.80	–0.45	132.00	99.75	2,464
Nov 06	101.75	103.25	101.75	102.40	0.15	132.75	101.75	551
Est vol 2,434		prev vol 2,976			open int 25,863: +627			

transport, there is a demand to hedge freight rates. The Baltic Exchange in London, a centre for arranging bulk shipping, produces indexes of bulk maritime shipping rates, but Euronext ceased trading a futures contract on the Baltic rates index because of lack of volume. Freight futures are traded on the Norwegian Futures and Options Clearinghouse and on the New York Mercantile Exchange.

Exchanges are also developing other non-physical contracts that may be used to hedge commodity prices. The Chicago Mercantile Exchange, for example, began offering contracts on temperatures, useful for hedging agricultural or energy prices, in 1999.

Reading commodity futures price tables

Many newspapers publish data summarising the previous day's commodity trading. Table 8.7 illustrates a typical newspaper price table for a commodity futures contract.

According to the heading, this table reports trading in orange juice futures on the New York Board of Trade (NYBOT).

The following line provides two essential pieces of information. First, one contract covers 15,000lb (6,804kg) of juice. Second, prices are listed in cents per lb, equivalent to 0.454kg. A listed price must therefore be multiplied by 15,000 to obtain the price of a contract in cents, then divided by 100 to obtain the price in dollars.

The first column lists the delivery months for which there has been active trading. These are not necessarily the only months available. Many contracts permit trading for delivery months several years into the future, but there is frequently little or no trading for more distant months and therefore no information to publish. The next four columns list the price of the first trade for each delivery month on the previous day (open), the high and low prices for each delivery month, and the official closing price (settle). As there are often many trades at various prices in the final moments of trading, the settlement price does not purport to be the price of the day's final trade. It is usually a weighted average of the prices of trades immediately before the close of trading, as computed by the exchange. Note that the market is in contango.

The column headed "change" is the difference between the settlement price on this day and that on the previous trading day. May orange juice is $0.0015 per lb lower, so the value of one contract has declined $22.50 since the previous day. November juice is 15 hundredths of a cent higher, so a contract worth $15,337.50 at the previous close (15,000 times the price of $1.0225) is now worth $15,360 (15,000 times the price of $1.0240).

"Lifetime high" and "lifetime low" are the highest and lowest prices at which contracts for that delivery month have ever traded, and show that orange juice for future delivery in all four contract months is about 30% cheaper now than it was a few months ago. "Open interest" gives the number of contracts that are still active. Although many other contracts have been sold, in most cases the buyers have liquidated them by buying or selling offsetting contracts. According to these numbers, most trading in orange juice futures occurs within a few months of delivery. The line at the bottom lists the total number of orange juice contracts traded this day and the previous day, the total open interest in all delivery months (including those not listed in this table), and the change in the number of open contracts from the previous day.

Financial futures markets

Financial futures, a comparatively recent innovation, have become extremely popular instruments to hedge the risks of interest-rate changes, exchange-rate movements and share-price changes. The first financial futures, traded on the Chicago Mercantile Exchange in 1972, allowed businesses to control the risks of exchange-rate changes. Hundreds of contracts now trade on exchanges around the world. Global turnover stalled in 1999, but resumed extremely rapid growth in 2001; worldwide turnover increased 162% from 2000 through 2004. Growth has been especially rapid in Europe, where financial futures were slower to develop than in the United States (see Table 8.8). Trading volume in financial futures now dwarfs volume in com-

Table 8.8 **Turnover of exchange-traded financial futures ($ trillion)**

	1996	1998	2000	2002	2004
All markets	269	319	318	502	832
North America	120	152	151	278	441
Europe	86	116	112	179	337
Asia, Australia, New Zealand	60	48	52	41	48
Other markets	3	3	3	3	6

Source: Bank for International Settlements

modity futures. All the world's most heavily traded futures contracts involve financial instruments.

Interest-rate futures

The most important category of financial futures allows financial institutions and bond investors to hedge the risk that changes in interest rates will affect the value of their assets. Trading in interest-rate futures accounts for over 90% of all financial futures trading.

The first interest-rate contract, introduced on the Chicago Board of Trade in 1975, allowed financial institutions to hedge the risk that changes in interest rates would alter the value of their portfolios of residential mortgages. The first Treasury-bill contracts traded in 1976. The success of these contracts led to the creation of financial futures exchanges in Europe during the 1980s. The 3-month Eurodollar contract at the Chicago Mercantile Exchange, tied to interest rates on dollar deposits outside the United States, and the Bund contract on Eurex, based on German government bond yields, now have more than twice the trading volume of any other futures contracts. But the market is diverse, with exchanges in Australia, Canada, Malaysia, Spain and dozens of other countries trading contracts on local-currency interest rates. Figure 8.1 on the next page traces the growth of the market.

Initially, interest-rate futures were used mainly to hedge changes in long-term interest rates. More recently, contracts on short-term rates have become popular and now account for more than half of all trading in interest-rate futures. Although hedgers use interest-rate futures to limit their losses if rates change, many speculators have found interest-rate futures an efficient way to bet on anticipated interest-rate changes without owning bonds.

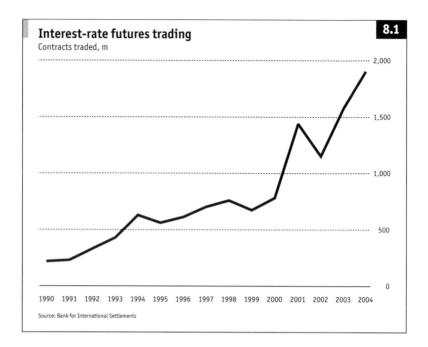

Interest-rate futures trading   **8.1**
Contracts traded, m

Source: Bank for International Settlements

To understand how interest-rate futures are used, consider the Treasury bond contract on the Chicago Board of Trade. This contract is based on a bond with a face value of $100,000 and a nominal interest rate, or coupon, of 8%, and the quoted price is per $1,000. In early 1999 such bond was trading at a price of about 125, so purchasing a single bond would have cost $125,000 (125 × $100,000). Assume that an investor expected long-term interest rates in September 1999 to be lower than in January of that year. It could have purchased a bond for $125,000 and held it to September, or it could have acquired one bond futures contract for September delivery, priced at 125.50, by making a down-payment of $2,700. Now suppose that a fall in interest rates had caused the price of the bond to rise 1%. The bond would be worth $126,250, and the September bond future, on its expiration, would be priced at 126.25. The owner of the bond would have:

> $1,250 in capital appreciation (1% of the price paid)
> + $5,333 in interest (representing payments of $8,000 per year over an eight-month period)
> = $6,583 total profit
> 5.27% return on the initial investment

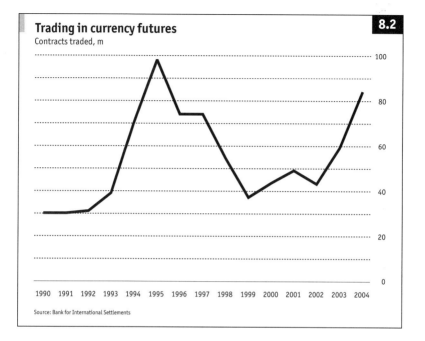

Trading in currency futures
Contracts traded, m

8.2

Source: Bank for International Settlements

The owner of the futures contract would have:

$750 in capital appreciation [(126.25 − 125.50) × 1,000]
− $144 forgone interest on the $2,700 down payment at 8% for eight months
= $606 total profit
22.4% return on the initial investment

Hence in a rising market the investor in interest-rate futures is able to earn a far better return than an investor in the underlying interest-rate-sensitive securities. Conversely, however, the futures investor in this example would have a much greater loss than the bond investor if interest rates were to fall.

Currency futures

Although exchange-rate contracts are the oldest financial futures, their popularity has remained modest (see Figure 8.2). There are two reasons for this. First, much currency hedging is now done with the use of derivatives contracts that are not traded on exchanges. These contracts are discussed in Chapter 9. Second, the stabilisation of exchange rates among 12

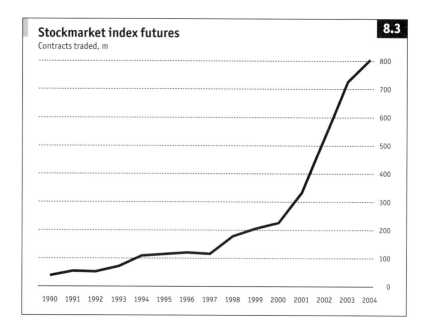

Stockmarket index futures `8.3`
Contracts traded, m

European countries in advance of the creation of a single currency, followed by the launch of the euro on January 1st 1999, eliminated the demand for contracts on the exchange rates among countries in the euro zone.

Much currency futures trading now occurs on markets in emerging economies. The Budapest Commodity Exchange in Hungary trades futures contracts on exchange rates between the Hungarian forint and the dollar, the pound sterling, the yen, the euro and the Czech koruna. The South African Futures Exchange offers contracts on the rand/dollar exchange rate. The contract on *real*/dollar exchange rates traded on the Bolsa de Mercadorias & Futuros in São Paulo is by far the most widely traded currency futures contract.

Stock-index futures
Contracts on the future level of a particular share index have proven enormously popular among portfolio managers. Their growth has gone hand-in-hand with the growth of tracker or index equity funds (discussed in Chapter 6) as they offer a nearly exact hedge for a share portfolio that is constructed to mimic the index. Figure 8.3 shows the growth of the index futures market.

The most popular stock-index futures are those on the Standard & Poor's 500 index in the United States, the Dow Jones/Euro Stoxx 50 index and the NASDAQ index. Other important contracts are based on the DAX-30 in Germany, the CAC-40 in France, the Financial Times Stock Exchange Index in London, the Nikkei 225 index in Japan, the Ibovespa in Brazil, the KOSPI in South Korea and the Australian All-Ordinaries Index. A futures contract on the most famous stockmarket indicator of all, the Dow Jones Industrial Average of 30 shares on the New York Stock Exchange, began trading only in 1997 because the index's owner previously opposed its use in futures trading. Stock-index futures are also traded on many smaller exchanges. The Australian Stock Exchange, for example, offers contracts on the ASX 50 and ASX 200 share indexes, and the Oslo Stock Exchange trades futures on its OBX share-price index.

Share-price futures
Many stock exchanges trade futures contracts on the prices of individual shares. A contract based on the future share price of China Telecom, for example, trades on the Hong Kong Futures Exchange. Although many similar contracts exist, few are notably successful as in most cases trading in the underlying equity is not lively enough to sustain interest in a futures contract. Futures on individual shares were permitted in the United States only in 2000; their introduction was delayed for many years because of opposition from stock exchanges, which did not welcome a competing product, as well as fears that speculators could trade share-price futures to circumvent limits on borrowing to buy shares.

Other financial futures
Exchanges have experimented with many different types of contracts to increase demand for futures trading. A contract on corn yields, offered on the Chicago Board of Trade, is based on the US Department of Agriculture's estimates of yields per acre (0.4ha) and allowed farmers and crop insurance companies to hedge the risk of a poor harvest; however, the contract was abandoned because of a lack of interest. Other insurance-related futures contracts are under discussion in the United States and Europe. A futures contract based on the US consumer-price index was abandoned for want of interest in 1988, but more recently futures contracts on inflation-indexed US Treasury bonds have filled a similar role. There are also continuing efforts to create contracts based on indexes of property prices.

Table 8.9 **DAX (Eurex)**

Month	Open	High	Low	Settle	Prev close	Change
03/06	5,110.00	5,139.00	5,050.00	5,053.50	5,025.00	+28.50
06/06	5,132.00	5,166.00	5,108.50	5,120.00	5,041.50	+78.50
09/06	5,172.50	5,172.50	5,172.50	5,172.50	5,060.50	+112.00

Reading financial futures price tables

Price tables for financial futures can be harder to understand than those for commodity futures, because the basis for determining prices is not always clear. Consider, for example, Table 8.9.

This table reports futures trading on the Deutsche Aktienindex (DAX), an index of German shares, which is traded on the Eurex exchange. On this trading day investors were more optimistic about the future course of German share prices. To understand the impact upon futures prices, however, it is necessary to consult the contract specifications published by the exchange, which do not accompany the published table. These reveal that the contract is valued at €25 per DAX index point. At this day's closing price, one March DAX contract would cost (5,053.50 × €25), or €126,337.5.

The DAX contract obviously cannot be delivered in a physical sense, but must be settled in cash. Suppose that a March DAX contract were to trade at the closing price, and that both the buyer and the seller were to hold the contract until the delivery date – in this case, according to the contract specifications, the third Friday of March. Suppose further that the DAX index on that date were to close at 5,100.00. The seller of the futures contract, who is short the DAX, would have a loss of [(5,100.00 – 5,053.50) x 25], or €1,162.5, and the buyer of the contract would have a gain of equal amount.

Clearance and settlement

Initiating a futures transaction requires two parties, a buyer and a seller. No trade is possible unless both parties agree to the terms. Once the bargain has been struck, however, the parties have no further responsibilities to one another. The exchange itself acts in place of the buyer for every seller and in place of the seller for all buyers. This facilitates trading in two important ways. First, either party to the original transaction is free to terminate its obligations by taking an offsetting position, without the consent of the other party. Second, no investor need worry about the reliability or solvency of any other investor. The exchange guarantees that those whose contracts gain in value receive their money and collect the sums owed by owners of money-losing positions. The organisation that accomplishes this is the exchange's clearing house.

The first step in the clearing house's work is clearing, the process of determining precisely what trades have occurred. This is often difficult on an exchange with floor trading, but it is critical to the smooth functioning of the exchange. As soon as the trade has been completed, the floor broker is supposed to record the details of each transaction, including the commodity, quantity, delivery month, price and the broker on the other side of the transaction. This information is written on cards or slips of paper immediately after each trade, and is then time-stamped by an exchange employee. The time stamp, along with videotapes of trading activity, is critical to reconstructing events in case the parties disagree about the terms of the trade, or if an investor subsequently complains about improprieties.

Exchange employees key the information from the floor broker into a computer, which transmits it to the two futures commission merchants whose floor brokers made the trade. The futures commission merchants must then reconcile the data with the reports of the clerks who took and confirmed the customers' orders. Frequently there are "out trades", about which the two futures commission merchants have conflicting information: in the hectic trading pit, a broker may have mistakenly sold a contract when he thought he was buying a contract, or may have mistakenly written down the wrong number of contracts. Although the exchanges have greatly improved their clearing systems, it is not unusual for 3–4% of a given day's trades to be out trades, which the exchange must investigate and reconcile.

The clearing process is far easier on electronic exchanges, because all the relevant information is available on the exchange's trading system at the time the trade occurs. There is thus no opportunity for incorrect information or data-entry errors to enter the system except when brokers enter mistaken bids through typing errors. Trades can often be cleared shortly after they are agreed.

Once the clearing process has been completed, the clearing house and the banking system can proceed with settlement, the process of matching payments with futures-market positions. Settlement is a far more complex process on futures exchanges than on stockmarkets, because of the exchange's role in ensuring that market participants live up to their commitments.

A margin of security

Before buying or selling a futures contract, an investor is required to deposit a down-payment, known as a performance bond or initial margin, with the futures commission merchant. If the futures commission merchant is a clearing member of the exchange it must, in turn, place variation margin or settlement variation on deposit with the clearing house. If it is not a clearing member, the futures commission merchant must maintain an account with a clearing member, which takes financial responsibility for its trades.

The minimum initial margin required of an investor is set by the exchange, although the futures commission merchant can require a larger amount. The exchange also sets a lesser maintenance margin or variation margin, the minimum the investor is required to have on deposit at all times. The amounts depend on the contract and on whether the investor is a hedger or a speculator. In 2005, for example, the initial margin required of a speculator in the Chicago Mercantile Exchange frozen pork bellies contract was $1,620 per contract and the maintenance margin was $1,200, at a time when the value of one contract was about $28,000. Margin requirements are often lower if an investor has bought and sold different months of the same contract, so that some positions are likely to increase in value if others decline. The idea is that the investor should always have sufficient margin on deposit to cover potential losses.

Marking to market

As part of the settlement process following each day's trading at most exchanges, the futures commission merchant recalculates the margin required of each investor. Each investor's contracts are marked to market, or revalued based on the latest settlement price. If an investor's holdings have lost value, money from the investor's account is transferred into the accounts of investors whose holdings have gained in value. Each clearing member's entire customer portfolio is marked to market in the same way. If the total value of all its customers' contracts declines, the clearing member must pay additional variation margin to the clearing house. Conversely, money is transferred from the clearing house into the accounts of clearing members, futures commission merchants and individual customers whose contracts have gained in value.

Margin calls

In this way, every participant in trading at the exchange is forced to recognise all gains or losses after each day's trading. The clearing house itself, at least in theory, is protected from loss because each clearing member is responsible for keeping its own customers' accounts in balance. The initial margin keeps an individual investor from running up large unrecognised losses and then defaulting on payment. If the amount in a customer's account falls below the maintenance margin, the futures commission merchant issues a margin call, demanding that the investor immediately deposit enough funds to meet the initial margin. The futures commission merchant will liquidate the investor's contracts if the funds are not forthcoming. Conversely, if the amount in the account rises above the initial margin, the investor may withdraw the excess, use it as margin for other futures trades, or simply leave it on deposit.

Even then ...

This system, unfortunately, is not foolproof. Clearing members are often subsidiaries of diversified financial firms, and it is possible that the financial problems of its parent could cause a clearing member to collapse. The clearing member is supposed to keep investors' funds strictly segregated from its own trading accounts so there will be no loss to investors should the firm collapse, but firms in financial distress may be tempted to violate this rule. Despite these shortcomings, however, exchange clearing houses have generally worked well. The biggest scandal in exchange-traded futures was the $2.6 billion loss suffered by Sumitomo, a Japanese trading company, in 1996. This sum was lost as a result of improper trading on the London Metal Exchange, one of the few exchanges that did not require investors to meet variation margins with cash on a daily basis. It appears that exchange rules and the clearing-house structure protected futures-market investors from loss in the October 2005 bankruptcy of Refco, which owned one of the largest US futures brokerages.

Cross-margining

Some exchanges have recently begun to allow cross-margining, in which investors are effectively allowed to use a single account to trade on more than one exchange. Gains in contracts on one exchange may then be used to offset losses on another exchange in determining the amount of margin required, generally reducing the amount of money the investor needs to keep on deposit. The ability to offer cross-margining is one of the main factors encouraging co-operative agreements among exchanges.

Delivery

As a contract approaches its delivery date, the issue of physical delivery must be resolved. For the buyer of a futures contract, physical delivery means taking possession of the underlying assets; for the seller, it means providing those assets. The specifications of some contracts, particularly financial futures, do not permit physical delivery, and even when it is possible investors rarely desire it. Only 1–2% of all futures contracts lead to physical delivery. Most futures investors choose cash settlement, either before or on expiry, and receive the current market value of the underlying assets rather than the assets themselves.

If the seller of an expiring contract wishes to deliver the commodity, it must provide the exchange with notice of intention to deliver several days before the contract expires. The commodity must be transported to and unloaded at a delivery point acceptable under the contract specifications, at the seller's expense. Exchanges maintain approved warehouses for this purpose.

If the buyer of a futures contract wishes to take physical delivery, it must notify the exchange at the time of contract expiry. Even in the rare event that both the buyer and the seller of a contract want physical delivery, the buyer will not receive the particular goods delivered by the seller. Instead, the exchange will determine the order in which buyers may take possession of commodities that have been delivered to it.

Trading strategies

Investors in the futures markets often pursue complex strategies involving the trading of different futures contracts simultaneously. The following are among the best-known strategies for futures trading:

- **Basis trading.** Also known as exchange of futures for physicals, this involves the simultaneous purchase of the asset underlying a futures contract and the sale of an offsetting contract in the futures market, or vice versa. An investor who has bought the physicals and sold the futures is said to be long the basis; one who has bought futures and sold physicals is short the basis. The goal of the strategy is to profit from changes in the relationship between the spot price of the physicals and the price of the futures contracts.

- **Dynamic hedging.** This involves constant changes in a futures position in response to changes in the price of the underlying asset and the rate at which the price of the underlying asset is changing.
- **Index arbitrage.** When someone seeks to capitalise on moment-to-moment changes in the price relationship between a share index and the futures contract on that index, by simultaneously buying the shares in the index and selling the futures, or vice versa.
- **Spreads.** A spread is a position constructed in the expectation that the relationship between two prices will change. There are many varieties. An intra-commodity spread involves contracts in two different commodities with approximately the same delivery date and could be used to speculate, for example, that cattle prices will rise more quickly than hog prices over the next three months. An international spread might bet that the difference between petroleum futures prices in New York and in London will widen or narrow. A quality differential spread concerns the price difference between two qualities of the same commodity, such as the northern spring wheat traded in Chicago and the hard red spring wheat traded in Minneapolis.
- **Straddles.** A straddle is a type of spread that involves purchasing a contract for one delivery month while selling a contract for another delivery month of the same commodity, thereby betting on a change in the relationship between short-term and longer-term prices. A bear spread is a straddle arranged with the intention of profiting from an expected price decline but limiting the potential loss if the expectation proves wrong. This is accomplished by selling a nearby delivery month and buying a more distant month. A bull spread is the reverse operation, designed to profit from a rise in prices while limiting the potential loss by buying contracts for a nearby delivery month and selling a more distant month.
- **Strips.** A strip, also called a calendar strip, is the simultaneous purchase or sale of futures positions in consecutive months.

Measuring performance

The prices of particular physical commodities may vary greatly over time. In general, however, the prices of many physical commodities rise or fall in response to general economic conditions. When world economic growth is strong, there is greater demand for metals, timber, petroleum and other products used in construction or manufacturing.

The prices of various petroleum futures contracts rose sharply in 2005, in response to higher world oil prices, while the prices of cocoa, sugar and grain contracts declined.

Several indexes attempt to track the movement of commodities prices overall. The best known are those published by *The Economist*, the Commodities Research Bureau, the *Journal of Commerce* and Goldman Sachs, an investment bank. Investors who wish to speculate on or hedge against movements in the average price of commodities can trade futures contracts on the Goldman Sachs Commodity Index (GSCI) at the Chicago Mercantile Exchange.

The performance of futures contracts over time cannot be measured in any aggregate way. In an individual case, one investor's profit from having purchased a contract will be offset by another investor's loss from having sold the contract. Besides, investors who use futures contracts to hedge are concerned not about the performance of the contract itself, but about the performance of their overall investment, including the asset hedged. If it reduced the investor's risk, a futures contract that lost money is frequently deemed to have been a worthwhile investment.

9 Options and derivatives markets

THE SIMPLE PRINCIPLE of market economics, that prices serve to bring supply and demand into balance, is familiar to everyone. But although markets for most things work well most of the time, on some occasions they work quite badly. Petroleum prices may soar, hurting airlines that have already sold tickets and now must pay much more than expected to operate their jets. The Australian dollar may suddenly drop against the yen, leaving an importer in Melbourne stuck with a shipload of Japanese electronic equipment that will be prohibitively expensive to sell. A German bank may unexpectedly report that a big borrower has defaulted, and its falling share price could cause a painful loss for an investment fund that had favoured its shares. The name for such price movements is volatility.

To a lay person volatility seems random and unpredictable. In truth, individual price movements usually are random and unpredictable. Yet over time average volatility can be measured, the probability of price movements can be estimated, and investors can determine how much they are willing to pay to reduce the amount of volatility they face. The derivatives market is where this occurs.

The term derivatives refers to a large number of financial instruments, the value of which is based on, or derived from, the prices of securities, commodities, money or other external variables. They come in hundreds of varieties. For all their diversity, however, they fall into two basic categories:

- **Forwards** are contracts that set a price for something to be delivered in the future.
- **Options** are contracts that allow, but do not require, one or both parties to obtain certain benefits under certain conditions. The calculation of an option contract's value must take into account the possibility that this option will be exercised.

All derivatives contracts are either forwards or options, or some combination of the two.

Derivatives have come to public attention only in the past few years, largely because of a series of spectacular losses from derivatives trading. Under various labels, however, derivatives contracts have been employed for thousands of years. The earliest known use was by a Greek philosopher, Thales, who reached individual agreements with the owners of olive presses whereby, in return for a payment, he obtained the right to first use of each owner's press after harvest. These options on all his region's pressing capacity, Aristotle reports, gave Thales control over the olive crop. Derivatives have been traded privately ever since, and have been bought and sold on exchanges since at least the 1600s.

The next section deals with exchange-traded options contracts. Over-the-counter derivatives, whose usage now dwarfs that of exchange-traded derivatives, are discussed later.

Exchange-traded options

Until the 1970s there were no option markets. Although some speculators arranged option trades privately, regulators regarded options trading as a dubious and even dangerous activity, intended mainly to defraud innocent investors. This characterisation was not far from the mark, as options trading was completely unregulated. Option trading came of age only in 1973, when officials in the United States approved a plan by the Chicago Board of Trade, a futures exchange, to launch an options exchange. The Chicago Board Options Exchange (CBOE) began by offering options on the shares of 16 companies.

Since then, as investors have increasingly turned to financial markets to help manage risk, option trading has become hugely popular. The face value of contracts traded on option exchanges worldwide rose from $52 trillion in 1996 to $71 trillion in 1998, fell back to $62 trillion in 1999, and then soared to $312 trillion in 2004.

Underlying every option

The world's many option exchanges compete to offer contracts that will be attractive to investors. Every option is based on the price of some instrument that is not traded in the option market. This instrument is known as the underlying. Each contract has a precisely defined underlying, a standard size and a variety of expiration dates, typically monthly or quarterly.

Puts, calls – the long and the short of it

Although the exchange sets the ground rules for each contract, an option is created only when two parties, a buyer and a writer, strike a deal. The buyer pays the writer a premium, determined by market forces, in return for the rights inherent in the option. These rights take one of two basic forms. A put option entitles the buyer to sell the underlying at an agreed price, known as the strike price, for a specific period of time. A call option gives the buyer the right to purchase the underlying at the strike price. In other words, the buyer of a put, who is said to be long the put, expects the price of the underlying to fall by a given amount, and the writer, who is short the put, thinks that the price of the underlying will fall less or not at all. Conversely, the buyer of a call anticipates that the price of the underlying will rise above the strike price and the writer thinks it will not.

Winners and losers

If the price of the underlying changes as the buyer expects – that is, if the price falls below the strike price (in the case of a put) or rises above the strike price (in the case of a call) – the option is said to be in the money. Otherwise, the option is out of the money. If oil is trading at $45 per barrel, for example, a call option at 46 is out of the money and not worth exercising, as it is less costly to purchase the oil in the open market than to purchase it at the strike price; if the oil price rises to $47 per barrel, however, the option will be in the money and will almost certainly be exercised. Note, however, that an in-the-money option is not necessarily profitable for the buyer or unprofitable for the writer. The buyer has paid a premium to the writer, and unless the difference between the strike price and the market price of the underlying exceeds the premium, it is the writer, not the buyer, who comes out ahead.

Types of options

The underlying may be almost anything that is actively traded in a market where the current price is continuously available and indisputable. For this reason, options markets often operate on the same schedule as the markets where the underlying instruments are traded, and close when the underlying stops trading. The most widely traded types of options are as follows.

Equity options

An equity option entitles the owner to buy or sell a certain number of common shares (100 is standard in most countries) in a particular firm. An equity option is not a security of the firm on whose shares the options are being traded; the firm itself does not issue the options and receives no money for them, and the owner of the options does not receive dividends or vote on company business. If an option is eventually exercised, the owner will end up acquiring or selling the underlying shares. Equity options offer a far more economical way to speculate on share prices than purchasing the underlying shares. They may also be used to hedge positions, as when an investor owns shares and purchases a put option so as to be assured of a price at which the shares may be sold.

Index options

An index option is based on an index of prices in some market other than options. Share-price indexes are most popular, but any index will suffice as long as its value is continuously determined in a market. Thus options are traded on the Goldman Sachs Commodity Index (Chicago Mercantile Exchange), a US municipal bond index (Chicago Board of Trade), the Reuters/Commodity Research Board Index (New York Board of Trade) and the South Korean stockmarket index (Korea Futures Exchange). Each option is based on the index times a multiple. The Chicago Mercantile Exchange's option on the Standard & Poor's 500 Stock Index, for example, is valued at $250 times the index. This means that if the s&p is at 1,300, one contract has a nominal value of $250 × 1,300 = $325,000. The nominal value, although large, has little practical importance; a market participant stands to lose or gain only the gap between the strike price and the market price of the underlying. If an investor purchases an s&p 1,300 call and the index reaches 1,305, the owner's gain and the writer's loss from the price change will be 5 points × $250/point, or $1,250. Unlike options on individual equities, an index option cannot be settled by delivery, as the index cannot be purchased. The owner of the profitable call would therefore receive a cash payment rather than stock, and the writer would make a cash payment rather than handing over shares.

Worldwide turnover in stockmarket index options reached $51 trillion in 2004, compared with less than $19 trillion in 2000.

Interest-rate options

These come in two varieties:

- **Bond options** are based on the price of a government bond, which moves inversely to interest rates. Their nominal value is set equal to the current market value of bonds with a specified par value; the Bund option traded on Eurex, a European exchange, is based upon a German government bond with a face value of €100,000.

◪ **Yield options** are based on an interest rate itself, but because interest rates are typically low the nominal value of a yield option is often set by deducting the interest rate from 100. Thus the nominal value of one option on Euro LIBOR, a short-term inter-bank interest rate, is equal to €1m × (100 − the rate), and the nominal value declines as the interest rate rises.

Interest-rate options offer a less costly way to speculate on interest-rate movements than the purchase of bonds. An investor who owns bonds can use interest-rate options to protect against a loss in value, and one who has chosen not to buy bonds can use options to avoid forgoing profits should bond prices rise. Interest-rate options are usually settled in cash. Worldwide turnover in interest-rate options was $260 trillion in 2004, compared with $47.4 trillion in 2000.

Commodity options

Options are traded on many commodities, from greasy wool (Sydney Futures Exchange) to gas oil (International Petroleum Exchange). If the underlying commodity is continuously traded, such as gold, the option may be based directly on the commodity's price. Most commodities, however, do not trade continuously in markets where there is a single posted price. It is therefore necessary to base most commodity option contracts on futures-market prices, as these are posted and trade continuously. For example, as actual bags of Brazilian coffee may change hands irregularly and in private, the arabica coffee option on the Bolsa de Mercadorias & Futuros in Brazil is based on the market price of arabica futures rather than the price of actual coffee. Commodity option contracts can usually be settled either in cash or with an exchange of the underlying commodity. (For more detail on commodity futures, see Chapter 8.) An estimated 5.9 million commodity option contracts were outstanding worldwide at the end of 2004.

Currency options

Currency options are based on the exchange rate between two currencies. Their nominal value is the amount of one currency required to purchase a given amount of the other; thus the nominal value of one Canadian dollar option on the Philadelphia Stock Exchange is the

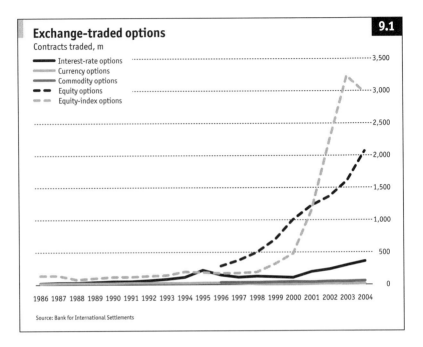

Exchange-traded options `9.1`

Contracts traded, m

— Interest-rate options
— Currency options
— Commodity options
■ ■ Equity options
▬ ▬ Equity-index options

3,500
3,000
2,500
2,000
1,500
1,000
500
0

1986 1987 1988 1989 1990 1991 1992 1993 1994 1995 1996 1997 1998 1999 2000 2001 2002 2003 2004

Source: Bank for International Settlements

amount of US dollars required to purchase C$50,000. The price of an option, however, may be expressed differently. Philadelphia's Canadian dollar options are priced in US cents per Canadian dollar. To sort through this confusion, assume that an investor owned a 66 Canadian dollar call and the Canadian dollar strengthened to 67. The owner could exercise the call and earn:

$$[(US\$0.67 - US\$0.66) \div C\$1] \times C\$50,000 = US\$500$$

As well as options on currencies, some exchanges trade option contracts based on exchange-rate futures. In general, however, interest in exchange-traded currency options has been weak as market participants have favoured over-the-counter derivatives instead. Although the value of currency options trading rose sharply in 2004, currencies make up only a tiny part of the worldwide options business.

Figure 9.1 shows the worldwide trading volume in the main types of options.

New types of options

Growing competition from the over-the-counter market has made option exchanges introduce two important types of new products:

- **LEAPS**, an acronym for long-term equity participation securities, are simply a form of long-term option. Whereas regular options usually expire within a 12-month period, LEAPS may have expiration dates up to three years in the future.
- **Flex options** are a way for traders to customise the contracts they trade to meet the needs of big institutional users. Usually, this involves setting an expiration date other than the ones that are standard for the option, or setting a strike price between two prices offered on the exchange, or both.

Gains and losses

On balance, an option contract produces no net gain or loss. Rather, one party's gain is necessarily equal to the other party's loss. The premium represents the maximum loss for the buyer and the maximum gain for the writer. A put owner's maximum gain – and writer's maximum loss – occurs when the underlying loses all value. There is theoretically no limit to the potential profit of a call owner or the loss of a call writer, as the price of the underlying can increase without limit. To limit their losses, some investors prefer to write calls only when they already own the underlying security – so-called covered calls – rather than riskier uncovered or "naked" calls.

To see how this works, consider options in Pfizer, a drugs manufacturer whose shares are listed on the New York Stock Exchange. One day in 1999, when Pfizer shares traded at $140, the September 1999 Pfizer 135 put option traded on the American Stock Exchange at $9.50. That is, in return for a premium of $950 ($9.50 per share times 100 shares) the buyer obtained the right to sell 100 shares of Pfizer at $135 on or before the third Friday in September, the expiration date, and the writer committed itself to purchase shares at that price. Had Pfizer shares failed to fall below $135 over the period, the put option would have expired worthless, leaving the writer with a $950 profit. Had the shares fallen to $130, the buyer of the put option could have earned $500 by purchasing 100 Pfizer shares on the stockmarket and selling, or putting, them for $135. Counting the initial $950 premium, however, the buyer would have suffered a net a loss of $450. The breakeven point, at which neither the buyer nor the writer would have made a profit, was $135 − $9.50 = $125.50.

At any share price below $125.50, the put would have returned a profit to the buyer of the option. The buyer's maximum profit would have occurred had Pfizer shares lost all value. The shares would then have been obtained for $0 and put at $135, thus earning a profit of

$$[100 (\$135) - 100 (\$0)] - 100 (\$9.50) = \$12,550$$

and the writer would have lost the identical amount.

Styles

Options are traded in three basic styles:

- **American-style options** can be exercised at any time before their expiration date. The owner of an American-style call, for example, can exercise the option whenever the price of the underlying shares exceeds the strike price.
- **European-style options**, in contrast, can be exercised only at or near the expiration date. If the price of a share were to rise briefly above the strike price but then to fall back before the expiration date, the owner of an American-style call could exercise it at a profit, but the owner of a European-style call could not. The exchange determines whether its option contracts will be American or European style, although some exchanges trade both simultaneously.
- **Capped options** have a predetermined cap price, which is above the strike price for a call and below the strike price for a put. The option is automatically exercised when the underlying closes at or above (for a call) or at or below (for a put) the cap price.

Expiration dates

The date on which an option contract expires is set by the exchange. Most contracts have four expiration dates a year, the number being limited to create as much trading volume as possible in each contract. The exchange usually staggers the expiration dates of various options to keep overall trading volume fairly constant through the year. Some contracts with heavy trading have monthly expiration dates.

Triple-witching days

In the case of equity-index options, contract expiration dates are often marked by heavy trading of options and shares. Several times a year equity options, equity-index options and equity-index futures expire at the same time. These Fridays have become known as triple-witching days. During the 1980s triple-witching days were marked by extremely heavy trading and sharp price movements near the close of stockmarket trading, but this phenomenon has become far less severe in recent years.

Motivations for options trading

Investors choose to trade options for one of five main reasons:

- **Risk management.** Options can allow the user to reduce or eliminate certain kinds of risks while retaining others. An engineering company signing a contract to supply automotive components at a fixed price might purchase calls on aluminium on the London Metal Exchange, thus locking in the price of an important raw material without using its capital to amass a stockpile of aluminium.

- **Hedging.** An option contract can be used to reduce or eliminate the risk that an asset will lose value. For example, an institutional investor with a large holding of German government bonds, known as Bunds, might buy Bund puts on the Eurex exchange. The puts would allow the investor to continue to own the bonds, profiting from interest payments and possible price appreciation, while protecting against a severe price drop.

- **Leveraged speculation.** Many investors favour options because a given amount of money can be employed to make a greater bet on the price of the underlying. Consider, for example, an investor that expects British share prices to rise. Purchasing each of the 100 shares in the Financial Times Stock Exchange Index (the FTSE 100) would require a large amount of cash. Investors in options, however, are required to pay only the premium, not the value of the underlying. Thus, for the same amount of money needed to buy a few shares of each firm in the FTSE, the investor could acquire enough FTSE options to earn a much larger profit if the index rises. (Of course, the owner of the options, unlike a shareholder, would receive no dividends, and would profit only if the stock index reached the specified level before the expiry of the options.)

- **Arbitrage.** Arbitrageurs seek to profit from discrepancies in prices in different markets. Options arbitrageurs watch for changes in an option's premium or in the price of its underlying, and buy

Table 9.1 **The leading option exchanges, contracts traded (m)**

Exchange	Abbreviation	Country	1998	2001	2004
Korea Futures Exchange	KFX	South Korea	32	855	2,529
Euronext[a]	Euronext	France/UK/Netherlands	134	454	477
Eurex	Eurex	Germany/Switzerland	103	277	381
Chicago Board Options Exchange	CBOE	US	196	307	361
International Securities Exchange[b]	ISE	US	...	65	361
São Paulo Stock Exchange	BOVESPA	Brazil	40	70	235
American Stock Exchange	AMEX	US	98	205	203
Chicago Mercantile Exchange	CME	US	43	96	138
Philadelphia Stock Exchange	PHLX	US	38	101	133
Pacific Stock Exchange	PAC	US	59	57	103

a Euronext owns the former MONEP, MATIF and LIFFE exchanges, to which the 1998 and 2001 amounts refer.
b Started trading in 2000.
Source: Exchange reports

when one seems out of line with the other. Price discrepancies are usually extremely short-lived, so an arbitrageur may open a position by purchasing an option and then close the position by selling the option within a matter of minutes.

◪ **Income.** Many large investors write options that are covered by holdings in their portfolios to obtain additional income. For example, an investor owning thousands of shares in Deutsche Bank, valued at €47 per share, might write Deutsche Bank 55 calls. If the bank's shares do not reach the strike price, the investor receives a premium; if they do reach the strike price, the investor must sell the shares on which it has written options but will still enjoy €8 per share of price appreciation plus the premium. Thus writing covered options is a low-risk, income-oriented strategy, quite unlike writing uncovered options, which can be risky.

Option exchanges

Dozens of exchanges around the world trade option contracts. In some cases, stock exchanges also trade option contracts; in some cases, futures contracts and option contracts are traded on the same exchange; in other cases, an exchange may specialise almost exclusively in options. In almost every country there are option contracts based on the local stockmarket index and on the exchange rate of the local currency. Table 9.1 lists the exchanges with the largest amount of option trading. The contract on the South Korean stock index, traded on the Korea Futures Exchange, is by far the most widely traded option contract in the world.

Competition and the cost of technology have forced many option exchanges to merge, to join forces with equity or futures exchanges or to form alliances. The Euronext exchange has brought options trading in Belgium, France, the Netherlands, Portugal and the UK under a single roof. Various American option exchanges have been involved in merger talks, as have option exchanges in Australia, Malaysia and other centres. Canadian financial exchanges agreed in 1999 to centralise option trading in Montreal, and the Swiss and German exchanges merged. The big financial firms, which are present on all the main exchanges, strongly favour such consolidation to reduce their costs.

In the past, a particular option was typically traded on a single exchange. Exchanges are increasingly competing head-to-head. Options on euro interest rates, only slightly different from one another, trade in London, Frankfurt, Paris, Madrid and elsewhere, and several European exchanges have been developing commodity option contracts to compete with those traded on American exchanges. In the United States, regulators have forced the option exchanges to abandon the practice of trading each equity option on only one exchange, and in August 1999 US exchanges began competing directly to offer the lowest-cost trading in equity options. This led to the creation of a new, all-electronic exchange, the International Securities Exchange, which began trading in the United States in 2000. The option contract on NASDAQ 100 stock index tracking shares, known as the QQQ option, initiated on the American Stock Exchange in 1999, now trades on at least five other exchanges and is among the most heavily traded contracts.

How options are traded

Options can be traded either by open outcry or electronically. Open-outcry trading occurs on an exchange floor, where traders gather in a pit or ring. A ring may be devoted to a single contract or to several different ones, depending upon the volume. In either case, puts and calls for all of the available expiration months and all available strike prices are traded simultaneously, and traders quote the premium they would charge for a particular expiration month and strike price. On an electronic trading system, bids and offers are submitted over computer links, and the computer system matches up buyers and writers.

Table 9.2 **Understanding an option price table**

Option/Strike		Exp.	Call Vol.	Call Last	Put Vol.	Put Last
Intel	25.00	Jul	−136	5.60	1,946	1.75
28.55	25.00	Oct	−11	6.50	1,480	2.35
28.55	27.50	Mar	−592	1.95	2,995	0.85
28.55	27.50	Apr	170	3.00	3,569	1.75
28.55	30.00	Mar	7,003	0.60	7,245	2.10
28.55	30.00	Apr	4,842	1.55	26,479	2.90
28.55	30.00	Jul	3,975	2.80	2,625	3.90
28.55	32.50	Mar	3,800	0.20	30,159	4.00
28.55	32.50	Apr	5,345	0.75	28,140	4.50
28.55	35.00	Mar	3,410	0.05	267	6.30
28.55	35.00	Apr	4,100	0.30	165	6.40

Obtaining price information

Price information about option contracts is readily available from electronic information systems and on websites operated by the exchanges. Option prices can change quickly, however, and investors who are not privy to the most recent information about bids and offers are at a distinct disadvantage.

Newspaper price tables provide summaries of the previous day's trading in the most active options.

Table 9.2, in the style used by *The Wall Street Journal*, reports on trading in options on the shares of Intel Corporation. The previous day's closing share price, in the left-hand column, was $28.55. The second column gives the various strike prices available on that option. The exchange normally creates new strike prices at regular intervals, so if Intel shares were to fall significantly there would be new prices added at 22.50 and 20. As indicated by the column headed "Exp.", almost all of the trading was for options expiring in March or April. Although market participants are permitted to trade options expiring up to nine months ahead, trading for distant months is typically light or non-existent.

Just before the close of trading on this date, a March Intel 30 call could have been purchased for a premium of $0.60. Prices and premiums are given per share; the buyer of such a call would have paid $60.00 for the right to buy 100 shares of Intel at $30 each. This was a popular option: 7,003 March 30 calls were purchased on this day. As is normally the case, options at strike prices more distant from the current market price, at $32.50 and $35.00, were far cheaper than options close to the money. The number of calls traded above the current price was greater than the number of puts traded below the strike price, indicating that investors were generally expecting Intel shares to move higher before March.

Factors affecting option prices

Unlike bond and equity traders, option traders are not concerned with fundamentals, such as industry structure or the earnings of a particular firm. Rather, option-market participants focus on the relationship between the value of an option, as expressed by the premium, and the price of the underlying asset. One reason option markets were slow to develop is that it was difficult to know what constituted fair value. The value depends heavily on the likelihood that the option will be exercised, but not until 1973, with the publication of the Black-Scholes option-pricing model, did it become possible to attach precise quantitative estimates to this likelihood. Several pricing models, including refined versions of Black-Scholes, are now in widespread use. As a result, option trading has become a highly mathematical affair in which traders rely on massive amounts of data and intensive computer modelling to identify particular options that are attractively priced.

The main variables option traders use to evaluate prices are described below.

Intrinsic value

The intrinsic value of an option is simply the extent to which the option is in the money. If a company's shares are trading at 110, the 105 call has an intrinsic value of 5, because immediately upon purchase the call could be exercised for a profit of $5 per share. The premium must be greater than the intrinsic value or the writer will have no incentive to sell an option. If an option is presently out of the money, its intrinsic value is zero.

Time value

The longer the time until an option expires, the greater is the likelihood that the purchaser will be able to exercise the option. This time value is reflected in the option's price. In Table 9.2, for example, March Intel 30 puts traded at 2.10, whereas July Intel 30 puts were trading at 3.90. The substantial price difference, equal to $1.80 per share, is the time value the market places on the additional four months before expiration of the July put. Market professionals devote great effort to calculating the rate of time decay, denoted by the Greek letter θ (theta), which is the rate at which an option loses value from one day to the next. As an option approaches its expiration date, its time value approximates zero.

Volatility

Volatility refers to the frequency and magnitude of changes in the price of the underlying. It can be measured in a number of different ways, of which the most common is the standard deviation of daily price changes over a given period of time. To see why volatility matters so much for the price of an option, consider two different shares trading at £12. If one frequently rises or falls by £2 in a single day and the other rarely moves by more than 50p, there is a far greater probability that the more volatile share will reach any given strike price, and all options on that share will therefore have higher premiums than options on the other share.

One of the difficult issues options traders must face is deciding how much history to incorporate in their analyses of volatility. One firm might offer to write a given option for a lower premium than another firm because it looks at the volatility of the underlying asset over a longer period of time. Of course, it may well be that both firms' estimates prove wrong, as future volatility may prove to be quite different from past volatility. The expected volatility of any option also has a term structure that can be calculated; the volatility of a particular call expiring two months hence would probably not be identical to the volatility of that same call expiring in five months' time. Students of the market can derive a firm's expectation of the future, known as implied volatility, from the premiums it quotes.

Delta

Represented by the Greek letter δ, delta is the change in the value of an option that is associated with a given change in the price of the underlying asset. If a 1% change in the price of the underlying currency or stockmarket index is associated with a 1% change in the value of the option, the option would have a delta of 1.00. The delta of a put option is the negative of the delta of a call option on the same underlying. Delta is not constant, but changes as the price of the underlying changes. With all other things remaining the same, an option with a low delta will have a lower premium than one with a high delta, because a change in the price of the underlying will have little effect on the option's value.

Gamma

Represented by the Greek letter γ, gamma is the rate at which an option's delta changes as the price of the underlying asset changes. Gamma is calculated as the change in delta divided by the change in the price of the underlying. A positive gamma means that a small change in the price of the underlying will cause a larger change in the value of the option than delta alone would predict. A negative gamma means that the rate of change in delta gets smaller as delta gets further away from the starting point.

Rho

Represented by the Greek letter ρ, rho is the expected change in an option's price in response to a percentage-point change in the risk-free interest rate – normally the interest rate on government bonds.

Vega

Also known by the Greek letter kappa (κ), vega refers to the change in an option's price, expressed in currency terms, in response to a percentage point change in volatility. A high vega, other things remaining the same, would make an option more costly.

Hedging strategies

Most options-market trading occurs as part of investors' broader strategies, often involving multiple types of financial instruments. The simplest strategy is a basic hedge, in which an investor purchases an asset and simultaneously buys a put option on that asset, guaranteeing a price at which the asset can be sold if its market price drops. Many strategies are far more complex.

Covering yourself

Writing covered calls or puts is a risk-minimising strategy. Covered means that the writer of the options already owns the underlying. To write a covered put, the writer would have to have a short position in the underlying, having borrowed the asset and then sold it in the expectation that the price would fall before it needed to replace the asset it had borrowed. Suppose, for example, that the writer sells short a share that is trading at $50 and must repay the share three months hence. The writer might then sell puts on the same shares with a strike price of $45. If the share price drops below $45, the writer may lose money on the put but make money by purchasing the shares it shorted at a much lower price. If the share price drops below $50 but stays above $45, the writer earns a premium on the put, which cannot be exercised, as well as making money on the short sale. If the share price rises modestly, the writer will lose money on the short sale of shares, but may earn enough from the premium on the unexercised put to cover that loss. Only a large increase in the share price would cause the writer to lose money. Similarly, writing covered calls involves writing calls on assets the writer owns, or is long on.

Baring all

The opposite strategy is to write naked calls or puts. Naked means that the writer has neither a short nor a long position in the underlying. Naked options offer the potential for higher returns than covered options, as the writer is spared the expense of investing in the underlying. However, writing naked options is a risky activity. The potential loss for the writer of a naked put is the difference between the nominal value of the option at the strike price and zero. The potential loss for the writer of a naked call is unlimited, because, at least in principle, there is no upper limit governing how high the price of an asset can climb.

Straddling

A straddle positions the investor to benefit either from high price volatility or from low price volatility. A buyer who is said to have a long straddle simultaneously takes put and call options expiring at the same time at the same strike price. For example, if the Deutsche Aktienindex (DAX) is now trading at 5,085, an investor might purchase both a May 5,100 DAX put and a May 5,100 DAX call. The straddle would pay off if the DAX either falls or rises substantially. On the downside, for the straddle to be profitable the DAX would have to fall far enough below 5,100 that the investor's gain would more than cover its premiums. On the upside, the DAX would have to exceed 5,100 by a wide enough margin to pay the premiums. At any DAX value between those two points the investor would lose, even though one of the two options would be in the money. However, the writer who is said to have a short straddle profits as long as the DAX remains between those two points; the writer loses only if the index becomes more volatile than anticipated, marking a larger loss or a larger decline.

Spreading

A spread position involves two options on the same underlying, similar to a straddle, except that the put and the call expire at different times or have different strike prices.

Turbo charging

A turbo option involves the purchase of two options with different strike prices on the same side of the market, such as calls at both 55 and 60 or puts at both 40 and 35. This strategy enables the investor to earn dramatically higher returns if the price of the underlying moves far into the money.

Dynamic hedging

Dynamic hedging involves continuously realigning a hedge as the price of the underlying changes. It is widely used by large institutional investors. One of the most popular variants is delta hedging, which attempts to balance an entire portfolio of investments so that its delta is zero. The hedge is said to be dynamic because as the stocks and/or bonds in the portfolio change in value, the options position must also be changed to maintain a delta of zero. The investor must therefore continuously buy or sell options or securities. Critics charge that dynamic hedging destabilises financial markets. Keeping delta at zero often requires the investor to sell the underlying asset at a time when its price is falling or to buy when the price is rising, making market swings sharper. Portfolio insurance, a dynamic heading strategy that purported to protect against declines in the value of stock portfolios, was briefly popular in the 1980s until a key assumption underlying the strategy – that it would always be possible to purchase new options as share prices changed – proved incorrect.

Clearing and settlement

Each option exchange operates or authorises a clearing house, a financial institution set up to ensure that all parties live up to their commitments. Once a trade has been completed, exchange rules normally require the buyer to deposit enough money with an options broker to pay the entire premium; the writer will receive the premium payment through its broker. Each broker, in turn, has an account with the clearing house, and must have enough money on deposit at the end of each day to cover the cost of the transactions it has handled. Settlement occurs when the money from buyer and writer passes through the clearing house.

Once the trade is made, there is no further connection between the buyer and the writer. Instead, the exchange itself steps in as the counterparty for each trade, removing any risk that the owner of a profitable position will fail to collect from the owner of a losing position. In most cases, the exchange's clearing house requires that each option position be marked to market each day. This means that any change in the option's market price is reflected as an increase or decrease in the value of the customer's position, and the customer will be asked to deposit additional funds if the position has lost value. If the customer fails to comply, its positions will be liquidated. The buyer of an exchange-traded option thus has no need to worry about the reliability or creditworthiness of the writer.

Terminating options

An option can be terminated in several ways. The most common is by selling or buying an offsetting option. For example, the owner of a March 1.60 sterling put on the Philadelphia Stock Exchange would write a March 1.60 sterling put; the offsetting positions would be closed out, with the investor recording a gain or a loss depending upon whether the put it wrote had a higher premium than the one it bought. Similarly, an investor who is short a call would close out the position by buying the identical call.

Another way to terminate an option is by exercising it. The owner of an American-style option may exercise it whenever it is in the money, but is not obliged to; the owner of an equity call at 55 may exercise as soon as the shares reach 55, or may hold on to the option in the hope that the stock will go even higher (and take the risk that it will fall back below 55, taking the option out of the money). Depending on the contract, the exchange will settle with the investor in cash or by exchanging the underlying. The exchange may force an investor with an opposing contract to settle. The owner of a General Motors put, for example, might wish to exercise the put, but the exchange will not want to own those shares. It will therefore select the writer of a similar General Motors put, usually at random, and require the writer to accept and pay for the shares.

Alternatively, the option can be held to expiration. Some option contracts, including all index contracts, are settled at expiration for cash, with the holder of a money-losing position paying the exchange, and the exchange in turn paying the holder of a profitable position. Many equity and commodity options, however, are settled with the exchange of the underlying. Investors often wish to close out contracts before expiration to avoid other costs, such as stockbrokerage commissions and commodity storage fees, which they may incur if they hold the option until expiration.

Over-the-counter derivatives

The fastest-growing part of the financial markets in recent years has been the over-the-counter market for derivatives. Over-the-counter derivatives are transactions occurring between two parties, known as counterparties, without the intermediation of an exchange. In general, one of the parties to a derivatives transaction is a dealer, such as a bank or investment bank, and the other is a user, such as a non-financial corporation, an investment fund, a government agency, or an insurance company.

In principle, derivatives are similar to exchange-traded options. Most derivatives involve some element of optionality, such that the price depends heavily on the value attached to the option. Many of the same mathematical procedures used to determine the value of options are therefore employed in the derivatives market as well. Unlike exchange-traded derivatives, however, over-the-counter derivatives can be customised to meet the investor's requirements.

As recently as the late 1980s, the market for over-the-counter derivatives barely existed. The business burgeoned in the 1990s as investors discovered that derivatives could be used to manage risk or, if desired, to increase risk in the hope of earning a higher return. Derivatives trading has also been controversial, because of both the difficulty of explaining how it works and the fact that some users have suffered large and highly publicised losses. Some observers have been alarmed by the sheer size of the market. The notional principal, or face value, of outstanding currency and interest-rate derivatives increased from just $3.5 trillion in 1990 to $217 trillion in 2004 (see Figure 9.2 on the next page).

Although the market is large, such figures seriously exaggerate its size. A currency derivative covering $1m-worth of euros has a notional principal of $1m, but the counterparties' potential gain or loss depends upon the amount of the euro's fluctuation against the dollar, not the notional value. The banks that are the most important players in the derivatives market have positions whose notional value is many times their capital, but as many of these positions cancel one another out the amount that a bank could potentially lose from derivatives trading is far less than the

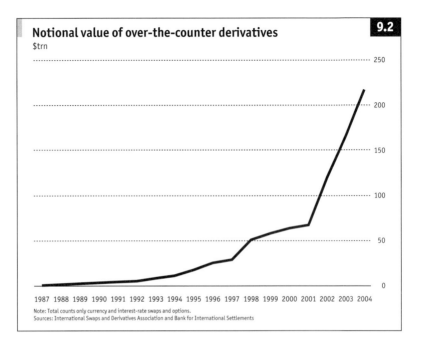

Notional value of over-the-counter derivatives

9.2

$trn

Note: Total counts only currency and interest-rate swaps and options.
Sources: International Swaps and Derivatives Association and Bank for International Settlements

notional value of its derivatives. On average, according to estimates by the International Swaps and Derivatives Association, a trade group, the potential loss from derivative positions is about 1–2% of the notional value of the positions. The gross market value of over-the-counter derivatives outstanding at the end of 2004 was only $9 trillion, and their net value – the amount that would have had to change hands had all the contracts been liquidated – was about $2 trillion.

The risks of derivatives
Over-the-counter derivatives pose certain risks that are less significant in the markets for exchange-traded options.

Counterparty risk
For all exchange-traded options, the exchange itself becomes the counterparty to every transaction once the initial trade has been completed, and it ensures the payment of all obligations. This is not so in the over-the-counter market, where derivatives are normally traded between two businesses. If the seller of a derivative becomes insolvent, the buyer may not be able to collect the money it is owed. For this

reason, participants in the derivatives market pay extremely close attention to the creditworthiness of their counterparties, and may refuse to do business with entities whose credit standing is less than first-class. A large and growing share of derivatives transactions is secured by collateral, offering protection to one counterparty in the event the other defaults.

Price risk

A derivatives dealer often customises its product to meet the needs of a specific user. This is quite unlike exchange-traded options, whose size, underlying and expiration date are all standardised. Customisation has advantages; for example, a firm expecting to receive a foreign-currency payment might seek a currency derivative that expires on the precise day the payment is due, rather than buying an option that expires several days earlier. But customised derivatives also have disadvantages. In particular, a user wishing to sell out its position may be unable to obtain a good price, as there may be few others interested in that particular derivative.

Legal risk

Where options are traded on exchanges, there are likely to be laws that clearly set out the rights and obligations of the various parties. The legal situation is often murkier with regard to over-the-counter derivatives. In recent years, for example, several sophisticated corporate investors have brought lawsuits charging that they were induced to buy derivatives so complex that even they could not fully understand them. In other cases, transactions entered into by government entities have been voided by courts on the grounds that the entity was not empowered to undertake such a transaction.

Settlement risk

The exchange makes sure that the parties to an option transaction comply with their obligations within strict time limits. This is not the case in the over-the-counter market. Central banks in the biggest economies have been trying to speed up the process of settling claims and paying for derivative transactions, but participants are still exposed to the risk that transactions will not be completed promptly. A particular concern is netting, the process by which all of the positions between two counterparties can be set off against each other. Without netting, it is possible that party A will have to make good on its obligations to party B, even though party B is unable to make good on its own obligations to party A. It is not clear whether netting can be legally enforced in all countries, leaving the possibility that a market participant will suffer losses despite having profitable positions.

Types of derivatives
Forwards
Forwards are the simplest variety of derivative contract. A forward contract is an agreement to set a price now for something to be delivered in the future. One type of forward, a futures contract, is traded in standardised form on exchanges (as discussed in Chapter 8). Over-the-counter forward contracts are similar to futures, but can be designed with the specific size and expiration date the user desires. A particular advantage of forwards is long maturity. Most futures contracts are highly liquid only a few months ahead, so they are not useful for a customer concerned about exchange rates or commodities prices two or three years hence, whereas a forward contract can be arranged to mature further into the future. A forward contract need not involve any option features.

Interest-rate swaps
An interest-rate swap is a contract between two parties to exchange interest-payment obligations. Most often, this involves an exchange of fixed-rate for floating-rate obligations. For example, firm A, which obtained a floating-rate bank loan because fixed-rates loans were unattractively priced, may prefer a fixed payment that can be covered by a fixed stream of income, but firm B might prefer to exchange its fixed-rate obligation for a floating rate to benefit from an anticipated fall in interest rates. In a simple swap, firm A might pay $30,000 to exchange its obligation to make payments for two years on a $1m notional amount at 1% above the London Inter-Bank Offer Rate (LIBOR) for firm B's obligation to pay interest on $1m at a fixed 7% rate. The notional amounts themselves do not change hands, so neither party is responsible for paying off the other's loan.

The value of an interest-rate swap obviously depends upon the behaviour of market rates. If rates were to decline, the swap position held by firm B would increase in value, as it would be required to make smaller payments over the next two years; and firm A's fixed-rate position would lose value because the rate is now far above what the market would dictate. However, if rates were to rise, firm A's side of the swap would be worth more than firm B's.

Table 9.3 **Notional principal of single-currency interest-rate derivatives ($bn)[a]**

	1998	2001	2004
Australian dollar	118	260	609
Canadian dollar	747	781	1,474
Danish krone	297	83	210
Euro	16,461	26,185	75,443
Hong Kong dollar	32	128	258
Japanese yen	9,763	11,790	23,276
New Zealand dollar	3	0	9
Norwegian krone	395	238	470
Pound sterling	3,911	6,215	15,166
Swedish krona	939	1,057	2,212
Swiss franc	1,320	1,362	3,234
US dollar	13,763	27,422	59,724
Other currencies	2,192	1,917	5,256

a Not adjusted for double-counting.
Source: Bank for International Settlements

Around half the notional value of interest-rate swaps is owned by banks, and half by other users. Financial institutions are the main end users, for purposes such as hedging mortgage portfolios and bond holdings. Table 9.3 shows the distribution of interest-rate derivatives by currency.

Currency swaps

Currency swaps involve exchanging streams of interest payments in two different currencies. If interest rates are lower in the euro zone than in the UK, for example, a British company needing sterling might find it cheaper to borrow in euros and then swap into sterling. The value of this position will depend upon what happens to the exchange rate between the two currencies concerned during the life of the derivative. In most cases, the counterparties to a currency swap also agree to exchange their principal, at a predetermined exchange rate, when the derivative matures.

The market for currency swaps is much smaller and more diverse than that for interest-rate swaps. The notional value of currency swaps used by financial institutions, for example, is barely 5% of the notional

Table 9.4 **Notional principal of foreign exchange derivatives, by currency ($bn)** [a]

	1998	2001	2004
Australian dollar	206	273	1,092
Canadian dollar	594	593	1,172
Danish krone	73	24	120
Euro	7,658	6,368	11,936
Hong Kong dollar	89	463	605
Japanese yen	5,319	4,178	7,083
New Zealand dollar	10	0	18
Norwegian krone	48	155	140
Pound sterling	2,612	2,315	4,349
Swedish krona	419	551	1,175
Swiss franc	937	800	1,461
Thai baht	28	5	2
US dollar	15,810	15,410	25,998
Other currencies	2,221	2,218	3,997

a Not adjusted for double-counting.
Source: Bank for International Settlements

value of those same institutions' interest-rate swaps. The overall market has grown far more slowly than that for interest-rate swaps.

Table 9.4 shows the notional value of currency swaps outstanding, by currency. As each swap involves two different currencies, the total value of swaps outstanding is only one-half of the sum of the value of swaps in each currency. The average size of a currency swap exceeds $30m.

Interest-rate options

This category involves a large variety of derivatives with different types of optionality. A cap is an option contract in which the buyer pays a fee to set a maximum interest rate on a floating-rate loan. A floor is the converse, involving a minimum interest rate. A customer can purchase both a cap and a floor to arrange a collar, which effectively allows the interest rate to fluctuate only within a predetermined range. It is also possible to arrange options on caps and floors. A swaption is an option that gives the owner the right to enter into an interest-rate swap, as either the fixed-rate payer or the floating-rate payer, at a predetermined rate. A spread option is based on the difference between two interest rates in the same currency rather than on the absolute level of rates; such an option might be used to protect an investor in long-term bonds, for example, against the risk that the yield curve will steepen and the bonds will lose value relative to short-term bonds. A difference or "diff" option is based on differences in interest rates on comparable instruments in different currencies.

Interest-rate options can also be built into fixed-income products, making them respond to interest-rate changes in ways different from normal securities. Inverse floaters (also called reverse floaters) are interest-bearing notes whose interest rate is determined by subtracting an index from a fixed rate, giving a formula such as 10% – six-month LIBOR; the investor thus receives less interest (and the value of its position declines) when interest rates rise, in contrast to most floating-rate securities. Multiple-index floaters have interest rates that are based on the difference between two rates, and step-up coupon notes have interest rates that increase if the security has not been called by a certain date.

Commodity derivatives
Commodity derivatives function much as commodity options, allowing the buyer to lock in a price for the commodity in return for a premium payment. Commodity options can also be combined with other sorts of options into multi-asset options. For example, an airline might feel that it could withstand higher fuel costs at most times, but not at a time of economic slowdown, which depresses air travel. The airline might therefore purchase a derivative that would entitle it to purchase aviation fuel at a specified price whenever a key interest rate is above 7% (at which point the economy is presumably slowing), but not at other times.

Trading in commodity derivatives is small relative to trading in interest-rate and currency derivatives. At the end of 2004, the notional value of all commodity derivatives outstanding was $1.4 trillion. Gold accounted for one-fifth of this amount; undisclosed "other commodities", presumably mainly oil, made up almost all the rest.

Equity derivatives
Over-the-counter equity derivatives are traded in many different ways. Synthetic equity is a derivative designed to mimic the risks and rewards of an investment in shares or in an equity index. For example, an American firm wishing to speculate on European telephone-company shares

could arrange a call option on a synthetic basket whose value is determined by the share prices of individual telephone companies. Synthetic equity can be used, among other purposes, to permit an investor such as a pension fund to take a position that it could not take by purchasing equities, owing to legal restrictions on its equity holdings. Step-down options on shares or equity indexes provide for the strike price to be adjusted downwards either at a specific date or if the price of the underlying falls to a predetermined level. Total return swaps are interest-rate swaps in which the non-floating-rate side is based on the total return of an equity index.

Credit derivatives

Credit derivatives are a comparatively new development, providing a way to transfer credit risk, the risk that a debtor will fail to make payments as scheduled. One type of credit derivative, a default swap, provides for the seller to pay the holder the amount of forgone payments in the event of certain credit events, such as bankruptcy, repudiation or restructuring, which cause a particular loan or bond not to be serviced on time (see Chapter 4). Another way of achieving the same end where publicly traded debt is concerned is a swap based on the difference between the price of a particular bond and an appropriate benchmark. If a given ten-year corporate bond loses substantial value relative to a group of top-rated ten-year corporate bonds, its credit standing is presumed to have been impaired in some way and the swap would cover part or all of the owner's loss, even if the company does not default on its debts.

Structured securities

These are synthetic securities created from government bonds, mortgages and other types of assets. The "structure" refers to the fact that the original asset can be repackaged in forms whose components have very different characteristics from one another, as well as from the underlying. The value of such securities depends heavily on option characteristics. For example, the owner of an interest-only (IO) security receives the interest payments, but not the principal payments, made by the issuer of the underlying security; if the issuer is able to prepay the underlying security before its maturity date, the value of the interest-only portion may collapse as no more interest payments will be received. The owner of a principal-only (PO) security, however, would applaud prepayment, as it would receive the principal to which it is entitled much sooner.

Table 9.5 **Notional value of derivatives outstanding, by type ($bn)**

	Interest-rate swaps	Currency swaps	Interest-rate options[a]
1987	683	183	...
1988	1,010	317	327
1989	1,503	435	538
1990	2,312	578	561
1991	3,065	807	577
1992	3,851	860	635
1993	6,117	900	1,398
1994	8,816	915	1,573
1995	12,811	1,197	3,705
1996	19,171	1,560	4,723
1997	22,291	1,824	4,920
1998	36,262	2,253	7,997
1999	43,936	2,444	9,380
2000	48,765	3,194	9,476
2001	58,897	3,942	10,879
2002	79,120	4,503	13,746
2003	111,209	6,371	20,012
2004	147,366	8,217	27,169

a Includes caps, floors, swaptions and other instruments.
Sources: International Swaps and Derivatives Association; Bank for International Settlements

It is not possible to determine the notional amount of each type of derivative that is outstanding or that has been written in a given year. Table 9.5 compares the growth in the three most popular types of over-the-counter derivatives.

Special features used in derivatives

Many derivatives of all types use multipliers as ways of increasing leverage. An interest-rate swap, for example, many provide that the party agreeing to pay a floating rate will pay not LIBOR plus 2 percentage points but rather the square of LIBOR minus 5%. Under this arrangement, if floating rates drop the square of (LIBOR − 5%) will plummet and the owner's payments will diminish rapidly. However, a small increase in floating rates could cause a sharp increase in the square of (LIBOR − 5%), and the owner of the floating rate position could owe significantly higher interest payments. Many of the large reported losses on derivatives transactions have come about because of multipliers of this sort embedded in the derivatives.

Another common arrangement in derivatives is a path-dependent option. Unlike a regular option, which pays off only if it is in the money at expiration (in the case of a European-style option) or when exercised before expiration (in the case of an American-style option), a path-dependent option has a pay-off that depends on its behaviour throughout its life. A simple path-dependent currency derivative might pay off only if the euro trades above $1.20 for seven of the 14 days before expiration. A more complex variant could conceivably require that the euro trades above $1.15 on July 1st, above $1.175 on October 1st and above $1.20 on January 1st; unless all three of these conditions are met, the exchange rate will not have followed the agreed path and the owner will not receive a payment.

Pricing derivatives

As with exchange-traded options, the prices of over-the-counter derivatives are determined mainly by mathematical models. The factors affecting prices are much the same: the level of risk-free interest rates; the volatility of the underlying; expected changes in the price of the underlying; and time to expiration.

Imagine a simple interest-rate swap, in which a manufacturing company wishes to exchange payments on $1m of debt floating at LIBOR + 3% for a fixed payment and an insurance company wishes to swap a 7% fixed-rate payment on $1m of principal for a floating rate. Before engaging in such a transaction each party, whether on its own or with the help of outside advisers, must develop a view of the likely course of interest rates over the relevant period. If they both judge that rates are likely to drop significantly, they may agree that over time the holder of the floating-rate position will probably pay less than the holder of the fixed position, so the insurer would pay a premium to the manufacturer in order to obtain the position it expects to be less costly. If they both think that interest rates will rise, they may agree that the manufacturer should pay a premium to the insurer for the opportunity to lock in a fixed rate. The precise amount of premium one party demands and the other agrees to pay will depend upon their estimates of the probable pay-offs until the derivative expires.

For "plain vanilla" derivatives, such as a simple swap, there is a large and liquid market and little disagreement about pricing. For more complicated derivatives premiums can be harder to calculate. In some cases, the premium can be determined by disaggregating one derivative product into several simpler ones and summing the prices. Many customers, even sophisticated companies, have difficulty reckoning a fair price for highly complex derivatives. They often rely on the pricing models of their bankers, which can lead to upset if, as often happens, the derivative does not perform precisely as the model expected. Many users are required to account for their derivative positions at current market value at the end of each quarter, booking a gain or a loss if the instrument has changed in value. Values, which are best described by the price at which the instrument could be sold, are often provided by banks, and unanticipated price drops can force owners to book losses.

The price a bank or other dealer will charge for a particular derivative will depend partly on the structure of the many derivative positions on the dealer's books. Dealers generally seek to minimise the risks of derivatives by hedging their own positions. They can hedge a derivative by buying an offsetting derivative from another dealer or by arranging a transaction with another customer. A dealer may offer a favourable price for a derivative that exposes it to loss if oil prices rise if it already holds a derivative exposing it to loss if oil prices fall, as the combination of the two positions would leave it in a neutral position with regard to oil-price changes. A customer whose proposed transaction would increase the dealer's risks might be offered a much less attractive price.

Settling derivatives trades

Trades in the over-the-counter derivatives market are settled through the banking system, according to standards established by each country's banking authorities. Central bankers, under the aegis of the Bank for International Settlements in Basel, Switzerland, have made a concerted effort to reduce the time within which the parties to a derivatives transaction must exchange contracts and money. Given the magnitude of derivatives positions, the failure of a major bank with many unsettled trades could cause the immediate failure of the banks with which it has been trading. Market forces have mitigated this risk to some extent, as banks are increasingly reluctant to trade with other banks whose creditworthiness they suspect; the weakness of Japanese banks in the late 1990s and early 2000s, for example, forced many of them to retreat from the market. Despite these advances, banking experts still consider unsettled derivatives trades to be one of the main factors that could threaten the stability of the world's banking system, and regulators continue to push banks to settle trades more quickly.

Derivatives disasters

Derivatives have made it possible for firms and government agencies to manage their risks to an extent unimaginable only a decade ago. But derivatives are far from riskless. Used carelessly, they can increase risks in ways that users often fail to understand. As individual derivatives can be quite complex and difficult to comprehend, they have been blamed for a series of highly publicised financial disasters. In some cases, the dealers have been accused of selling products that were not suited to the users' needs. In other situations, the problem has been not with the instruments themselves, but with the financial controls of the organisation trading or using them.

Metallgesellschaft, a large German company with a big oil-trading operation, reported a $1.9 billion loss in 1993 on its positions in oil futures and swaps. The company was seeking to hedge contracts to supply petrol, heating oil and other products to customers. But its hedge, like most hedges, was not perfect, and declines in oil prices caused its derivative position to lose value more rapidly than its contracts to deliver oil in future gained value. The company's directors may have compounded the loss by ordering that the hedge be unwound, or sold off, before it was scheduled to expire.

Procter & Gamble, a large American consumer-products company, and Gibson Greetings, a manufacturer of greeting cards, announced huge losses from derivatives trading in April 1994. Both companies had purchased highly levered derivatives known as ratio swaps, based on formulas such as:

$$\text{Net payment} = 5.5\% - \frac{\text{Libor}^2}{6\%}$$

If the resulting number is positive, the dealer must make a payment to the user. As interest rates rose early in 1994, however, the numerator rose geometrically, drastically increasing the users' losses. Procter & Gamble admitted to losing $157m, and Gibson's loss was about $20m. Both firms recovered part of their losses from the dealer, Bankers Trust Company. In both cases, the firms' derivative investments were made in violation of their own investment policies.

Barings, a venerable British investment bank, collapsed in February

1995 as a result of a loss of $1.47 billion on exchange-traded options on Japan's Nikkei 225 share index. Investigation subsequently revealed that the bank's management had exercised lax oversight of its trading position and had violated standard securities-industry procedures by allowing a staff member in Singapore, Nick Leeson, to both trade options and oversee the processing of his own trades, which enabled him to obscure his activities. Mr Leeson subsequently served a prison term in Singapore.

Orange County, California, suffered a loss ultimately reckoned to be $1.69 billion after Robert Citron, the county's treasurer and manager of its investment fund, borrowed through repurchase agreements in order to speculate on lower interest rates. In the end, about $8 billion of a fund totalling $20 billion was invested in interest-sensitive derivatives such as inverse floaters, which magnify the gains or losses from interest-rate changes. These derivatives were designed to stop paying interest if market interest rates rose beyond a certain point. This large position was unhedged, and when the Federal Reserve raised interest rates six times within a nine-month period in 1994 the value of the fund's assets collapsed.

Sumitomo, a Japanese trading company, announced total losses of ¥330 billion ($3 billion) from derivatives transactions undertaken by its former chief copper trader, Yasuo Hamanaka. Mr Hamanaka, known for being one of the leading traders in the copper futures and options markets, was accused of having used fraud and forgery to conceal losses from his employer, while continuing to trade in an effort to recoup the losses. Inadequate financial controls apparently allowed the problems to mount unnoticed for a decade. After Sumitomo's huge losses were revealed in 1996, Mr Hamanaka was convicted and sentenced to a prison term.

Derivatives played a role in the financial crisis that crippled Thailand in the summer of 1997. Many investors misjudged the country's situation because the Thai central bank reported holding large foreign currency reserves. The central bank did not report that most of these reserves were committed to forward contracts intended to support the currency, the baht. Once the baht's market value fell, the bank suffered huge losses on its derivatives and its reserves were wiped out. A year later several American and European banks reported significant derivatives losses in Russia after a sharp fall in the country's currency led to the failure of several banks and caused local counterparties to derivatives trades to default.

Accounting risks

Many problems such as these can be attributed to inadequate financial controls on the part of firms using derivatives. But the difficulty of applying strict and consistent accounting standards to derivatives positions makes it difficult for investors to assess a company's condition. Furthermore, derivatives may provide a means for users to avoid restrictions on their activities. For example, a firm that has stated that it will not purchase foreign equities could purchase a derivative that mimics the behaviour of foreign equities, exposing the firm and its investors to the same risks as if they did own foreign equities. Inadequate disclosure often makes it difficult for investors to determine whether a given firm is in fact using derivatives to circumvent limits on its activity.

Index

Figures in *italics* refer to tables, those in **bold** refer to figures.